The Model Company Town

The University of Massachusetts Press
Amherst, 1984

The Model Company Town

Urban Design through Private Enterprise in Nineteenth-Century New England

John S. Garner

Copyright © 1982, 1984 by John S. Garner
All rights reserved
Printed in the United States of America
Library of Congress Cataloging in Publication Data
Garner, John S., 1945–
The model company town.
Bibliography: p.
Includes index.
1. Company towns—New England—History—19th
century. 2. Company towns—New England—History—
19th century—Case studies. 3. City planning—New England
—History—19th century. 4. City planning—New England—
History—19th century—Case studies. 5. Hopedale (Mass.)
—City planning—History—19th century. 6. City planning
—Massachusetts—History—19th century. I. Title.
HT123.5.A11G37   1984   307.7′67′0974   84-8636
ISBN 0-87023-442-0
Publication of this book has been assisted by a
generous grant from the Merrimack Valley Textile Museum,
North Andover, Massachusetts

To Lloyd and Juanita Garner

Contents

Acknowledgments

This book originated as a dissertation at Boston University, where it was read by David D. Hall and Sam Bass Warner, Jr., of the Department of History. To them I am especially indebted. Michael G. Conzen, Walter L. Creese, and John W. Reps also read the manuscript during its years of revision, offering suggestions and encouragement. I have further benefited from lengthy conversations with Lewis Mumford and J. B. Jackson. A willingness to share their expertise in the fields of history, geography, architecture, and urban planning provided me with a much broader understanding of my subject.

Two classic studies kindled my interest while a student and ultimately shaped my approach. John Coolidge's *Mill and Mansion: A Study in Architecture and Society in Lowell, Massachusetts, 1820–1865* (1942) and Walter L. Creese's *Search for Environment: The Garden City, Before and After* (1966) remain unsurpassed. It was my good fortune to have taken a course with the former and to have become a colleague of the latter.

Indirectly, Cecil D. Elliott, George Chamberlain, Alan K. Laing, and Abbott Lowell Cummings prepared me for this task through their courses in architectural history, though they are not to blame for my perverse interest in industrial landscapes.

The Merrimack Valley Textile Museum of North Andover, Massachusetts, under the direction of Thomas W. Leavitt, furnished many of the illustrations and provided a most generous and necessary grant for their inclusion. The Maps Division of the Library of Congress also furnished several photographs and my friend Scott Wedeking provided one other. Maps, plans, and elevations of buildings were drawn by the author.

Finally, I must thank my wife, Susan, who does not share my interest in company towns but instead continues to provide a most welcome diversion from all things prosaic.

It comes at no small sacrifice to our democratic form of government and free enterprise economy that private and unrestricted land development so often results in poorly conceived and socially disruptive urban environments. Nowhere was the lack of planning, design, and management more evident than in the nineteenth-century industrial town. Little thought was given to environmental issues as businesses prospered and factories expanded. But one type of industrial town, despite its other failings, proved to be an exception.

Though born of the "age of enterprise" and once a symbol of exploitation and repression, the "model company town" also embodied positive advances in planning and architecture. It was a forerunner of the garden city and new town in that it imposed long-range planning goals for controlling growth and avoiding decline. Its purpose was to provide and then to maintain a productive environment for the interest concerned. The idea has been around for some time, but it has never been widely adopted. Designed communities tend to limit personal initiatives in land speculation and construction. Though this sometimes produces good architecture, it also restricts certain kinds of business and employment. The result usually benefits the controlling interest more than the individual worker or tenant. But during the middle decades of the nineteenth century, the negative and visibly corrosive aspects of the Industrial Revolution, stemming from a lack of planning, called attention to the need for taking comprehensive measures in hand. For a time, at least, the model company town served as a favorable alternative to other types of industrial settlements.

In America the company town appeared first in the Northeast, especially in New England, and elsewhere thereafter. Its history is tied to the beginnings of the Industrial Revolution and the rise of the factory system. Though barren in soil and harsh of climate, New England contained some of the first experiments in American town planning and management, and as agriculture gave place to manufacture it became a proving ground for later industrial settlements. Although the industrial town in general, and the company town in particular, never rivaled in significance the great mercantile ports, the pattern they established was more pervasive and perhaps more representative of the American urban experience of the nineteenth century.

To describe this urban achievement, the text has been divided into two parts: the first part addresses the image and meaning of industrialism in town building and surveys a group of New England towns to arrive at a composite view of their design features and development strategies. The second takes an in-depth look at one of these towns, Hopedale, Massachusetts, and analyzes in detail the forces that shaped it. Emphasis has been placed on the built environment. Maps, illustrations, and photographs help to present an accurate image of town development while clarifying different phases of construction. Workers' dwellings and landscape improvement receive special attention because of their prominence and tangible merit. What is stressed most is the causal effect of design and supervision in long-term environmental maintenance. In this regard, special attention has been given to the built environment in interpreting urban history.

To harness waterpower for factories, to excavate or drill for metals and minerals, or to mill timber, entire towns were constructed by single businesses. Each laid streets and built houses to accommodate a work force. Some of these towns were superior to others and therefore termed "models." One of these was Hopedale, a small communitarian settlement purchased in its entirety in 1856 by George and Ebenezer Draper, who founded the Draper Company. The Drapers made textile machinery to supply cotton mills with spinning and weaving equipment. Although two small shops and several dozen houses had already been built, they proceeded to expand these and to build a town of their own design. Expansion continued until 1916, after which the business declined and construction ceased. Not until the 1950s, however, were the houses sold off; and much of the town still remains with the enterprise, which became a division of Rockwell International in 1967. The Draper family controlled every aspect of the business and the town, including decisions regarding planning and architecture. They took pride in their manufacture as well as in their town and were of the opinion that attractive surroundings drew the best workers. They employed two landscape architects, Warren Henry Manning and Arthur A. Shurcliff, to lay out subdivisions and a park in the period 1886–1916. Manning and Shurcliff were former associates of Frederick Law Olmsted and among the founders of the American Institute of Planners. Fred Swassey and Robert Allen Cook, among several architects employed by the Drapers, designed a variety of handsome buildings. Hopedale received from them a practical as well as an attractive landscape, and their initiatives in urban design were carried forward in later years in new-town experiments. A result of this professional employment, to cite one example, was that the Draper Company dwellings received awards from international housing congresses held at trade fairs in France, Belgium, Italy, and the United States.

If, in instances, the model company town would seem to appear as a "New Jerusalem" among otherwise "dark satanic mills," then of course the subject will have been misrepresented. There was nothing saintly about Hopedale or other towns of its type. Despite the sentiment of some observers, these places were hardly "industrial paradises." But neither were they as grim and oppressive as sometimes depicted. Workers were probably better off in company housing than in city slums. And despite the big-brother implications of paternalism, many employers made a genuine attempt to attract, satisfy, and retain skilled labor. What is more, initiatives in architecture and planning with long-term benefits emerged from the best of these places.

JSG
Urbana, Illinois
1984

Chapter 1
Introduction

The model company town was constructed and afterward supervised by a single business enterprise. In America the earliest were built by New England manufacturers during the middle decades of the nineteenth century. Thereafter, they appeared elsewhere, though they continued to be built for industrial purposes. No one knows exactly how many single-enterprise towns once dotted the United States; twenty-five hundred would be a rough estimate based upon federal labor and census reports. The century 1830–1930 experienced the greatest activity in their development: the first fifty years saw them built along the river valleys of the Northeast, and the second fifty years witnessed a more vigorous and extensive establishment upon the Piedmont in the South and across the mineral plains, mountains, and forests in the West. A few of these towns were labeled as models by visitors, journalists, and labor officials. What distinguished these few from other single-enterprise towns were their appearance and administration, resulting from comprehensive measures applied to design and management and thereby creating prosperous, yet pleasing environments. They managed to combine manufacturing with what appears to have been attractive and healthful working and living situations for wage-earning men, women, and their families. To achieve this combination, however, required a reinvestment of a portion of their industrial profits in their surroundings to ensure long-term benefits for all concerned. This study proposes to examine the architectural and social fabric of several of these towns and to assess their achievement.

Visual sources can provide information that would be difficult to obtain from tabulated statistics or written accounts. Buildings and their spatial arrangements reveal urban patterns and depict social customs. They may also document physical changes that periodically take place; photographs and drawings and, of course, existing buildings offer an exact record of space and time. These images and artifacts of the built environment can be helpful in providing an understanding of urban history.[1]

The company town lends itself to visual analysis because its composition can be easily perceived and reduced to a single image: spiraling smokestacks form silhouettes against rows of identical houses. Carnegie's Homestead, one of many towns built for the steel industry, produced such an image. Founded in the 1880s, Homestead, Pennsylvania, possessed all the visual features usually associated with a company town, and its gray and forbidding landscape became the setting for a notorious episode in labor history. Moreover, it helped to shape our present thinking about company towns.[2] Although these places differed considerably from one industry to another, each has been cast alike to convey one image. "The Insensate Industrial Town," in Lewis Mumford's *Culture of Cities* (1938), illustrates well the combining of literary and visual sources taken from several towns to create one image. For Mumford (and others),[3] the company town symbolized the destructiveness of the Industrial Revolution or "paleotechnic" era. His argument depends upon the social anomie caused by exploitative businessmen and their utter disregard for the environment. In effect, his criticism created a type that came to represent all single-enterprise towns. Many were wretched places and justly criticized, though all did not strip and sear the environment as did "Coketown" or morally debase the people who built and worked there.

To the contrary, it can be argued that the principles of design and planning praised by Mumford in garden cities and new towns were first employed in company towns. To support this assertion, however, requires a visual as well as a documented investigation of towns other than those of the steel-making industry. In the conclusion of his book, Mumford observes that the designer should provide an environment "broad enough and rich enough never to degenerate into a 'model community.'"[4] Although his reference is to an ideal solu-

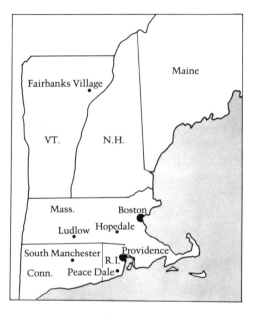

1. Five model company towns in New England, founded between 1830 and 1870.

tion or utopia, he would likely include the model company town. On this point, there is no argument. Environments should not be designed to produce stereotypes. But as an alternative to other industrial towns of the nineteenth century, the model company town offered the worker and his family favorable conditions in a number of instances.

Hopedale and Ludlow, Massachusetts, South Manchester, Connecticut, Peace Dale, Rhode Island, and Fairbanks Village at Saint Johnsbury, Vermont, represent a few of a number of company towns that developed into model communities throughout the United States. Because of their relative proximity in location and time (founded in New England between 1830 and 1870), because of the ease with which they may be grouped and compared, and because so much remains of the original towns, they form the basis of a group study (fig. 1). Though information about company towns is usually confined to company records, advertising brochures, or a history of the manufacturer, these five towns were mentioned in labor reports, architectural and engineering journals, popular magazines, and newspapers. Moreover, they were often cited as a group or in reference to one another. Two very important government studies, Carroll D. Wright's *Report on the Factory System of the United States* (1883) and Albert Clarke's *Report of the Industrial Commission* (1901), provide the best evidence for singling out these towns and labeling them as models. Factories, houses, stores, town halls, libraries, and parks were designed to promote the enterprise and to serve the work force. After establishing the physical plant, these companies directed programs for building upkeep and ground maintenance. They published accounts outlining methods of operation, finding that concern for the welfare of labor was good for business. Plant officials and workers maintained a rapport that permitted them to resolve problems relating to company and community affairs. This was unusual for the time. As a result, strikes were avoided throughout the nineteenth century in each of these towns. At a time when management and labor were embroiled in a struggle over working conditions, contemporary journals interviewed these exceptional companies to determine and publish the reasons for their conciliatory attitude and social benevolence. Company agents like Dutcher of Hopedale and Stevens of Ludlow responded by listing community goals that required both employer and employee to contribute.[5] The image cultivated by the company advertised its product at international trade fairs and associated marketing quality with the town. Visually distinct and attractive, these model company towns stand in contrast to other industrial towns that bypassed such measures and therefore became blighted through custodial negligence and managerial apathy.

More than other countries, the United States lent itself to building company towns. The ingredients were a vast expanse of unsettled land rich in resources, a government that took a laissez-faire attitude toward business, and the mass migration of labor (domestic and foreign), both skilled and unskilled. Even at the edge of the frontier, industry played a vital role in urban expansion.[6] Though the majority of company towns engaged in extractive and raw processing industries, some of the earliest produced textiles or made machinery. In one hundred years, between 1814 and 1914, the United States became the largest producer, processor, and transporter of raw materials in the world,[7] and the company town played a part in this rise to industrial hegemony.

Different types of industrial towns

To avoid confusion, distinctions should be drawn among mill villages, industrial communitarian settlements, company towns, corporate towns, garden cities, and new towns. The first two rarely attained the size either to qualify as towns or to require long-term, comprehensive measures regarding site planning and maintenance.

Some did set a precedent for later manufacturers through their technical organization and industrial management. In New England and the Mid-Atlantic states, the mill village became commonplace during the early years of the nineteenth century. Even toward the end of the eighteenth century a few textile mills had begun production.[8] Several dozen cottages, loosely assembled around a mill building, often situated no farther than a few miles downriver from a similar site, represented the typical layout. Few are as picturesque as Harrisville, New Hampshire, described by John B. Armstrong in *Factory under the Elms*, which because of its state of preservation and natural setting has become an attraction for tourists. In *Rockdale: The Growth of an American Village in the Early Industrial Revolution*, Anthony F. C. Wallace has provided a detailed account of the families, technologies, and character of these small and amorphous developments. More complex in structure, though similar in size with populations rarely exceeding several hundred, were industrial communitarian settlements. These utopian experiments flourished in the period 1840 to 1860 and were influenced primarily by the French social theorist, Charles Fourier, though the Shaker settlements date from the 1790s. Those settlements that sustained their faith with a well-organized industry, like Oneida, New York, and Amana, Iowa, grew for a time and prospered. Members shared in the ownership and wealth of these settlements to a varying degree. The few that weathered the best held fast either to one ideology or to one enterprise. But most disbanded before growing into towns, so that development rarely extended beyond several buildings and the immediate grounds. In *Seven American Utopias: The Architecture of Communitarian Socialism, 1790–1975*, Dolores Hayden describes the best developed among these and analyzes their building programs.[9]

Company towns were developed, administered, and owned in their entirety by a single enterprise. Those which were comprehensive in design with a physical layout that included landscaping, community facilities, safe and sanitary factories, good houses, and programs for maintenance have been labeled as models. This appellation was used consistently after 1850,[10] though both in Britain and America the phrase "model industrial village" or "model village" was preferred to "model company town."[11] But these were not villages, either in size, with populations averaging twenty-five hundred to five thousand, services, or governance. To their administrators, as well as to visitors who investigated and wrote about them, they were models by example. Model company towns need not have been preplanned, though planning in later phases of development was in response to industrial expansion. Much of the interest in model conditions came after initial construction. Each exhibited care in maintaining buildings and landscapes as a result of personal supervision by resident administrators and owners. The goal of these companies was to protect their industrial investment through comprehensive planning and site control and to secure employees by offering attractive working and living conditions. Stanley Buder's study, *Pullman: An Experiment in Industrial Order and Community Planning, 1880–1930,*[12] gives a thorough account of the best-known model company town; though Pullman, of which more will be said later, was in some ways an anomaly.

Corporate towns, such as Lowell, Lawrence, and Holyoke, Massachusetts, and Manchester, New Hampshire, to cite a few, differ in both magnitude and type of development. These large multienterprise towns, founded between 1820 and 1850, which grew to populations in excess of ten thousand, were initially planned by a single authority. But this initial period quickly ended. Orderly development ensues only when a single enterprise exercises control over an entire town site; and this was not the situation in the corporate town, where many companies, each acting independently, were permitted to build with little or no coordination. The founding interest eventually became a land and utility company, abandoning site supervision through lease or sale to other businesses or developers. A destruction of order—not order—resulted, as the quality of their environments rapidly deteriorated. Studies of corporate towns have focused primarily on economic and social conditions, and Constance M. Green's *Holyoke, Massachusetts: A Case History of the Industrial Revolution in America* is a pioneering example of this approach. However, because of its environmental history, *Mill and Mansion: A Study in Architecture and Society in Lowell, Massachusetts, 1820–1865* by John P. Coolidge remains the classic study of industry and urban form in the first of these towns.[13]

The garden city combined communitarian principles with industry to create an alternative to the industrial city in Britain and other countries in Europe. Although industry would provide economic support, it was neither industrially oriented nor profit-motivated. Emphasis was placed on site planning and housing; the public came first, the enterprise second. Ebenezer Howard, a court stenographer who later in life turned social reformer and town promoter, conceived the idea and set forth the principles in his book *Garden Cities of Tomorrow*.[14] Howard's garden cities never successfully materialized in America, however, though some industrial and suburban satellites emulated portions of his first experiment at Letchworth, England.[15] Letchworth (1903) contributed significantly to the knowledge of what model towns could be, though it remains that little has been built in the United States on that pattern. Howard's "town-country magnet," a euphemism for alleviating city slums by bringing industry to the countryside, was hardly novel. Model company towns in Britain and America had tested this principle a generation before. The relationship between these earlier industrial developments and the garden city in Britain has been revealed by Walter L. Creese in *The Search for Environment: The Garden City, Before and After*.[16] What these earlier types did not provide was a regional planning framework. Howard's garden city did, with a pilot scheme that could be extended to the building of many satellite towns around large industrial cities. For this reason, he has been credited as the founder of new-town planning.[17] Howard further believed that resident stockholders should own their garden city in shares and then lease parcels of land to industry. But few industrialists in Britain were willing to accept his proposition. Spoiled by cheap land, low taxes, and an abundance of resource sites, American industrialists developed their own estates.

Rather than English garden cities with regional planning programs, satellite towns (many of which were company towns) cropped up indiscriminately in areas bordering or within a few miles of cities large and small. Those founded by industries, like Indian Hill near Worcester, Massachusetts, built in 1912 by the Norton Grinding Company, provided a place to work as well as to live and were economically self-sufficient.[18] Others, financed by realty or philanthropic organizations, such as the Russell Sage Foundation's experiment at Forest Hills Gardens (1908–11), Long Island, New York, were merely dormitory communities and totally dependent upon the city. Though private enterprise built the first of these towns in the decade before World War I, the federal government began erecting war housing communities in 1918 for migrants who worked in industrial cities engaged in shipbuilding and armaments. Later, the government's Tennessee Valley Authority and Greenbelt towns, begun in the 1930s, culminated public participation in financing the development of satellite towns.

Company towns, corporate towns, and garden and satellite cities each differed in organization and purpose, though all were designed and planned in various phases of construction. The model company town managed to maintain site control throughout development because of its simple organization, single-enterprise economy, and relative isolation, whereas the others did not. As a result, the opportunity for creating and maintaining a model town was greater.

All types imposed some measure of social order, however. Social order (conformity in the behavior patterns of a town's inhabitants)[19] varied from place to place; but in each town a degree of social order existed and could be easily perceived. It resulted partly from common working and living routines and partly from common cultural values. In addition to these, social order was affected by the physical design of the landscape. The spatial treatment and site arrangement of buildings and grounds can influence behavior by establishing patterns of personal activity through movement or confinement.[20] Factories, houses, and community facilities were clearly defined and carefully stratified. They established the worker's routine as he walked among these buildings along determined paths at fixed intervals. Though workers in other types of towns also followed routines, their patterns were not as invariable or as visually delimited as in the single-enterprise town. The design and placement of buildings could in this way affect and alter social behavior. Not only the disposition of buildings and grounds but also factory layouts could have an effect upon the productiveness of the enterprise and the efficiency of the work force. It was no accident that Frederick Winslow Taylor, the proponent of scientific management, conducted some of the first time-motion efficiency studies in model company towns.[21]

A regard for social behavior in environmental design still survives. It is most evident in the new towns constructed since World War II, developed for a specific life style and social echelon. But to ascribe the origin of new towns to preplanned towns in general is simply inadequate. New towns, like company towns, stem from a single enterprise.

In America new towns appeal largely to middle-income families bent on leaving the city, whereas in the countries of Great Britain and northern Europe they have served as a partial remedy to the urban dilemmas of the working class. These countries—especially England, France, Sweden, and Finland—have promoted new towns to alleviate chronic housing shortages and other problems attending crowded industrial cities. England alone built twenty-nine new towns between 1946 and 1978, and others are being planned.[22] The return to new towns in America has been identified as a means of controlling suburban growth,[23] though not because our core cities are too crowded or short of housing. The reason is simply to build better suburbs that are relatively free of congestion and crime. Moreover, the need here for new towns on the order of Reston, Virginia, and Columbia, Maryland, begun in the 1960s, is less pressing than in other countries. Since 1945 many Americans have been able to obtain a foothold in the suburbs, though admittedly in poorly designed tract housing. Government financed or insured home mortgages have made possible a dispersion of urban dwellers, leaving the centers of old cities to the immigrating poor.[24] No new towns are being planned for them or for the low-income employed.

It can at least be demonstrated that the model company towns and the garden and satellite cities that followed them attempted to solve some of the problems caused by the Industrial Revolution by providing itinerant labor with adequate housing in planned environments. Designed for low-income workers, they provided a timely alternative to large industrial cities and projected an image of responsible design that can still be seen amidst their streets and across the fronts of their factories and cottages.

Outline and procedure

This study is presented in two parts. The first part surveys the model company town in New England and lays a framework for evaluating the meaning of image and order through town planning, architecture, and administration. The second part constitutes an in-depth study of one town, Hopedale, Massachusetts, and examines in detail the mechanisms of a once creditable industrial environment.

In New England, a relative isolation together with an emerging industrial landscape distinguished the company town from other small towns and agricultural villages. Because of the need for power to run textile machinery, trip-hammers, forges, and saws, the company developed a site isolated from large coastal cities and sometimes distant from trade routes in order to tap a river or stream. Its location and single-enterprise economy encouraged only those businesses which supported the company to settle. The lack of potential growth simply did not attract outside investment. Independent merchants and grocers might sell to company employees, but their stores were usually rented from the company. The appearance of closely built factories and houses contrasted with less densely settled farming communities, which operated on a very different scale. Even when viewed from far away, the company town presented a distinct image.[25]

In effect, the nature of a single-enterprise economy controlled and restrained physical size and shape. Town development was rarely accidental or haphazard; careful consideration was given to a site before industrialists invested capital to begin construction or to carry forward later expansion. Financial responsibility and developmental authority rested in each case with one family, which directed the operation. Whether or not the business survived depended on the inventive ability of the company to keep its product marketable. Labor procurement and transportation costs also figured in the town's potential for growth.

Site development was governed by the size of the factory, its work force, and supporting facilities. None of the towns studied attained a physical radius of over one mile, and populations rarely exceeded five thousand. Laid out at a time when automobiles were unknown and when streetcars were still a novelty, they relied on pedestrian traffic to establish distances between places of residence, employment, commerce, and recreation. No place was located too far away to be reached on foot, and vehicular nuisances were minimized. These distances, relative to so many small towns, later became a planning criterion—the "neighborhood unit." Clarence Perry, a planning administrator of the Russell Sage Foundation, defined the neighborhood unit in 1927 as a population no larger than five thousand, inscribed in an area of half an hour's walking radius. He found this unit compatible with the needs of a community without having to duplicate services or to rely on some form of transit.[26] These limits were used in planning the Greenbelts and some of the British new towns. But with the acceptance of the automobile, this emphasis on pedestrian movement proved rather naive.

For the employer, the town's internal organization and economy were simple. One enterprise owned the real estate and employed the work force. When production slowed in the factories, the slack could be taken up either by cutting back on workers' hours or by laying men off.[27] But layoffs were to be avoided, since lost jobs resulted in a loss of tenants. Living in a single-enterprise town meant working for *the company*; losing a job meant leaving rather than changing employment. To the employer, it could mean additional cost for new recruitment. Therefore, a special effort was sometimes made, as in Hopedale in 1884, to prorate manufacturing, enabling production to continue during slowdowns without loss of employment.[28] Companies without tenants, in larger towns or cities where pools of labor made hiring and firing easy, did not share the same compunction to maintain steady employment. Workers were laid off whenever profits dipped below a competitive ceiling. The result caused unemployment and precipitated migration between jobs, neighborhoods, and cities during financially unstable times.[29]

The invasion and succession of migrating waves of workers were less appreciable in the model company town than in the corporate town because of its single-enterprise economy. Statistical evidence from property valuation and census reports supports this finding.

Workers with families often stayed in one place long enough to take root.[30]

Missing from the street scenes of model company towns were the anonymous faces depicted by Winslow Homer in sketches of working men and women treading to and from factories, as illustrated in large corporate towns like Lawrence. At Fairbanks Village, for instance, the Fairbanks brothers knew their employees on a first-name basis. Horace Fairbanks told his workers, "You should come to me as to a father."[31] Though some workers may have recoiled from such paternalism, others probably took comfort from it. When the Reverend Jonathan Baxter Harrison visited a large corporate town and wrote about what he experienced, he discovered a less paternal attitude on the part of employers. When walking the streets of this corporate town of "about 50,000 population," he was haunted by the stares he received from workers on their journey home from work. Approaching them, he noticed an "instinctive shrinking and drawing together for self-defense which is shown by wild animals in similar circumstances." He was troubled by the way members of "their class" met him with suspicion and hostility. After examining their living and working circumstances, he concluded:

> It is not enough that people who have money and culture pay the operatives their wages. That is not all that justice requires. . . . There is far too little fraternal interest in them,—too little disposition to share their burdens, and to help them to make the best of their life.[32]

Harrison was not advocating equality but asking employers to assume paternal responsibility. To him, and to some industrialists in company towns, paternalism provided what was missing.

Although opinions varied as to the worth of paternalism, there obviously was a time when industrialists needed to exercise greater responsibility in the treatment of labor. Muckrakers like Upton Sinclair, Ida M. Tarbell, Richard T. Ely, Edith Elmer Wood, and Graham Romeyn Taylor criticized paternalism only insofar as it impinged on personal liberties. Ely first challenged the concept of paternalism in 1885 in Pullman before the strike but was otherwise impressed by the town's physical planning and architecture.[33] Other writers have been split between approving the goals of paternalism and approving the methods, at least as exemplified by Pullman. In some measure, paternalism may have been justified as a means of carrying out planning objectives and of implementing social programs during a period in which government exercised little responsibility.

In exercising control over the buildings and grounds, companies devised ways to encourage employees to partake in the upkeep of their towns and to show pride in the appearance of their houses by establishing prizes for the best-maintained premises, especially for yards and gardens. The communal gardens envisioned by architect Elbert Peets for Greendale, Wisconsin, begun in 1936, can actually be found in the model company towns. Campaigns for physical recreation and cultural uplift, influenced partly by the gymnasium and Chautauqua movements at the end of the nineteenth century, were also supervised and encouraged by companies.[34] To be sure, this was partly public relations work, though it had a salutary effect.

Community facilities such as parks, playgrounds, lyceums, and libraries symbolized another interest in social improvement. They represent the philanthropy of the manufacturer. Without them, workers were deprived of places to go for recreation and education.[35] They provided an alternative to the factory and home and represented a resource that most towns of similar size simply could not afford. In instances, the landscaping and architecture of these facilities were exceptional, as still to be seen in the H. H. Richardson buildings at North Easton.[36]

"Village improvement societies," stemming from a conservation movement begun in New England during the 1850s, were another expression of paternalism. Some industrialists developed an abiding interest in the landscape of their towns. Through village improvement, measures were taken to protect the environment and to conserve resources. There was cause for concern, for these towns depended on their sites for water and fuel. They did not permit the erosion of riverbanks by the removal of trees or the pollution of waterways with industrial refuse. Instead, they initiated programs for environmental protection and experimented with waste adaptation. Through landscaping, houses and community facilities could be placed in proximity to the factories without adverse effects. In contrast to other industrial towns, the landscape served as a foil between the factories and houses as a result of responsible site planning. Land berms and trees were implanted to shield residential areas from the noise and sight of the factories. In some instances, industrialists made a point of bringing nature into the factory yard with an idea in mind to make working conditions more attractive. Village improvement combined interests in both conservation and philanthropy.

Company housing could be studied separately from the company town, since it formed a constituent part of many industrial towns and cities. It is in fact an ancient solution to the problem of shelter.[37] In America it connotes a type of housing labeled by reformers as alien and undemocratic, for it signifies opposition to an almost sacred quest, the supposed right entitling heads of families to secure their domain.[38] Though independent ownership of single-family houses has been a cause célèbre in American history, the goal remains elusive. Beginning with the Massachusetts Bay colonists, attempts were made to allocate house lots and farms. Later, the Homestead Act and land runs that followed the opening of western territories again tried to make possible a kind of universal home franchise by giving away land to those who would inhabit it. And since World War II the extension of credit and availability of government-insured mortgages have made homeowning a reality for many families. However, the trend toward ownership may have a limited future as economic inflation, interest rates, and job mobility increase.[39] What is more, the young, the old, and the poor can no better afford the obligations of home ownership today than in the past. Company housing, like any rental housing, had certain advantages. Rents were adjusted to one's ability to pay, and company house crews made regular inspections for repairs. Though low rents often reflect low wages, an overall comparative ratio of rents to wages finds that families in company towns spent less of their income on housing than did their counterparts in larger cities.[40]

The necessity of furnishing homes to those who could not or otherwise would not manage shelter fell to the company. At the wage level of most workers, it would have taken them years to purchase a house, and owning a house in a single-enterprise town raised the question of what to do if unemployed and forced to move. Therefore, the company rented several types of houses, varying in style, size, and rent; and, through uniform construction, these houses were often suitably proportioned in terms of workingmen's needs.

Decent housing again depended upon the paternal interest of the company. South Manchester, Peace Dale, Fairbanks Village, Ludlow, and Hopedale were owned and supervised by resident families who took a personal interest in site planning and building maintenance. Paternalism not only affected labor relations but provided housing and other amenities as well.

One town, above others, exemplifies a significant achievement in industrial organization, housing, and site management. Hopedale, Massachusetts, offers a paradigm by which other industrial towns, as well as model company towns, can be compared. It represents the best of its type: not only was it able to provide a pleasant environment for its inhabitants, but it also retained a model image and social order through professional design and site maintenance. In terms of development, it accomplished some of the environmental objectives that the designers of garden cities and new towns set out to achieve.

Founded in 1842 as a religious commune, Hopedale was purchased in 1856 by the E. D. and G. Draper Company. For the next one hundred years it operated as a company town; and only in the past twenty-five years has the business changed hands and the houses been sold. This divestment came by merger with the North American Rockwell Corporation (now Rockwell International) and not because the original business failed. Fortunately, Hopedale retains much of its early appearance, and it is in the topography of the town's streets and buildings that its significance lies.

Among the seventy or more religion-inspired communitarian settlements that briefly flourished during the middle decades of the nineteenth century, Hopedale Community (1842–56) numbered among the longer-lived. Initially, thirty-two men and women banded together on January 27, 1841, in Mendon, Massachusetts, a small farming and manufacturing town located two miles southwest of the present site of Hopedale, and pledged support to a covenant establishing "an order of Human Society based upon the sublime ideas of the Fatherhood of God and the Brotherhood of Man, as taught and illustrated in the Gospel of Jesus Christ."[41] On April 1, 1842, they crossed over the Mendon hills and into "the Dale," a secluded valley that lay between Mendon and Milford about thirty miles southwest of Boston. Descendants of the original settlers sold the membership a 258-acre farm in the Dale—to which the word "hope" was prefixed before they christened their venture. At first all participants in the community, men and women, were paid equally from the dividends earned from their joint stock investment in farming and manufacturing. But in time production lagged and tempers flared over work roles and responsibilities. Eventually, in 1847, payment was made on an individual basis by the amount of labor each member performed. Although the community suffered from dissenting factions throughout its existence, it managed to attract three hundred people and to acquire six hundred acres of water and land prior to 1856.

The original covenant optimistically left questions of conduct to personal recognizance. Yet, as time passed, rules of conduct were imposed (coincidental to an expanding and ever more heterogeneous membership). The rules undermined the mirth and spontaneity that went into performing chores and also complicated the easy union that characterized the charter group. The reason for the rules was to stabilize social order. Some individuals needed to be taken in hand, while others struggled under a tighter control. Though rules were imposed to govern individual and group behavior, almost none pertained to business.[42] A few members sought financial rewards beyond those available through farming: capital was needed to construct homes and schools, improve lands, and purchase a library and printing press. Farming provided only food—and meager fare at that. Moreover, some arrivals did not wish to spend their hours tilling the rocky soil that covered the site, land better suited to foraging livestock than cultivating fruit and vegetables. The more enterprising members started new businesses or continued old ones brought to a new location. Within a small building known as the "mechanic shop," Ebenezer and George Draper worked at making textile machinery, while other men made boxes for hats and shoes, sawed lumber, and operated a forge. The Drapers' business succeeded, but the others failed. Had the membership pooled its resources into one endeavor, the venture might have stood a better chance; yet measures taken to strengthen the community's economy by following one line of business weakened social equity, and those favored members able to purchase large shares in the community had more of a say than others in the way things were done. The result vitiated the society and brought an end to the community.

Between 1856 and 1916, from the time the company began building until development leveled off, will be the period brought into focus.

During this period the business climbed to an eminent position in the textile machinery industry and the town's present topography was laid. As with other company towns in New England, Hopedale grew in stages and not all at once. But additions were planned and superintended throughout.

To examine in detail the planning, architecture, and society of Hopedale necessarily involves a thorough understanding of the enterprise and its product. But it is the town and not the product that is of principal interest. Though methods of manufacture and marketing are instrumental in the ultimate success or failure of the product, profit margins provide only a partial index to the quality of the site or to the management of the town.

Before examining Hopedale, a framework will be laid that entails a certain amount of exploration in towns of similar stature and of shared importance to the history of single-enterprise, new-town development. They will provide a context both for evaluating Hopedale and for examining the ingredients of comprehensive design. These ingredients—houses, utilities, streets, and community facilities—are much the same, basically, in recent new towns as they were a century ago in company towns. Behind each was an enterprise responsible for planning and development. The present emphasis is placed upon housing instead of industry, but entire building sites still require comprehensive planning and design to be successful. In the nineteenth century, large-scale manufacturing, brought to undeveloped sites, precipitated the need for long-range planning, social organization, and environmental maintenance. Industrialists were the first in a position to undertake such comprehensive measures. And company towns represent the earliest attempts to carry out these measures. Nowadays, land developers and mortgage bankers have replaced industrialists in new-town promotion. Though large industrial plants continue to influence residential development because of their location and employment, direct involvement in housing and community planning has been avoided. If in the beginning, however, places like Hopedale produced good working and living environments, the reasons should be determined; and if what they contributed was of importance, it should be recognized—indeed, expounded.

Part One
The Model Company Town
Chapter 2
Morphology

Although New England produced a variety of industrial settlements, from small mill villages to large corporate towns, the preconditions for development were much the same for each. The rise of industrialism and the expansion of trade created the commerce necessary for these towns to evolve. At first, development was hampered by primitive machinery, a shortage of skilled workers, and remote locations. But in time advancements in technology, availability of immigrant labor, and access to transportation overcame these limitations. However, it was the introduction of the factory system and specialization that combined to produce a distinctive type of industrial town. What distinguished model company towns from other industrial towns were important differences in operational scale, planning, ownership, and management. South Manchester, Peace Dale, Fairbanks Village, Ludlow, and Hopedale represented this new and distinctive urban form. Maps, aerial drawings, and photographs attest to the salutary visual results achieved by these towns, where the relationship between environment and society was productive and responsible. Visitors assaying the towns found them exemplary among enterprises furnishing housing, parks, and community facilities, and reports by government bureaus for labor and commerce supported their observations.[1] What is more, the relative merit of their urban design, which can still be seen and experienced, was not lost on later new-town developers.

Technological and economic advancements

By 1830 New England's economy had made a shift from mercantilism to industrialism, and many of the smallest towns and villages acquired some manufacturing enterprise as a supplement to agriculture or trade. The production of clothing goods was by far the most widespread industry. Four of the five towns studied were occupied in making cottons, woolens, silks, and textile machinery. The fifth town emerged with the invention and manufacture of platform scales. Though the textile industry dominated the economy of many settlements, some towns became known for their cordwainers and hatters, and still others specialized in making firearms and timepieces, providing rope and other naval stores, building ships, smelting ore for cast iron, smithing farm implements, and quarrying granite and firing brick. A Massachusetts survey of manufacturers in 1837 disclosed that 294 towns produced in sum sixty-eight varieties of manufactured goods.[2] From Massachusetts alone, in 1830, the value of cotton products derived from textile factories amounted to nearly half the value of all raw cotton exported from the South.[3] By 1870 the sale of cotton products in Massachusetts tripled that sold by the state's nearest competitor, neighboring Rhode Island, and was six times greater than that produced by Pennsylvania, the most competitive textile state outside New England.[4] Even though New England lagged behind other regions in agricultural production, it achieved prosperity and political clout through industry. Following Jefferson's embargo, imposed against trade with England and France (1807–9), the enactment of an "American system" of tariffs between 1816 and 1857 had further encouraged manufacture while protecting New England's economy.[5] While Boston, Newport, and Portsmouth remained chiefly mercantile cities, small inland towns beckoned their capital and labor through industry.

Manufacturing towns flourished in the decades immediately after 1830, a period Walt Rostow has named the "takeoff."[6] With technology, capital, and trade sufficient to sustain rapid economic growth, the Industrial Revolution was now well underway. Though just an initial phase in a sequence leading to the formation of a modern economy, the takeoff and subsequent "drive to maturity" encouraged specialization with the advent of the factory system. Both of these were requisite to the development of the single-enterprise manufacturing town, which appeared first in response to the textile industry.

In 1830 very few towns were single-enterprise in organization and management. Those with a large business, like a cloth manufacturer, usually supported a few smaller businesses as well. Small crafts duplicating services performed in other towns lingered well into the first decades of the nineteenth century when local economies were isolated and independent. Moreover, limited improvements in machinery kept small crafts distributively competitive. Mendon, Massachusetts, near the future site of Hopedale, contained in 1837 some eight cotton mills, four woolen mills, one furnace for iron castings, two scythe manufactories, one plow manufactory, one hat manufactory, and dozens of independent boot and shoe and wagon and harness makers for a typical New England town of population 3,657.[7] Extreme examples of this kind of early manufacturing diversification were also found outside New England, where in Lancaster, Pennsylvania, as early as 1786, 234 of 700 families were listed as manufacturers.[8] Nearly all were employed in household crafts.

Specialization replaced household crafts by consolidating manufacture in one town or region; and the company town became the manifest expression of this process. Specialization awaited the completion of a transportation network within at least regional limits and an accessible trade arrangement whereby raw materials could be procured from one site, manufactured at another, and sold at yet another. Edward C. Kirkland's *Men, Cities, and Transportation* (1948) traces this process in New England. Moreover, there had to be enough of a demand in products to justify the risk of expending large sums of capital to industrialize. Except in those instances when merchants banded together to share costs, the financing of a specialized factory site or a factory town posed a serious risk. Jefferson's secretary of the treasury, Albert Gallatin, had said that "the want of a sufficient capital was one of the most prominent of those causes impeding the growth of manufacturers in the United States."[9] With tariffs and trade assurances by the 1830s, more capital began to flow as demand for national goods increased. Demand encouraged the movement toward specialization with incentives for improved machinery to raise production, opening new markets and increasing competition in old ones.

The factory system derived from a chain of advancements in technology leading to specialization.[10] The factory system brought to one site all operations of manufacturing. It revolutionized the textile industry in New England and vastly increased the number of employees working in one location. Eventually, towns developed around one factory, populated with factory workers and their families. Though the British were first to improve textile machinery and had erected spinning mills in the 1770s,[11] they encountered difficulty in adopting the system since weaving had traditionally been a cottage industry. Weavers hesitated to leave the independence afforded by their cottages; forcing them and other skilled artisans to accept the routine of the factory proved difficult, and the struggle persisted in some Lancashire and Yorkshire towns throughout the nineteenth century.[12] New England, on the other hand, with a shortage of skilled labor and with no long-established working traditions in the textile trades or intransigent minorities of artisans, accepted the factory system without a struggle.

In 1814 the Boston Manufacturing Company of Waltham, Massachusetts, a textile mill financed by a group of merchants known as the Boston Associates and guided by Francis Cabot Lowell, combined power spinning with power weaving to found the factory system in America. According to Bishop's history of manufacture, this was the first application of the factory system in the world.[13] Whether it was the first in the world is debatable. Tench Coxe, Hamilton's able lieutenant, in addressing the "Friends of American Manufacturers" in Philadelphia in 1787, had revealed that, "strange as it may appear," machines "also card, spin, and weave by water in European factories."[14] Yet these processes were usually performed independently and housed separately in countries abroad. Cartwright's invention of the power loom in 1785, together with Crompton's spinning-mule, which combined Hargreaves's and Arkwright's inventions, removed the final obstacle to establishing the factory system. But it took about twenty-five years to iron out the minor technical problems in these inventions, and some intrigue was involved in exporting the technology. What happened at Waltham was the practical combination of all textile processes within one plant, putting to use British technology and modifying it to meet American conditions.[15] The next step was finding enough workers to operate the machinery, which could be extended considerably through the application of waterpower and by increasing the size and output of the factory. In 1787, the year of Coxe's address, attempts had been made to automate textile spinning in Philadelphia and in Beverly, Massachusetts (by horsepower); but not until Samuel Slater perfected waterpower "spinning" at Pawtucket, Rhode Island, in 1793 did the textile industry get off to a sure start.[16] Moreover, the building erected in Pawtucket was large enough to employ a dozen hands. By 1831 the average number of employees working in a cotton manufacturer's establishment had risen to sixty; in 1880 the number had climbed to 287.[17] By necessity, the advent of manufacturing towns populated by the employees of a single enterprise awaited improvements in technology and an acceptance of the factory system.

Power to operate factories lay in New England's bountiful supply of water from inland rivers and streams. Though sometimes distant to established cities and markets, the river valleys of the Blackstone, Merrimack, and Connecticut provided numerous power sites on which to build factory towns. Operators of gristmills and sawmills had harnessed the power from these rivers and their tributaries as early as the seventeenth century, so that by 1830 waterwheels were a common sight.[18] Though small streams were sufficient to operate a gristmill, large quantities of swift-moving water were needed to power factories turning elaborate machinery. Limited advantage could be obtained from a small stream by constructing a dam and reservoir and then channeling the water through a millrace to strengthen and accelerate the current; but little else could be done to improve a weak site. Searching for suitable places in which to construct factories dispersed manufacturers throughout New England along its undeveloped river valleys. The centrifugal flow of industrial expansion continued in the textile industry until 1850. After 1850, however, expansion ebbed in the wake of specialization and increased competition as a result of centralization: in New England the number of cotton textile establishments declined from 570 in 1850 to 564 in 1860, 508 in 1870, and 439 in 1880, though total production increased.[19] Concurrent with a decline in the number of establishments was a decline in the population of many rural agricultural and mixed-economy villages.[20] Yet prior to 1850 the pursuit of waterpower and new industries had encouraged the building of new towns.

The location of power sites created topographic problems in terms of land development. Dams, embankments, and reservoirs had to be built before factories could commence production. If more than one factory were contemplated, the industrialist had to plan and space them apart in a line along the fall of a river or canal, limiting the extent of development. Depending upon the width of the valley or the contour of the surrounding terrain, the settlement about the factory either fanned out or stretched along one or both sides of the river. Good power and building sites were not always compatible, and many towns, built to harness the water, were awkwardly planted on irregular sites with houses precariously pitched on steep grades. Building towns in such locations required forethought and planning.

The alternative to building a town around a power site was to find another source of power and bring it to an already established town, and the only alternative to the fixed source of water was steam. Had the portable steam engine been perfected and sources of fuel been available in the beginning, the company town in New England might never have emerged. New England used steam power sparingly, though elsewhere it was largely responsible for setting the Industrial Revolution in motion. Rhode Island's Samuel Slater explained in 1833 that "The amount of water power still unoccupied is very great. With such a redundancy of this natural agent, the more expensive one of steam has been, so far, very little used and only under particular circumstances of location and business."[21] Though waterwheels would continue as the chief motive for manufacturing during the first decades of industrialization because of New England's bountiful rivers and streams, the improvement and American manufacture of steam engines together with the excavation of soft coal from western Pennsylvania for fuel provided an alternative source of energy by the 1830s. However, the cost of mining and shipping coal by barge, ship, and rail to New England caused the price of fuel to be financially prohibitive, especially for small towns in the hinterland.[22] So reliant were industrialists on waterpower that the government published a special report on it in 1885, giving a historical, geographical, and statistical account:

> It is probably safe to say that in no other country in the world is an equal amount of power utilized. . . . Such is the energy developed by our rivers, streams, and brooks, of which we are using but little over half of one per cent. Could it all be utilized, the power afforded would probably be more than sufficient to turn all the machinery on the globe.[23]

Not until the decade 1870–80 did the number and horsepower of steam engines used throughout the states equal and surpass that of waterwheels. During that decade, however, the percentage increase of waterwheels and steam engines rose disproportionately a respective 8 and 40 percent.[24] Nonetheless, only two New England states, Massachusetts and Rhode Island, made the crossover from water to steam at that period. The percentage of total power generated by Vermont's factories slipped very little in dependence upon water, from 88 to 83 percent between 1870 and 1880, indicative of the fact that many New England towns remained fixed to their water resources throughout the nineteenth century. And manufacturing continued to be carried on in sometimes isolated places, distant from the centers of market.

To a lesser extent, transportation occupies a place in the development and later growth of the company town. Routes for shipping raw materials and manufactured goods connected larger towns and cities first by road and then by rail. New England's rivers and streams were usually unnavigable for barges or commercial packets, except along coastal estuaries, and the prospect for digging canals through to New York seemed geographically impractical. But in 1835 the Boston and Providence Railroad brought a new era to transportation and economic growth.[25]

Although the railroad spread rapidly throughout New England during the 1840s and 1850s, it came too late to affect the location of most towns built for commerce. In fact, its logistic implications were minor in regard to settlement. Most of the track laid before the Civil War stretched between the larger cities, while small farming villages and manufacturing towns were left to make connections as best they could. Company teamsters regularly drove wagonloads of manufactured goods to the nearest railheads until a spur line could be built.[26] Ludlow and Fairbanks Village were fortunate in lying within a few miles of main lines in the mid-1840s; but Peace Dale, thirty miles south of Providence, did not receive access (to the Narragansett Pier Railroad) until 1876, after many years as a successful enterprise.[27] Hopedale waited until 1889 before it received a small electric railroad, the Grafton and Upton, which ran to Worcester.[28] South Manchester, on the other hand, was better situated in being two miles south of a junction on the New York and New England Railroad. The main line was laid in 1854, and the South Manchester spur was tied into it in 1869.[29]

The railroad came after initial commitment to site development and was thus a secondary consideration insofar as building layout was concerned. The lack of rail service prevented a major improvement in factory power by supplementing water with steam, since getting coal or even wood in sufficient quantities was limited without a direct line or port. The time lag in gaining rail access permitted these company towns to plan streets and build factories and houses without the imposition of a track, which frequently bifurcated the plans of later towns. In terms of commerce and town planning, the introduction of the railroad brought only latent changes in the operation and appearance of the company town in New England.

From industrial village to company town: four examples

By midcentury, a rationally laid and visually distinct type of industrial village had begun to replace the solitary mill with its random assortment of cottages. Some of these villages, in turn, formed model company towns. To assert the model company town as a type that differed from other towns, it is necessary to describe a representative sample.

Picture, for example, the view from a hilltop that lies inland and distant from the activity of a busy port. From this hilltop it is easy to scan the valley below. A narrow though swiftly flowing river follows the contour of a ravine before widening into a small lake above a dam. In the background are mostly frame buildings, though some are brick or stone. Interspersed among them are oak, elm, hickory, and maple trees. The scene could be reminiscent of a Currier and Ives lithograph commemorating an annual season; yet something is different. A group of small factories figure more prominently in this landscape than the traditional meetinghouse with its steeple. And the noise of water falling from the dam is suppressed by the droning sound of machinery. A smokestack by a foundry sends a plume of smoke into the air. Nearby the factories are clusters of small houses, which are alike in detail—too similar in appearance to account for a native building type. The landscape opens at intervals to reveal the contours of a park or cemetery. Everything appears tidy and well kept. Overall, an impression of order, routine, prosperity, and propriety is inescapable. The following towns could be introduced by such a general sketch, even though they are distant to one another and vary in manufacture and site.

SOUTH MANCHESTER, CONNECTICUT

Cheney Brothers Manufacturing Company at South Manchester illustrates such a scene as described above. The enterprise commenced in 1838 with the construction of the first factory and one small boardinghouse. Gradually it expanded from a village of twenty-five hundred people in 1870 to a town of more than five thousand by the turn of the century.[30] It was the first company town to place equal emphasis on producing a good environment while manufacturing a good product. The landscape of South Manchester was a garden in comparison to the back-lot appearance usually described in factory towns. Industrialists, labor economists, and social reformers cited South Manchester because of its appearance and administration as a factory town worthy of emulation.[31] The author of one article wrote: "Here in this little village are gathered the materials to furnish an epitome of the industrial and social development of the country during this century."[32] This 1872 observer pictured the model company town in much the same light as did proponents of the "Garden City in America" a generation later.

The Cheney family's history on the site went back to the mideighteenth century, when in 1753 three brothers owned adjoining farms in Hartford County fifteen miles east of the capital. One brother, Timothy Cheney, built a saw, grist, and fulling mill on the bank of a stream that ran through his property, while another, Silas, experimented with growing an orchard of mulberry trees.[33] To host a silk culture, mulberry trees had been planted in Virginia as early as 1627 and grown in Connecticut by 1763. Efforts to establish the culture in Connecticut encouraged some speculation in the production of raw silk, but the plant never thrived in the New England climate. Attempts were made to revive the culture in the 1830s with a stronger tree, the *Morus multicaulis*. In 1833 three of Silas Cheney's grandsons established a nursery and profited so well from the sale of these trees during the "*Morus multicaulis* craze" of 1836 (when saplings sold for seven dollars a dozen) that they were able to purchase fifty thousand dollars' worth of machinery to process and weave silk.[34]

Having set up the machinery, Charles, Ward, and Frank Cheney proceeded with the first application of the factory system to the manufacture of silk in America. Not until the 1830s had silk reeling and weaving machinery been perfected for power operation.[35] In 1840 the effects of a depression and a plant blight had destroyed the market for trees, but the brothers found a way to secure raw silk from the Orient and to survive as manufacturers. With their attention focused upon the processing of silk, they began enlarging the factory and building a town. The Hop-brook stream, which powered the earlier gristmill, was next used to power a factory with one undershot wheel at the base of a six-foot dam. Another factory was constructed in the early 1850s and operated by two water turbines capable of producing forty horsepower. Steam power arrived later with the building of three new factories in 1872, which replaced the earlier frame buildings with long brick structures three stories in height. By this date, the brothers had united the family's landholdings to include one thousand acres, on part of which two hundred single- and double-family houses were placed for a work force of nearly a thousand.

2. View of South Manchester, Conn. (Boston:
O. H. Bailey, 1880). Note the abundance of trees
and the proximity of houses to factories.
Courtesy of the Maps Division of the Library of
Congress.

South Manchester (fig. 2) was not built for the purpose of real estate speculation; had it been, the site layout might have taken a more familiar and rectangular appearance. The Cheneys did not follow a formula or a set pattern in laying out their town; guiding them was the idea that the town was their home, and "we like it to look nice, that's all."[36] Interspersed between the houses of the workers were the homes of the family. In some respects, the town can be compared with the earliest New England villages, which functionally developed in the shape of "spinal or nucleated" sites depending on the terrain. One similarity was the town common: at South Manchester the common or green was not limited to one central enclosure about which a few houses were clustered but was an avenue of natural landscaping intersected by streets and as broad as 250 feet between cottages. It was in appearance a residential parkway.[37] In 1872 one main street skirted the town, separating the factories from the houses and community facilities. After 1838 the farm gave place to the town, though retained was an open terrain enhanced by groves of shade trees. In one corner of the site was a "wooded knoll which has been left an unchanged natural forest, traversed by picturesque walks."[38] Houses were kept well back from the streets, and the construction of fences was prohibited, so as not to interfere with the "parklike" setting. Within the housing area, minor streets were laid in contour with the land; gravel on top of a clay base served as paving, and wood planking was used for walks. Stylistic attention focused upon Cheney Hall, the town library and lyceum, a building constructed in 1849 from profits derived during the Mexican War from the sale of silk flags and gold braid. The attractive Italianate building lay in the residential park with a vista to the houses and grounds. Uniform construction and periodic maintenance established continuity in building design as a pleasant complement to the site.

South Manchester presented an image of disciplined space; variety in landscape checked the more formal arrangement of the buildings.

Moreover, there existed a scale proportionate in the total enterprise to the purpose of the individual buildings. In a clearing to one side lay the factories while, across the way, the workers' houses centered about Cheney Hall and a small meetinghouse. Each building occupied a well-chosen site in the visual organization of the town. In 1890, after sixty-two years of controlled development, the town was described as follows:

> It is not marked by the regularity of newness that characterizes Pullman; it is a well-grown, time-mellowed rural community, dwelling in a well-trimmed park, away from the clamor of the machinery with which it does its daily tasks. . . . The principal mill buildings—red brick, many-windowed—stand in a treeless, grassy spot near the railroad station. There is plenty of sunshine pouring into the rooms. . . . Almost immediately, however, one enters the thickly shaded place where the dwellings are. It is an essential feature of the village, one which cannot be made too clear, that the men and women—mostly women—do not look from their homes upon the walls of their workshop.[39]

The layout of South Manchester drew the attention of the Industrial Commission during its investigation of "Manufactures and Business" in 1901. Frank W. Cheney was questioned about the company housing, which occupied "a beautiful park surrounded by well-kept lawns and meadows and beautiful shade trees." When complimented on these "model" provisions, Cheney protested that "we [the company] are not in the model-village line. . . . We live here. This is our home, and, selfishly, we like to keep it in order."[40] His modest reply was probably intended to avoid appearing paternalistic, for the result of Pullman was well known. Yet the investigators were fascinated by the model layout and its effects upon the work force.

The attractive setting and thoughtful juxtaposition of buildings probably could not have been obtained without the supervision of a small and sustaining family of owner-managers who took a special interest in the enterprise and town. Even though the Cheneys had an office in Hartford, they made South Manchester their home. An abiding interest in the site avoided heedless construction, which would have detracted from the parklike setting and natural surroundings in which the buildings were placed.

PEACE DALE, RHODE ISLAND

Peace Dale occupies a site faithful to its name in a quiet valley near South Kingston, some thirty miles south of Providence and across Narragansett Bay from Newport. Rowland G. Hazard (1801–88) named the town for his wife, Mary Dale, and it became the home for several generations of his family. Hazard was principally an industrialist involved in woolen manufacture, but later in life he turned to politics and philosophy. He served in the state legislature of Rhode Island, worked as a founding member of the Republican party, spoke as an ardent abolitionist, and corresponded with John Stuart Mill.[41] Above all, he had a fascination for mechanical objects and a keen mind for business. Upon retirement in 1879, he left the enterprise he founded with a capital stock of $200,000. Apparently, the site had been occupied by the family as early as 1802, and in either 1814 or 1815 power looms were being employed there to weave coarse woolens.[42] It was not until 1848, however, that Hazard began to operate on a large scale with the completion of a new factory and with a work force other than his family. In that year the business was reorganized as the Peace Dale Manufacturing Company, specializing in fine woolens, such as shawls, worsted coatings, and cassimeres.[43]

With the completion of another factory in 1856 and yet another in 1872, the town continued to expand. Proceeds from the company were used to construct houses and public buildings for the workers, who numbered approximately 450 in 1885. The population of Peace Dale increased from little more than eight hundred in 1870 to over fifteen hundred by 1890.[44] A school was built in 1854 so that children would not have to walk to South Kingston, and in 1856 a library began distributing books from a house formerly inhabited by one of the family. The library was a special concern to Hazard, a self-educated man, and it was eventually placed in the new meetinghouse in 1872, where it remained until the construction of Hazard Memorial Hall in 1891. His grandson, also named Rowland G. Hazard, managed the enterprise from 1879 until his death in 1918. A museum composed mostly of Indian artifacts was his gift to the town.[45] In describing the relationship of the Hazards to their town, a government report noted:

> The Hazards have their homes in Peace Dale and make its material and moral prosperity their concern. Their residences are unpretentious, offering no occasion of envy to their employees. Rowland G. Hazard was a Quaker. It was his honorable ambition to make his business a blessing to all connected with it. His influence lives in the policy of the company and in the economic prosperity and moral wellbeing of its workpeople.[46]

This concern extended to the buildings and grounds and to the factories and workers' housing as well.

The appearance of Peace Dale has changed little since the turn of the century. A landscaped park with colorful flowers calls attention to the center of town. A stream passes through the park before reaching the mills, where it once operated turbines to power the machinery. The factories are three stories in height and constructed of local stone, conveying the image of a substantial industrial presence. The foursquare office building with its richly corbeled cornice, hipped roof with dormers, and massive chimney still exhibits the pride of this once thriving enterprise. A meetinghouse in the Romanesque Revival style sits off to one side of the group of factories and public buildings, though all of the larger buildings are tied together visually because of the consistency of materials—especially the buff-colored stone—and the careful site planning. The more prominent sites were reserved for the public edifices, and at the base of each ornamental evergreens were planted. Though the modest single- and double-family frame houses have long since been sold off, they appear to be well maintained. Despite the passing of time, Peace Dale has maintained the integrity of its earlier planning, and the Hazard family is remembered with affection.

FAIRBANKS VILLAGE, VERMONT

Fairbanks Village of E. and T. Fairbanks and Company lies immediately west of Saint Johnsbury Plain along the Passumpsic River valley. Saint Johnsbury was staked out as a township in northeastern Vermont toward the end of the eighteenth century through the efforts of a country squire and physician, Dr. Jonathan Arnold. The quietude of the small agricultural settlement lasted until 1815, when Joseph Fairbanks of Brimfield, Vermont, relocated with the purpose of building a gristmill on the banks of Sleeper's River, which skirted the township on the west. For the next fifteen years Fairbanks and his three sons, Erastus, Thaddeus, and Joseph P., operated their mill in grinding meal and in hammering iron for wagons and plows. But in 1830 they launched a new enterprise with the manufacture of a weighing device. Having had difficulty in judging the weight of wagonloads of grain at the mill, Thaddeus Fairbanks, the second-eldest son, invented the "platform scale." Now, instead of hoisting a weight to counterbalance, a load could simply be rolled into place. Thaddeus and his two brothers took out a patent in 1831 and reportedly were deluged with orders shortly thereafter.[47] Fairbanks Platform Scales were manufactured to nearly every size and use from the tiniest balance to huge weighing locks on the Erie Canal.[48] In later years, the brothers were honored at international trade fairs throughout the world for the precision and quality of their product.[49]

Factories, stores, and houses were put up by the company beginning in the 1830s and furnished with an aqueduct for fresh water and sewers for refuse by midcentury. By the end of the century, the company had constructed a gas plant and an electric generator to heat and light its homes. In 1870 the population amounted to nearly twenty-seven hundred, a number that would double by the turn of the century.[50] The company underwent enlargement in 1875 to accommodate an expanded plant and residential area. Seventy new houses of a double-family type were constructed for part of five hundred additional workers. To design the streets and houses, the Fairbankses employed a relatively unknown architect and landscapist named Lambert Packard, who had earlier received commissions for several community buildings.[51] Packard laid the streets to follow the turns in terrain imposed by the river valley. The company maintained all the land along a two-mile length of the river and landscaped it as a public park. This was a protectionary measure to avoid the cutting of timber along the banks and the obstruction of the river, which operated the factories.

The Fairbankses predominated in the business and social activities of Saint Johnsbury. Having acquired great wealth, the brothers gave unstintingly to the enhancement and social betterment of the village they built and the township in which they resided. Erastus's sons, Horace and Franklin, carried on the fortunes of the company while finding time for philanthropic pursuits. Horticulture, natural history, art, and literature each found a home at Fairbanks Village, where the brothers erected several fine buildings to house their collections. Open and free to the public, these facilities provided inhabitants of the village and township with opportunities for cultural enjoyment rarely accorded small towns. In 1841 Thaddeus erected an academy for instruction in general courses. By 1872 it had thirteen instructors, three hundred pupils, and a $100,000 endowment from the company. Horace Fairbanks built the Saint Johnsbury Athenaeum in 1871, "the first public free library with endowment in Vermont."[52] In 1890 brother Franklin built a museum for the village to contain his natural history collection. These community facilities seem to have been one dimension of an even broader interest in their town's environment. In addition to these, the brothers encouraged parks and grounds improvement to bring industry and society together in a harmonious relationship.

LUDLOW, MASSACHUSETTS

Ludlow, Massachusetts, like South Manchester, Peace Dale, and Fairbanks Village, presented the image of a model company town, though it developed differently and at a later period. Ludlow was a small manufacturing and farming village of several hundred people when the "Ludlow Associates" purchased fifteen hundred acres northeast of Springfield in 1868. The purchase included most of the existing village. In effect, a single enterprise was superimposed on the foundations of an earlier settlement, an undertaking not without precedent, as will be seen in Hopedale.

Years before, in 1848, Charles T. Hubbard had purchased a cotton textile factory[53] on the banks of the Chicopee River, which ran through Ludlow, but was unable to expand his operation until after the Civil War. Then, in partnership with his sons and two other men, Col. Cranmore N. Wallace and John E. Stevens, Hubbard founded the Ludlow Associates. The new enterprise began in a big way with a large acquisition of property, which protected their interests for later expansion. There were certain advantages in taking over and expanding an already established site. In addition to the earlier factory were buildings for immediate occupancy and industrial use; moreover, the village was near a railroad for transportation. First steps had been taken to harness the abundant waterpower that was available. An early historian of Ludlow recalled in 1868, at the time of the takeover, that the "village consisted of very few old tenement houses, one church and one single-room schoolhouse owned by the company, situated on two country roads." Within a decade, however, the condition of Ludlow changed markedly: "new streets were constructed, a number of new cottages and a six-room schoolhouse were built."[54] Then, between 1878 and 1900, the Associates further expanded the enterprise to include a library with clubrooms, "dining-rooms outside the works," and a hotel, plus 350 houses for twelve hundred of their eighteen hundred workers at the close of the century. During this period, the company built "seven miles of good streets . . . with gutters of concrete and sidewalks curbed with the same material" and provided "a public park," gas and electric plant, and waterworks.[55]

Boosting Ludlow's economy to finance such growth was the manufacture of burlap in supplement to cotton textiles. Burlap was the material used chiefly in baling raw cotton shipped from the South. Hemp had formerly been used in the manufacture of burlap, but a stronger, more elastic fiber was jute, a plant grown in the Orient. When the Ludlow Manufacturing Company could not get a sufficient supply of jute, it set up a plantation in East India to cultivate the plant and within a few years became both supplier and manufacturer, a protectionary procedure that Firestone and other companies would later follow.

The Hubbards' interest in site planning differed from the Cheneys'. Ludlow had not been a venerable family homestead like South Manchester. It had not been settled by the Hubbards. However, the pace of development at Ludlow forced recognition of the need for site control and building organization to meet the needs of factory expansion and production. When the company erected its first houses in the 1870s, several multifamily tenements were included; but the management quickly discovered a reticence among workers with families to live in them.[56] The workers preferred single- or double-family houses, even if it meant living elsewhere. Numbers of employees commuted from Springfield by train, though the inconvenience and expense of travel along with the higher rent discouraged some of the better-skilled workers. For these reasons and to keep the better-trained workers from leaving, the Ludlow Associates proceeded to build model houses rented at nominal sums. The original tenements were converted into boardinghouses for single men.

A policy of selling houses affected both control and site improvement: sold units eventually detracted from the appearance and maintenance standards set by the company. Why should the company have cared once the houses were sold? The answer was that it had a long-term investment in the site; many houses would continue to be rented, and property values needed to be protected. Agent Stevens observed:

> When we first began building the modern type of cottage . . . it was our policy to sell to any of our operatives who cared to buy, and as a matter of fact we did sell several cottages with lots of about one-quarter acre. We sold the cottages for about the cost of building, calling the land nothing, and making easy terms of payment. This plan, however, did not work out successfully for the reason that rules drawn up to promote the health and comfort of the community at large could not be enforced against individual holders. For this and kindred reasons we have ceased to sell cottages and, in fact, bought back at a premium those we sold. Our rents are made as low as can consistently be done, and are much lower than the prevailing rents in this neighborhood.[57]

A further examination of Ludlow's model houses will follow in chapter 4 to illustrate why the first U.S. commissioner of labor proclaimed them to be the best workers' cottages in America in 1880.

These model company towns, though responding to differences in manufacture and site conditions, were distinctly similar in type. Their developers treated all ancillary space around the factories as an integral extension of the enterprise. As a result, they managed to coordinate living and working arrangements. Even when winning recognition at trade fairs for the quality of their products, a regular event, these companies received honors (sometimes at the same fair) for their workers' houses and community facilities.[58] Economic and geographic limitations required experimentation in building factories and towns. The energy that had been applied to improving machinery and fabrics went into the organization and administration of entire towns. Before cities actively sought industries by providing modern industrial parks, furnished with utilities, access to highways, and nearby tracts of housing, a much larger commitment to environmental development fell to individual companies, whose towns represent important initiatives in this wholesale approach to meeting urban requirements.

From company town to new town

The development of comprehensively designed, single-enterprise towns continued into the twentieth century and survives today in somewhat modified forms. After 1870 big industries tended to concentrate in cities, reversing the centrifugal movement of the preceding period. New sources of energy, improved transportation, and an abundance of labor caused this reversal. However, a diminishing supply of land in the central city for large-scale plant construction, together with congestion, pollution, and high land costs, soon resulted in peripheral or satellite industrial developments.[59] Eventually, with these, new towns appeared.

Mentioned in the introduction were industrial satellites and new towns. Each possess design features in site planning, housing, and community facilities comparable to the earlier company town. Creese and Burke in their investigations of nineteenth-century town planning in Britain establish a connection between the model industrial village and the garden city.[60] A similar connection exists between the various types of single-enterprise towns in America. Common to all single-enterprise towns, whether built by private firms or government agencies, are the ingredients of (1) a central authority directing planning and construction, (2) a standard house type, and (3) community programs and facilities to edify newcomers while providing social diversion. Differences appear in technological advances and operational scale, but the approach to overall design has changed little. The elimination of physically prominent and centrally located factories constitutes the principal difference in the layout of the company town of the 1860s and the renascent new towns of the 1960s, since residential construction and public utilities are no longer dependent on local industry. Workers commute to jobs in nearby cities, and land companies in charge of development have based their sales strategy on places to live and escape from work. Despite these differences, a thread of continuity as regards comprehensive design stretches from the first company towns to new-town developments.

INDUSTRIAL SATELLITE TOWNS, THE GARDEN CITIES OF AMERICA

The distinction between company town and satellite town is in name only. Neponsit Garden Village (1907) and Indian Hill (1912), Massachusetts; Eclipse Park (1918), Kistler (1918), and Kohler (1915), Wisconsin; Firestone Park (1916) and Goodyear Heights (1913), Ohio; Alcoa (1919), Erwin (1914), and Kingsport (1915), Tennessee; Corey [Fairfield] (1909), and Kaulton (1912), Alabama; Torrance (1912), California; and Hershey (1903), Pennsylvania, to cite the better known, were single-enterprise industrial towns. The men who planned them were for the most part landscape architects with prior experience in designing company towns.[61] Popular periodicals and professional journals mistakenly labeled these places as American garden cities.[62] But they shared nothing in common with the English garden city except an affinity for small cottages and neatly trimmed hedges. Georges Benoît-Lévy, the French proponent of the *cité jardin*, even went so far as to include Aurora, New York, and Paterson, New Jersey, in his survey of America.[63] However much these places fall short of the principles laid down by Ebenezer Howard, they do represent a continuation of single-enterprise towns into the first decades of the twentieth century. All were founded by industrialists and provided homes to working-class families, though they were not part of a regional plan coordinated with a goal to relieving the population of larger industrial cities. In fact, most, like Goodyear Heights near Akron, developed by the Goodyear Tire and Rubber Company for three thousand of its employees and planned by Warren Henry Manning with houses designed by architects Mann and MacNeille, were eventually absorbed by their larger neighbors.[64] The objectives for which they were built are listed by their founders:

1. To select a location conveniently related to raw materials, markets, water or other power, or good industrial water supply, and having a favorable climate.
2. To attract a supply of labor, adequate in quantity and quality.
3. To stabilize the labor supply and minimize labor turnover by providing facilities for family life (in contradistinction to factory conditions) at a cost within the earning power of the workers. . . .
4. To escape the undue competition for labor in an existing community, the high land values and operating costs without commensurate return, and in general to have a more free hand, unhampered by adverse conditions due to past developments.[65]

The first three reasons echo conditions sought in founding the company town in New England, and the last one reflects a change in employment attitude because of "the undue dominance of 'organized labor'" after 1880. The company town as it lasted into the first decades of the twentieth century remained largely the product of a regional economy.

Its dissolution can be attributed mostly to economic and technical changes. The period between 1870 and 1920 has been associated with the rise of the big city and the maturation of a national economy.[66] Though the satellite town made its appearance during this period, the trend was toward centralization and agglomeration in both industry and urban development. Perhaps the best example of this trend can be seen in the steel industry. Until 1910 it had followed a course of decentralization, but within a decade the cycle reversed. Only a few of its industrial satellites have survived intact, let alone expanded. Gary, Indiana, is a notable exception. Many others lost their physical identity and political sovereignty as a result of annexation. The advent of new technologies, such as steam and hydroelectric power generation, no longer necessitated plant location near a natural water resource. And low-fare streetcars, interurban trains, and inexpensive automobiles like the Model T Ford eliminated the need for industrially developed housing estates placed in walking distance to factories. The future of single-enterprise towns lay not in the direction of traditional industrial expansion but rather outside the private market in the period between World Wars I and II.

GOVERNMENT TOWNS

Government objectives in new-town building have been threefold: to establish sites for national defense, to resettle urban dwellers, and to develop national resources. With each there has been a quasi-private objective usually resulting in private ownership after a period of government management. Despite the reticence on the part of government officials to interfere in the mechanisms of a free market, especially in something as prosaic as workers' housing and town planning, they recognized the limitations of private enterprise in initiating and carrying out large-scale projects. In 1918 Congress established the United States Housing Corporation to plan and build homes for some of the estimated 300,000 itinerant war workers who had been attracted to eastern industrial cities during the war. Of sixty-seven proposed housing projects, only twenty-seven neared completion when the war ended and money for construction was discontinued.[67] These projects either abutted cities as residential suburbs in places like Waterbury and Bridgeport, Connecticut, or were located as satellites a few miles away as in the example of Atlantic Heights near Portsmouth, New Hampshire. All were dependent upon the city for municipal services and functioned as residential communities. Enlightened as some of these war housing projects were in terms of planning, few successfully recovered from the transition from public to private when funds for maintenance were cut off and when the housing was divided up for private sale.[68] Planning lessons offered by these communities were forgotten when annexed by their larger neighbors; and, as a result of little or no zoning protection, these war housing developments can barely be distinguished within the built-up areas that later enveloped them.

The Greenbelt towns, as their name implies, tried to avoid suburban entrapment by means of a protective buffer. The Greenbelts emerged from the designs drafted by the Resettlement Administration (RA), which was founded in 1935 as one of several New Deal planning agencies. The Greenbelts qualify as the most interesting, yet least pragmatic of all government attempts at new-town development. Controversial and destined to draw fire from conservative opponents, they purported to show how crowded urban workers could be resettled into low-density communities located in areas peripheral to core industrial cities. Their approach to the urban problem was essentially one of abandonment, like earlier twentieth-century industrial satellites. Greendale, Wisconsin; Greenhills, Ohio; and Greenbelt, Maryland, moved too slowly under the aegis of government administration, mismanaging time, money, and design talent as construction dragged along.[69] Greenbelt, Maryland, which came nearest to completion, suffered through political infighting and administrative setbacks that stymied construction for lack of funds and time and again compromised the design program. Greenbelt would have combined industry, housing, and community facilities, protected by a surrounding park; however, after several clusters of houses, a school, and a few commercial shops were constructed, the entire project succumbed to the private auction block in 1954.[70]

In contrast to the Greenbelts were the Tennessee Valley Authority (TVA) towns, also a product of the thirties. Confronted then as now with an energy crisis, the government sponsored regional power sites and received congressional approval and public support. Though industrialists including Henry Ford once offered to finance the construction of hydroelectric power sites, such as Muscle Shoals, Alabama,[71] the threat of having private companies further monopolize electric utilities deterred this alternative to federal control, and, subsequently, the Depression put an end to the matter. The Tennessee Valley Authority Act passed Congress in 1933 during the halcyon days of New Deal diplomacy along with the National Industrial Recovery Act, which superintended the RA's Greenbelts. The purpose of the TVA was to rebuild the economy of a chronically depressed region by erecting power stations along the turbulent Tennessee River. The new construction sites would create thousands of jobs and relieve the economic plight of the region, eventually establishing a new labor base and social prosperity. This technological and economic boost to the region was President Roosevelt's own vision, though inspiration and guidance came largely from Sen. George Norris.[72]

The first TVA town, Norris, Tennessee, hardly differs in program or design from the company town. Construction began in 1934 and continued until 1956, completing the initial phase of planning. The town provided housing and services to the Norris Dam workers and their families and later furnished space for private industry. Without industry, the town would have withered after the dam was constructed. By 1936 Norris had attracted 1,350 people of a projected 5,000, and construction had already commenced on 350 dwellings. A mix of boardinghouses, duplexes, and single-family houses composed the first residential group. Most were furnished with running water, electric lighting and heating (a few burned coal), water closets, and baths, which made them even at this date examples of efficiency in workers' housing. Placed in one location and separate from the houses were buildings composing the civic center, which included a school with gymnasium and a commercial block.[73]

Streets followed the contour of the terrain, which sloped irregularly upward from the banks of the Tennessee River. Special care in paving avoided excessive land cuts, fills, and drainage problems while making the most of the aesthetic potential of the heavily forested site. The town covered part of a two-thousand-acre tract of pine forest; and because of the irregular surrounding terrain and natural beauty of the site, the plan received careful attention. Regulations were established to protect against unwanted development. Part of the TVA program stipulated that the power site should eventually be leased or sold to private interests, attracting industry and additional housing once the area reached completion of the first phase of growth. Nonetheless, no concessions were made that would spoil the site or risk it to the whims of future private developers. The pattern of growth received thoughtful study with streets laid in such a way that residential additions would spore from the end of several street terminals. Existing plots of houses conformed to the site in a manner that prevented subdividing. Restrictions were imposed to protect the site and to regulate admissible development.

Responsible for the administration and planning of Norris were Arthur E. Morgan, Earle S. Draper, and Tracy B. Augur, whose solutions had sources in common. Morgan, first chairman of the TVA, experimented with the model-community idea and later wrote a book entitled *The Philosophy of Edward Bellamy* (1945).[74] He coordinated plant operation with town organization, determining a need for community facilities in supplement of housing. "A benevolent labor policy formed an important part of the Norris community. Morgan insisted that there be a close and friendly relationship between labor and management."[75] Paternal supervision appeared with self-improvement courses, which placed men in classrooms during their idle hours and gave women lessons in homemaking, child study, weaving, and home furnishing. These educational activities took place in the school and library, located together on a plateau to one side of the residential site. Morgan recognized Norris's need for organized social activity because of a rapidly assembled transient population that would eventually move on to other jobs.

Both Draper and Augur were designers. Draper's town-planning experience came from fifteen years of designing company towns in the South. Among these his finest achievement was Chicopee, Georgia (1927), which fully embraced contour planning and low-density detached housing.[76] Other company towns designed by Draper include Biltmore, Lexington, and Pineville, North Carolina; Abbeville, Pacolet, Laurens, Whitmire, and East Spartanburg, South Carolina; and West Point, Georgia.[77] These places were emulative of the company town in New England and were developed by the textile industry, which had begun expanding to southern locations after 1880. Both Draper and Augur, the latter of whom wrote an M.L.A. thesis at Harvard in 1921 on the design of industrial towns,[78] were greatly influenced by another planner of company towns, John Nolen. Nolen laid out Neponsit Garden Village at Walpole, Massachusetts, for the C. S. Bird and Sons paper factory in 1909 before journeying to Tennessee in 1915 to design Kingsport.[79] Nolen, sometimes titled the "father of American town planning," designed many settlements and was a contributing figure along with Warren Henry Manning and Frederick Law Olmsted, Jr., in extending the number of designed single-enterprise towns from New England to points west. They also encouraged the government to support comprehensive planning and regional development.

What Norris obtained that the Greenbelts did not was operational autonomy and economic independence. Norris, like South Manchester, for example, managed to combine industry and housing in a parklike setting through careful planning. Its future lay within proscribed physical limits. Greenbelt and other strictly residential settlements, on the other hand, were dependent upon neighboring cities for employment and services. The result sacrificed internal stability and design control.

NEW TOWNS

Government-sponsored new towns contributed to the advancement of comprehensive planning and urban design. They met objectives unattainable through private enterprise. In more than a dozen new towns founded since the 1960s, studies in regional planning and site analysis reflect decisions or policies put to use in the Greenbelt and TVA towns. Founders of the Regional Planning Association of America (RPAA),[80] who supported these government endeavors, were inspired by the public's willingness to address social and environmental issues. Their appeal to regional planning and urban decentralization stems from Howard's garden-city program which, though broadly revised, was adopted in Britain with the passage of the New Towns Act in 1946.[81] But, unlike Britain and Europe, American government got out of the business of building towns and into the business of mortgaging them. This lesser role, which is more compatible with free enterprise, derived from the New Deal legislation of the thirties and survives today in the various entitlements of the housing acts superintended by the Department of Housing and Urban Development.[82] But, as British planner J. R. Atkinson wryly observed, "Everyone knows in the United States 'the least government is the best government' and that private initiative is all important.''[83] Private enterprise thus continues its historic and central role in new-town development.

The renascent new towns of the 1960s and 1970s in some ways return to the earlier mold, at least in their insistence on entrepreneurial control and single-enterprise development. Reston, Virginia; Columbia, Maryland; Jonathan, Minnesota; Irvine and Valencia, California; Woodland, Texas; and Park Forest South, Illinois, to cite the more successful, each pursues long-range building schedules of twenty-five to fifty years within a protected reserve of twenty-five hundred acres or more.[84] Their development strategies are more sophisticated than those of their industrial antecedents. Emphasis is placed on residential, not industrial, construction; shopping centers, schools, and libraries dominate the center of town; factories, if found at all, occupy a peripheral location beyond the park. Dependent on larger cities for employment, utilities, and services, they are economically and sometimes administratively subordinate to the metropolis. These new towns appeal to a broader cross-section of people, though they fail to offer an effective alternative to traditional urban development. As long as housing remains their chief attraction, less exclusive suburban developments with fewer amenities will attract greater numbers of residents.

Model company towns, industrial satellites, and government towns—now followed in turn by a later generation of new towns—have never posed a serious alternative to conventional urban development. Protectionary restrictions on land use through single-enterprise ownership places a limit on physical expansion and deters outside investment. Their contribution to urban history lies outside the mainstream of urban development. What they provide are examples of good site planning, landscaping, architecture, and environmental management.

Chapter 3
Paternalism

A means for shaping an industrial society that drew heavily on environmental planning and architecture as reinforcement was paternalism. Despite the resentment it may have fostered among workers, resulting from attempts at social engineering, paternalism was considered by many nineteenth-century businessmen to be a moral responsibility, protecting society while furthering business. Apart from administrative policies affecting company operations, a human factor also was involved. Anthony F. C. Wallace, for example, found among the leading families of Rockdale, Pennsylvania, a "Christian industrialism" emerging during the middle decades of the century.[1] Its underlying features included a pervasive evangelism, a Protestant work ethic, and a belief in the principle of noblesse oblige. It prompted employers to exercise responsibility not only in the internal affairs of their companies but in external matters as well.

In managing or regulating the affairs of employees living and working in a company town, some industrialists found paternalism a useful policy; and for a few, it became an obsession. At the outset it was a ploy to attract labor, but as the pastoral mill village grew more businesslike, paternalism shifted from procurement to management. This pattern was followed not only in manufacturing towns but also in places of extractive industry—mining towns, oil towns, and lumber towns—where it became a contributing factor in labor disputes over management practices.[2] As organized labor achieved some success in raising wages and lowering working hours, paternalistic policies became less benign and more coercive. The climactic struggle of the will of management over the will of labor was waged in the Midwest at Pullman, Illinois, now a Chicago suburb, in 1894. Soon after the Pullman strike, the light of paternalism diminished when critics assailed it as autocratic, feudal, and un-American—therefore doomed to failure.[3] But disputes over paternalism largely escaped the company town in New England; administered over a longer period of time and removed from the center of the labor movement, it was accepted or at least tolerated.

Long before the advent of Pullman, and prior to a time when laws obligated companies to observe safety and health standards, paternalism was viewed as a means to protect labor. During the first decades at Lowell, the mill girls were supervised through mandatory curfews, meals, lodging, and church service "to ensure their health and moral welfare," according to visitor William Scoresby in 1845.[4] In the beginning workers were attracted to industrial routine. A Chicopee weaver admitted that a diversion of "tastes led her away from her own people in the solitary little farm far away in the hills down to the social warmth and companionship of the factory, where labor is limited to working hours, and the everlasting requirements of livestock and dairy are not perpetually calling away youth and age alike from scanty rest and rare pleasure."[5] Paternalism was used at first to attract workers, particularly women, offering them protection while away from family and home. But once the supply of labor began to flourish, these procuratorial measures ceased. That is, they ceased in large corporate towns with the arrival of foreign immigrants.

The guiding hand

Some industrialists entreated workers by offering good wages and decent housing. This was especially true at the outset. Europeans had early suggested that the want of factory labor would keep America from industrialization. Two Frenchmen, Etienne Clavière and J. P. Brissot, dismissed America's industrial potential in 1795 with a treatise entitled *The Commerce of America with Europe*:

> The manufacture of cloths is in the number of those complicated manufactures which employ throughout the year a great number of workmen by the day; therefore it will not be suitable to Amer-

icans, so long as that class of men which produces these work-men shall be able to employ themselves more usefully in the clearing of lands, and in cultivation in general.[6]

A Scotsman, Thomas Tod, predicted much the same in 1782 after publishing *Consolatory Thoughts on American Independence*. Resigned to Britain's loss, Tod saw no danger in the allegation that American independence would tempt British workers to "emigrate to that country, and soon come to provide them in all manufactures, so that they will need none from Europe."[7] As long as American labor had land to clear and the potential for becoming a "landlord or free-holder," to which the lower class of manufacturers and merchants "are constantly aspiring," there was "little danger of them doing any thing extensive in manufactory."[8] Hamilton, Coxe, and, of course, Jefferson were well aware of these arguments; and when in 1823 Patrick T. Jackson of Boston and Lowell went scouting New England for mill hands, the carrot he offered was high wages and model living conditions. Not until 1836 did the Lowell manufacturers begin taking their workers for granted by reducing wages and refusing to negotiate.[9] Even in 1843 members of the Cheney family, who made up a large percentage of South Manchester's work force, labored overtime and accepted twenty-eight to forty-eight dollars for three months' labor in order to pay higher wages to their workers.[10]

Compounding matters for the remote industrial village or company town was the competition for labor it faced in larger cities. Skilled labor in New England received the highest wages in the nation, though as the century wore on wages and production did not increase commensurately. Though wages in 1880 purchased more in terms of manufactured goods than in 1840, even with a devaluation in specie, there was little satisfaction among textile workers in knowing that earnings for their labor during this interval increased only two-thirds in proportion to company profits.[11] Things had changed by the end of the century, however, after European immigrants had expanded the labor force and saturated industries like textile manufacture. Exploitation through wage reduction was accepted by workers driven off impoverished New England farms or forced to leave Europe, where similar work brought half the income. Many workers were thus caught up in the shift between larger industrial towns and were frequently in search of a job.[12] But company towns in out-of-the-way places off the beaten track still had to attract help by advertising in Boston and Providence papers.[13]

On the other hand, places like Fall River, which drew streams of British workers because of an easily accessible port of entry,[14] could be less concerned about labor treatment. What matter if workers left; there was a steady immigration. Furthermore, laws to protect labor against injury and overwork were laxly enforced. A Massachusetts report on the "hours of labor" (1866) found the most abusive instances of overwork in large industrial towns like Charlestown, New Bedford, and Fairhaven.[15] State general statutes passed in all the New England states largely after 1870 established minimum health and operational safety requirements. Yet the passage of a ten-hour-workday act in 1874, pertaining to women and children, had been anticipated by several company towns in New England. In them no child was permitted to work.[16] The small size and relative isolation of these towns do not appear to have given them a special opportunity to mistreat labor.

In time, the increased agitation and threat of organized labor affected paternal practices. Though early in the century paternalism was used to acquire labor, it eventually became a means of control or protection. Relatively few strikes had occurred in the United States between 1800 and 1880. Massachusetts reported the most, 159, of which only 18 had been successful.[17] But between 1880 and 1900 the situation changed radically: throughout the United States 22,783 strikes affected 117,405 business establishments,[18] and industrialists began seeking ways to avoid confrontation. Paternalism was tried as a means of accomplishing two objectives: "to anticipate tendencies toward the paralysis of industry by the withdrawal of employees acting in mass and to secure a still greater degree of productive interest and intelligence on the part of the individual workmen."[19] Books, pamphlets, and numerous articles were published to illustrate methods for improving labor and management relations. The first books were written as narratives, partly moralistic and partly biographical, such as Elizabeth Stuart Phelps's *The Silent Partner* (1871), which focused attention upon the need for better labor treatment by contrasting the lives of mill operatives with those of mill agents. *How They Lived in Hampden* (1884), written by Edward Everett Hale, extols the virtues of a small manufacturing community and its benevolent industrialist. During the 1880s, labor received the attention of the social scientist, and a new kind of literature appeared.

Carroll D. Wright, political economist and chief of the Massachusetts Bureau of Labor between 1875 and 1883, published a booklet entitled *The Relation of Political Economy to the Labor Question* (1882) after a lecture series presented by the Lowell Institute in 1879. Wright believed that America's material prosperity depended upon the health of its workers and their surroundings and that social science would provide valuable lessons in labor management. Foremost among the subjects that he believed social economists should understand were "sewerage, tenement houses, light and ventilation."[20] For him there was a moral at stake: capitalists guided solely by the profit motive would neglect the laboring population and destroy its work ethic. Britain stood as an example of what might happen in America if workers were sacrificed in exchange for power and wealth. However, he discovered that the experience "of the Cheney Brothers at South Manchester, Conn., of the Fairbanks Company in Vermont, of hundreds of others who have recognized the great fact of the Decalogue, testifies to the soundness of the doctrines which will be taught by the economists of the future";[21] that industrial ethics will ensure the "happiness and welfare" of the people. Wright also thought that such a benign interest in their workers on the part of employers would check ruthless competition and shorten the duration of economic depressions. In 1883 he became the first U.S. commissioner of labor and through his new office launched numerous investigations into laboring conditions.

Still another political economist, Nicholas Paine Gilman, pursued Wright's plea for reform with some managerial programs. His "Profit Sharing in the United States" suggested how industrialists could involve labor in the financial rewards of industry through the European invention of profit sharing. Several company towns tried profit sharing, the earliest of which as cited by Gilman was Peace Dale in 1878.[22] Profit sharing and later "cooperation" were then novel ways of bringing workers into the participatory role of stockholders. Yet another book published during the eighties was John Gibbons's *Tenure and Toil* (1888). In opposition to Wright and Gilman, Gibbons spoke cautiously about the rewards of the factory system because of the practice of tenantry. He argued that it was the right of every man to work his own land, insisting that the separation of labor from land ownership was the root of social evil, as evidenced by the history of feudal tenures in Europe. Like Henry George's *Progress and Poverty* (1882), which had appeared a few years earlier, Gibbons's study called for land tax reform. He further believed that employers should not be landlords and strongly criticized the example of Pullman, the most publicized model company town in America between 1885 and 1894.

Every device that the ingenuity of man can invent or suggest is employed by the owners to so completely meet the demands for material comfort and attractive surroundings that their employees, with their physical senses cloyed, will feel no stirring impulse within for social, moral, or mental growth that might breed discontent. But while this scrupulous attention to material details which so strongly combine to enhance the physical comfort of man is most admirable in conception and perfect in execution, yet there are phases of Pullman life that must be admitted are not only unpleasant, but which unfit a man to fully understand the obligations, perform the duties, and share the responsibilities of American citizenship.[23]

To Gibbons and others, the specter of Pullman cast an ominous shadow over industrial labor relations in which paternalism lay at the heart.

The argument he made against Pullman could have been lodged against the earlier New England towns, had they aroused similar attention. What distinguished them most from Pullman was their subtle use of paternalism and the innocent climate of labor, which changed radically after 1880. In making explicit his intentions as employer and landlord, George Pullman was never able to convey to his employees his interest in their well-being, and he rebuffed appeals to meet with labor leaders. Another difference was to be seen in Pullman's physical setting. Its red-brick buildings reinforced a rectangular grid plan set on a flat terrain, a physiognomy avoided in the New England towns where a less regular topography and the patina of age had softened their image. Pullman's houses appeared totally subordinate to the factories—if every bit as regular in feature.[24]

Pullman was an anomaly inasmuch as other company towns avoided its pattern. In New England not even the corporate towns quite compare with it. Not until Longview, Washington, was built in the mid-1920s was there another comprehensively designed company town that could match its size and pace of development.[25] Between January 1, 1881, and September 30, 1884, the population of Pullman grew from 4 to 8,513,[26] placing it in a class by itself. Wright, together with a delegation of several heads of state bureaus of labor, visited Pullman in 1885 and observed that the achievement was comparable to Krupp's work at Essen, Germany, Godin's familistère at Guise, France, and Salt's model village of Saltaire in Yorkshire, England. For precedents of type in America, Wright called attention to several New England towns:

> In all the countries named there have been many other experiments worth the careful study of all interested in social advancement. This is thoroughly true of our own country, and with justice we might call attention to the success at Peace Dale, R.I., at St. Johnsbury [Fairbanks Village], Vt., at Willimantic, and [South] Manchester, Conn.[27]

The "success" these earlier towns obtained brings out an important difference between them and Pullman. Buder's study of Pullman describes the town as an "experiment in social order" and documents the company's history and paternal policies.[28] He points out the irony resulting from a model physical environment with attractive and sanitary buildings and services and a completely controlled social environment—modern in one way, completely feudal in the other. Yet Buder provides no comparisons between the paternal measures taken in Pullman and those of other company towns. If paternalism failed in Pullman, did it succeed elsewhere, and for what reasons?

A condition for the success of paternalism that Pullman did not obtain was isolation. The geographic conditions that led to paternalism in the first instances later reinforced it. Spatial separation between towns can induce social introspection, and company towns acquired special advantages in shaping public opinion because of their isolation. Life inside and outside the factory was regulated by the company, since town and business were inseparable. Activities between neighboring towns, even a few miles apart, were restricted. Workers received the company's viewpoint first; and their children often took jobs without advantage of outside employment. An investigation of twentieth-century mill towns in the South indicated that such isolation caused an abnormal sense of pride in a company's image and product and a resignation to low wages and limited occupational mobility.[29] A disadvantage to labor in most instances, isolation did permit experimentation by management in the improvement of factory and housing environments. An endorsement of such isolation cites the advantages obtaining in two New England company towns:

> The Whitin Iron Works (Whitinsville, Massachusetts) and the Cheney Silk Mills (South Manchester) show the very great advantages of isolated manufacturing plants and resident owners and manager, each thoroughly familiar with some branch of the operations carried on. Isolation gives opportunity for beautiful surroundings, pure air, and agreeable living conditions, which made the workers healthy, happy, and contented.[30]

Proponents of garden cities would later agree in part with these sentiments. Moreover, isolation inhibited socially disruptive forces like organized labor. The endorsement states further that "it is extremely improbable that any 'labor agitator' can ever succeed in 'organizing' workmen of such an environment as that which obtains in Whitinsville and South Manchester." These towns provided no cause for disruption since their environments contained "the ideal condition for manufacturing purposes."[31] In fact, during the nineteenth century, no strikes occurred in South Manchester, Ludlow, Fairbanks Village, Hopedale, and Peace Dale.

Isolation in regard to paternalism made it easier for management to regulate other activities as well, such as temperance and politics. Alcohol abuse contributed to absenteeism and job instability and was in general socially disruptive. Temperance not only reduced absenteeism but also stabilized family conditions, protecting the interests of the employer. Liquor was banned in New England's company towns, but it was also prohibited in many other towns and cities.

In Springfield, Massachusetts, Ludlow's larger neighbor and a fast-growing mixed-economy city in the period 1830 to 1870, temperance laws were enforced not because its manufacturers insisted upon it but because the townspeople deemed liquor a social danger.[32] The only political boss in a company town was the industrialist. Because their employees formed a kind of pocket-borough constituency, many industrialists were elected to public office. Though a laborer might serve as a constable or clerk, it was his employer who held state and federal office, and some became governors and ambassadors. Isolation as a feature of company towns made all such elections easier to control.

Outwardly, paternalism was expressed in the landscape. As a response to "village improvement," programs were initiated to arouse interest in maintaining and improving town appearance. Workers and their families were encouraged to participate in home maintenance and gardening with companies awarding prizes for the best premises. The reasoning was partly to get everyone out in the sunlight and fresh air and to promote health and social intercourse through gainful exercise. Another goal, however, was to shore up appearances while enhancing the town image. A good image attracted publicity, which could bring attention not only to the town but also to its product.[33] What is more, it brought the employee into a kind of alliance with management, giving him a share in the responsibility for improvement. As an alternative to owning a house and lot, the employee and his family were encouraged and rewarded for taking care and pride in the company and town. In *Factory People and Their Employers*, Edwin L. Shuey, a labor relations expert, informs readers that

On the part of the employees, . . . opportunities for self-culture and encouragement to more beautiful surroundings have all contributed to make better citizens with higher ambitions and a fair recognition of the position and abilities of their employers.[34]

Shuey provides an example of "encouragement to more beautiful surroundings" in Peace Dale and describes it as "an instance of personal and family interest in the business and village alike," furnishing "organizations for the moral, social, and educational advantage of the town."[35] He highly commends the practice of awarding money in prizes for the best-kept front yards, backyards, window boxes, vacant lots, boys' vegetable gardens, and yards alongside railroad tracks. In one place he found prizewinners who received ten dollars in gold and a diploma, while those who placed last received only the diploma. The idea for such company-sponsored rewards originated at Ludlow, Hopedale, and Fairbanks Village, all mentioned in Shuey's book. He listed booklets that supplemented programs of yard and garden improvement, illustrating basic landscape practices. "A stretch of green lawn and a few flowers . . . go far toward making life worth living for the man of work. They give him a pride in the plant, and help to make him enthusiastic for its success."[36] Management played a decisive role, therefore, in design control through paternal programs enlisting company labor. Although such town-maintenance incentives never forced compliance among workers, their very existence set goals for which some families would strive.

Cultivating the industrial landscape

Environmental maintenance or conservation was not a burning issue during the nineteenth century, but neither was it entirely ignored. While industry tended to centralize in cities during the second half of the century, the small manufacturing and farming villages of New England experienced a decline in economy, population, and physical upkeep. Attempts to counter this decline began as early as the 1850s with "village improvement" campaigns in rural areas. Model company towns provided the setting for some of the more successful campaigns or efforts made in restoring natural surroundings and in producing attractive landscapes. They grew in population and thrived as businesses while managing to avoid manufacturing practices that elsewhere eroded landscapes and polluted rivers and streams. Their attention to maintenance was entirely self-serving: the Cheneys, Hazards, and Fairbankses depended upon area resources to power their mills and to provide shelter and fuel for their workers. They imposed measures protecting capital investment through site improvement. What is more, in addition to recognizing the salutary effects of conservation and good housing, they expressed the opinion that attractive and healthy surroundings produced "moral workers" who would be efficient and dependable.[37] Protecting business and ensuring future productivity required the maintenance of all resources controlled by the company.

Two company towns, South Manchester and Fairbanks Village, received praise from the Reverend B. G. Northrop, secretary of education for the state of Connecticut and a spokesman for village improvement. Northrop began campaigning in 1869 by visiting New England towns and lecturing on ways to preserve natural conditions.[38] Beset at first with public apathy, he managed to overcome skeptics and in a ten-year period helped to establish fifty improvement societies. Not until 1880 was he able to put his findings in order and write a book entitled *Rural Improvement*. Among a list of "Objectives of Rural Improvement Associations" provided in his book were these: "To cultivate public spirit and town pride," "Secure better hygienic conditions," "Improve public grounds," "Tree planting," "Better factory surroundings," and "Recuperate sterile lands." Commending South Manchester and Fairbanks Village as "models" of better factory surroundings, Northrop suggested:

An important work of rural improvement in many towns would be the betterment of the surroundings of their factories. Too frequently these grounds are disfigured with rubbish and made unsightly by neglect. . . . The influence of flowers, shrubbery, or neat and cultivated grounds upon operatives in refining their taste and promoting their happiness and content is too often ignored. There is, however, a goodly number of our manufacturers who show their interest in their hands by making their factory buildings and tenement houses inviting, comfortable, and healthful, and adorning the surrounding grounds.[39]

Like Ruskin, who in *Munera Pulveris* (1872) wrote that industrialists should not expect improvement among their workers before they themselves provided better living environments, Northrop furnished the instruction for implementing change. But to his dismay he discovered a number of "serious embarrassments in large and crowded manufacturing towns, especially where the factories are controlled by non-resident owners, more anxious for dividends than for the comfort and improvement of their workmen."[40] He refers, of course, to corporate towns and the avarice displayed by absentee landlords. What Northrop and his followers tried to do was to rectify the image and condition of industrial towns.

The beginnings of interest in rural conservation date to the eighteenth century, though it was not until the 1850s that organizations for village improvement gained popular support. Soon after the Revolution, "societies for promoting the arts" were established in Massachusetts, Pennsylvania, and South Carolina to inquire about agricultural and mechanical improvement of land and industry. Members read papers, issued reports, and offered prizes for imaginative solutions.[41] One society surviving this early period was the Massachusetts Society for Promoting Agriculture. Established in Boston in March 1782, it contributed essays on landscaping through the publication of annual reports, and it lasted long enough to celebrate a one-hundredth anniversary. As a state and regional organization, however, it did not address the needs of any one town, especially problems only broadly related to agriculture. In regard to local needs, village improvement societies responded. They usually gathered support as a community activity through the initiative of one influential person. In 1841 a spokesman for Fairbanks Village (by way of a local chronicle) entreated nearby residents of Saint Johnsbury Plain "to devote half a day to transplanting trees to ornament and beautify our village." The following day all turned out, "none excused except the lame and the lazy."[42] Trees once lost to farming, manufacturing, and shelter were to be replaced. Such early efforts usually arose off-handedly, though later activities would be organized with a goal to improve living and working conditions.

When Northrop visited South Manchester, the work of village improvement was already underway. In this "model factory village," he wrote, "a fine lawn laid out with winding concrete walks and adorned with shrubs and flowers fronts the mills, and usually each of the houses. No fence or visibly dividing line separates the front yards from the roads," giving the town "the appearance of an extended park" or "well-kept garden."[43] The creation of a landscape, open or accessible to pedestrian movement as well as to view and unspoiled by man-made barriers, was no accident of development but rather a matter of company policy. "No debris or rubbish is seen around or near any dwelling. There is evidently a public sentiment in favor of neatness and order that pervades the entire community and allows no dirty nooks to be found."[44] He concludes his tour of the company's premises with a description of the library and its contribution to the intellectual improvement of the employees, who expressed their appreciation for "the liberal methods" of the Cheneys in "promoting their well-being"; "Hence strikes and alienation between capital and labor are here unknown." In a later publication, Northrop encourages the founders of village improvement to begin with "open, gross and palpable improvements" and then, after these have had time to settle in the minds and emotions of the inhabitants, to pursue the organizing of free town libraries to further the goals of cultural and moral uplift.

Peace Dale owed its environmental improvement to an able administrator named Rowland G. Hazard II (1829–98). Although Hazard forsook college to take his place in the family woolen mills, he developed a fascination for study and discovered an interest in a wide range of subjects, which included the improvement of land and labor. Between managing the mills and pursuing philanthropic interests, he found time to write a half-dozen books, ranging in scope from metaphysics to finance.[45] The founding of an improvement society merely carried forward a family involvement in managing the business and town. Aside from bestowing care in claiming parkland along the riverbanks, he invested both thought and money in finding ways to make life more rewarding for his workers. He wanted them to cultivate interests and improve their minds during hours of idleness. But what says more about the condition of labor in Peace Dale was Hazard's personal belief "that the men whom he employed should be made to feel that they were not mere parts of a sharply driven money-making machine, but helpful members of a well-managed business organization, the successful working of which was of substantial benefit to themselves."[46] In addition to providing business incentives like profit sharing, he sought environmental improvements through site planning and landscaping, which can still be experienced when entering this small Narragansett town. The achievement, according to an observer in 1898, "has made that village in Rhode Island a leading text in works treating of industrial and social economics—and a place of pilgrimage for economists, ranging from Herbert Spencer downward, from many lands. It is the one mill-town in the English-speaking world where strikes do not occur."[47] Though in fact other mill towns also escaped strikes, few matched the environmental commitment in landscaping and philanthropy displayed by Hazard in Peace Dale. It took a central and pervasive figure to set a village improvement program in motion and steer it in the right direction, and the administrator of a company town had, if he chose to use them, the authority and wherewithal to better conditions.

Hazard, and other industrialists, recognized the protectionary and ameliorative aspects of landscaping. Landscaping provided a way to modify the relationship of site to building: wasted expanses of unimproved land containing factories and dwellings could be transformed into parks either to enhance or to shield existing structures. Factory yards could be made inviting to workers, visitors, and all who came in contact with the enterprise. In the company town, long-range planning objectives were easier to realize than elsewhere, because one family or company obtained site control. Natural spaces could be protected against speculative land use. Expansion of industrial and residential sites could be planned within areas set aside for their use, since both were developed by one enterprise. Landscaping could also effect visual unity where desirable instead of separation. It further permitted the placement of different types of buildings near to each other, while mitigating the nuisance of factory noise and congestion. Landscaping became the principal tool of village improvement.

ONE EXAMPLE AMONG MANY

To examine the impact of village improvement on a company town, it is worth turning to Fairbanks Village and the work accomplished there (fig. 3).

In 1855 the Fairbankses sponsored the Ornamental Tree Association and charged a one-dollar membership fee. Together with factory workers, farmers, and merchants, the Fairbankses planted new trees in place of those that had been cleared a half-century before,[48] at a time when open spaces were desired for safety and cultivation.

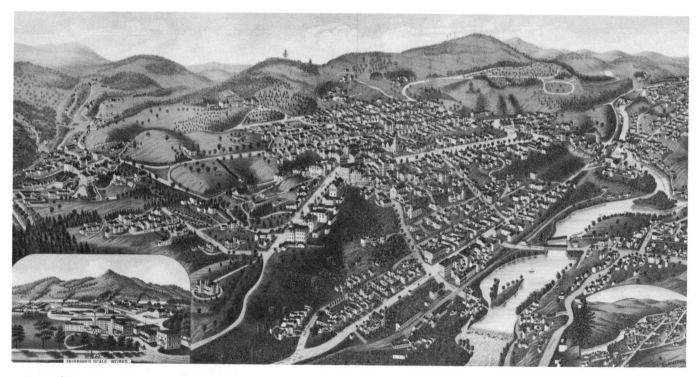

FAIRBANKS SCALE WORKS.

3. View of Saint Johnsbury, Vt., with inset of
Fairbanks Scale works (Brockton, Mass.: George
E. Norris, 1884). Fairbanks Village is located to
the west, or in the left half of the lithograph.
Courtesy of the Maps Division of the Library of
Congress.

Horticulture fascinated Franklin Fairbanks, friend of conservationist George Perkins Marsh, and his home estate was opened to the public as a park. Planting exotic fruits and trees and landscaping the grounds occupied much of his time outside the factory office. Underclyffe, his estate, was reportedly "surrounded with grounds and conservatories wherein bud, blossom, bloom and yield increase every kind of fruit and flower that grow in temperate or torrid zones. Bananas, oranges, lemons, cinnamon, pepper, cloves, breadfruit, etc."[49] were cultivated with pomiferous affection. Fairbanks invited his workers to stroll through his gardens and conservatories and encouraged them to cultivate gardens of their own.

The verdure enhancing the estates of the family found its way into the factory yards, which, by 1875, extended in area to ten acres and enclosed 272,183 square feet of building floor space. Interspersed between the foundries, workshops, storehouses, plow shop, saw and grist mills, and countinghouses were trees and flowers of myriad kind:

> Most of these buildings were embowered in maples and elms, surrounded with gardens, while all are well kept, well painted, mostly with white, betokening to a remarkable degree the presence of that grand trinity of human excellences, industry, sobriety and thrift. Look whichever way we may, nothing but a scene of singular beauty greets the eye.[50]

So read one enthusiastic account of the Fairbanks factory and grounds. An effort was made to secure and to protect a pleasant environment within the midst of a busy enterprise. The brothers intended that the working environment would be productive for them as well as ameliorative to those employed.

When Northrop visited Fairbanks Village, he inquired of the workers their opinion of the management. Many workmen replied, "They do everything on the square,"[51] and then praised the quality of work and high standards they set for themselves. Northrop concluded that "It is not strange that the workmen 'Hold on,'" some to work thirty and forty years. The transient laboring population was small. Most of the workers came from nearby farms and towns, and few of these were foreign-born. Differing somewhat from the job routine in the textile mills, the Fairbanks company managed several different shops worked by crews. Each crew, after receiving a purchase order, followed it through and enjoyed some occupational variety. Of $312,000 paid by the company in wages in 1875,[52] the average take-home pay per worker amounted to $624, or about $2 a day. Though equivalent to that of a common laborer in Boston, the amount was less than a city machinist would have received.[53] But what wage earners in Boston or Boston's nearby industrial towns did not receive that Fairbanks Village employees did was security after retirement. "Efficiency and faithfulness reap their proper reward. . . . the superannuated [are] pensioned; the widows and orphans of those who die in the harness are provided for."[54] In visiting the homes of the workmen, Northrop found to his surprise that many were furnished with pianos and with tapestries from Brussels.[55]

Fairbanks Village acquired some public attention for its model appearance, especially in regard to landscaping. Even readers of the *Boston Globe* were apprised of its attractions, as the paper called attention to a "model" environment: "where everybody is contented with his lot because its lines are cast in the pleasantest of places on earth . . . the joint product of four sources: Nature, Christianity, the Fairbankses and the Passumpsic Railroad."[56] The promotional slant of the article indicates the degree to which model company towns like Fairbanks Village impressed visitors with their attractiveness and paternal concern.

Fairbanks Village continued to serve as an example of the achievements of village improvement and industrial enlightenment. Parris Thaxter Farwell, author of *Village Improvement*, describes the City

Beautiful movement, which came to symbolize and embody progressivism in larger cities throughout America at the turn of the century. But Farwell credits the small town with maintaining social and environmental harmony. Citing Saint Johnsbury among other towns in his book, he said: "it is now a well recognized principle in the business world that attractive surroundings are a decided advantage for a business plant, and that the influence on employees of pleasant grounds, adorned with flowers and shrubs, tends to increase their pleasure in and loyalty to their work."[57] The association formed between work and environment cannot be overstated; it lay at the heart of social activity in the model company town.

THE SIGNIFICANCE OF VILLAGE IMPROVEMENT

Landscaping emerged as a science during the nineteenth century. Before then, it had been an art form used primarily in the layout of private gardens and cemeteries. This changed with the need for public parks and the application of civil engineering, geology, and horticulture. But professional landscapists had little impact before mid-century.[58] They were preceded, however, by businessmen, ministers, and women, who studied and wrote articles suggesting methods of village and grounds improvement.[59] Industrialists had the special advantage of being in a position to take landscape matters in hand. Eventually they hired professional designers but initially made landscape decisions themselves. Some were aware of the interest in picturesque or romantic landscapes of the period, which suggested the amelioration of industry through natural surroundings.[60] Of these industrialists who "must provide a town for workingmen," wrote Ida M. Tarbell, a few were "captured by the dream of building something, where health, beauty, freedom and prosperity should reign."[61] An understanding of both the natural and the industrial environment lay at the foundation of their "dream."

A point to be stressed is that the founders of these towns adopted village improvement as a means of maintaining attractive and viable environments. Their objective was to protect the business, and site maintenance was the key.

The timeliness and significance of village improvement were not lost on those concerned with the regional stability of New England, for such voluntary associations not only rendered villages "attractive and pleasing to the eye, by the planting of trees and shrubs, [and] the maintenance of orderly-looking and neat town ways" but also taught others to appreciate their heritage. Because of a loss of "able-bodied young men moving West" and the fear of "foreign populations" who share no "interest and affection" for the rural towns in which they settle, the entire region might suffer unless those in positions of authority took account. They could realize improvement "by infusing into the minds of the inhabitants a pride in the appearance and reputation of their town."[62] Industrialists took this reasoning to heart and made it part of their paternalism.

The concern over regional decline was justified. During the second half of the nineteenth century, profits from agricultural staples declined after vast acreages of machine-tilled land opened in the West, whence crops were also milled and shipped. More and more farmers sought extra work to support their families, and the village young moved to the cities to earn higher wages. Of Vermont's 238 towns, 158 reached their peak population in 1850.[63] While the number of manufacturers began to diminish as a result of industrial centralization and corporate aggregation, certain regions experienced a corresponding decline in population. The period Schlesinger outlines in *The Rise of the City, 1878–1898* could also have been termed the demise of the rural village. In the decade 1880 to 1890 the capital worth of urban areas doubled that of rural areas.[64] Furthermore, there was an apparent acceleration in population movement from city to city and from farm to city. But village population decreased slowly, as if by atrophy. An essay entitled "The Doom of the Small Town" suggested that a place "which loses its inhabitants loses also its energies and sinks into lethargy" and the decay of village life may go unnoticed.[65] Moreover, manufacturing, not just farming villages, suffers decline. Villages dependent upon the production of "farm implements, of brick and tile, cooperage, grist mills and flouring mills, foundries and machine shops, saw-mills and mills whose products are made from logs and bolts, the making of furniture, wagons, and carriages," all decline in number.[66] The essay draws on the census reports of 1880 and 1890 that indicated 3,144 of 6,291 townships had lost population.[67] The resulting desuetude brings to mind places like Sherwood Anderson's *Winesburg, Ohio* (Canton), where a family struggles for self-esteem against the background of an aging boardinghouse in a factory town.[68] In New England and elsewhere village life was beginning to pass by as settlers moved time and again in what Mumford termed "The Diaspora of the Pioneer."[69] Those who stayed behind had too much invested to leave, though they were aware of a need to conserve what remained. Large corporations absorbed and combined smaller companies, winnowing the least successful. Mergers and diversification, together with the financial panics of the late nineteenth century, did much to accelerate the passing of single-enterprise towns. Those surviving fought to protect their markets, and they were also concerned about the image of their premises.

Advice about maintaining small towns and rural environments came from those concerned with landscape architecture and sanitary engineering, such as Horace Cleveland, George Waring, and Nathaniel Egleston. Together, their books furnished the guidelines for village improvement during the 1870s.

Landscape Architecture presented Cleveland's belief that the founders of new villages in the western states should benefit from the example of New England towns by laying streets to follow land contours and avoiding the monotonous grid.[70] His principal objective, however, was to promote tree planting in the Midwest, to which he moved in the 1850s. A contemporary of Cleveland's and another New Englander, George Waring, delved less into matters of planting and more into procedures for building roads and laying sewers. *Village Improvement and Farm Villages* describes in detail street grading, paving, and subterranean drainage as well as the planting of hedgerows and ornamental trees. Such improvements were acted upon by many small towns, including company towns, as a reading of annual town reports will attest. Waring mentions the Laurel Hill Association but then outlines his own tenets for village improvement. He cautions his readers to go easy on embellishments and warns that ornate buildings detract from rural landscapes. He then calls upon the would-be builder and landscapist to make an improvement suited to the problem at hand.[71] Waring's advice was seconded and even quoted verbatim by the Reverend Nathaniel Egleston, who followed Waring's study with *Villages and Village Life*. Egleston found the beauty of villages, not in fine houses with formal grounds, but rather in the "cosiness, neatness, simplicity, and that homely air that grows from these and from the presence of a home-loving people." He believed that the earnest and wholesome qualities of the rural landscape should be reflected in the homes of the village dweller and that, accordingly, those in a position to exercise influence within a village should set the best example.[72]

Though the lessons passed on by Egleston, Waring, and Cleveland, together with Northrop, provided the first programs for village improvement, there had been earlier spokesmen who no doubt influenced those who led the movement. Guides to ornamental landscaping appeared in England and France during the eighteenth century, and the publications of Uvedale Price and John Claudius Loudon were widely distributed in the 1830s and 1840s. Not until 1841 did an American author treat landscaping as a matter of design. Even then, in *The Theory and Practise of Landscape Gardening*, Andrew Jackson Downing characterized landscaping as a matter of individual taste, as to be seen in a private residence or park.[73] Though Downing left village design to his eminent successor, Frederick Law Olmsted, he offered some advice on the treatment of "Our Country Villages" while editor of the *Horticulturalist* in 1850. He urged his readers to learn from the example of villages in Massachusetts, where interested citizens have "set about improving their own property." Furthermore:

> Every spring and every autumn should witness a revival of associated efforts on the part of selectmen, trustees of corporations, and persons of means and influence, to adorn and embellish the external condition of their towns.

What Downing says next reveals his understanding of both man and nature, implying that those less sensitive to the effects of beauty may derive pleasure from the "increased value given to the property thus improved, and villages thus rendered attractive and desirable as places of residence," making the argument for village improvement as an economic incentive.[74]

Less cogent reasons for examining rural landscapes may have been inspired by the literature and art of the middle decades. The prose of Emerson and Thoreau and the tales of Irving and Cooper need hardly be mentioned. The pastoral ideal intoned by American writers expressed the virtues of rural life. It seems reasonable to think that those interested in village improvement would have drawn inspiration from the literature of their day. Moreover, the recognition of American landscapes gave rise to a native school of painting. Artists like Durand, Doughty, and Cole idealized rural scenes. To be sure, industrialists pictured their villages in tabloid perspectives with bustling factories and bright machinery; but in the background loomed green hills and valleys. From within the Fairbanks Village Athenaeum, such landscape paintings as McEntee's *Scene among the Catskills*, Green's *Bay of Rhige*, and Coleman's *Crossing the Plains* paled before the sublime grandeur of Bierstadt's *Domes of the Yosemite*.[75] At least among some industrialists, the beauty of nature was not lost.

To measure the achievements of village improvement in New England and the rest of the country would be difficult. Toward the end of the century, when gathering momentum, it seems to have been eclipsed by the City Beautiful movement. When Charles Mulford Robinson published his pioneering study, *Modern Civic Art*, he discovered that many small towns had already accomplished their goals of the preceding century. Having emerged from a "more or less continuous series of spasmodic reform efforts" that secured electric lighting, street paving, and the piping of water and sewage, "industrial communities" moved forward from meager beginnings.[76] But after World War I small-town associations for civic improvement apparently fell by the wayside. The kind of improvement societies commended by Charles Eliot, Olmsted's student and designer of Boston's metropolitan parks, which "assist in the planting of the roadsides . . . and occasionally save from destruction a fine tree, or a bold ledge, or some other landmark of the neighborhood,"[77] now disappeared. Personal initiatives ended. Municipal agencies had begun to replace private groups, and new magazines like the *American City* published a thin "Town and Country" edition for rural needs. Activities performed by village improvement societies eventually became the responsibility of park, sanitation, and planning departments.

The architecture of philanthropy

Community facilities in the form of public buildings were prominent additions to company towns. Together with factories and houses, they established the overall character or urban design of a place. They also exhibit the most conspicuous evidence of paternalism. Given to the town by the industrialist and his family, they were usually dedicated in his name or in that of the company and intended for use by the work force. Aside from landscaped parks and grounds, the buildings represented the town's ultimate visual achievement and local distinction, consisting of schools, libraries, and town halls for the most part. Churches can also be placed in this category. However, since the donor was usually the industrialist, only his denominaton received a suitable meeting place. Denominational differences between management and labor undermined the symbolic importance of the church as a regulating force in maintaining social order.[78] Gone was the emotive power of the New England Congregational, one-faith village of an earlier period. Catholicism predominated among immigrant workers while their employers remained Protestant. Evangelism, where it existed, held greater personal appeal than traditional Congregationalism. The factory had replaced the church as the chief institution and center of town activity. Even health services, fire protection, and municipal offices were sometimes housed inside the factory and administered by the company. But community facilities emerged with a need to provide some space for social diversion outside the factory. Older towns achieved such diversion through the intermingling of established families for whom politics, recreation, and personal recognition enjoyed slow maturation. This kind of cultural tradition was unattainable in the company town with its ready-made, disparate population.

Hazard Memorial Hall in Peace Dale, Cheney Hall in South Manchester, the Fairbanks Museum, and the Town Hall and Brancroft Memorial Library in Hopedale represent interesting examples of buildings designed as community facilities. As focal attractions, they imparted the model image because of their architecture and prominent location near to the factories and houses of the employees. These buildings had an acculturative purpose. It was within the lyceum or town hall or from the steps of the library that commemorative orations were sounded: there crowds gathered on holidays to

4. The "Library and Reading-Room" in Cheney Hall, South Manchester, Conn. From *Harper's New Monthly Magazine*, 1872.

parade about and later enjoy a company picnic on the surrounding grounds. On less festive occasions, the "Sewing Society and Boys' Club" met, and instruction was offered in "well organized classes in manual training for boys and girls."[79] Next to the town hall, the school often received special attention, as indicated by annual town reports. Education had become a state requirement with a mandatory six to eight years of study by the middle of the nineteenth century.[80] By 1870 legislation in the six New England states prohibited the employment of children under fourteen years without a compensatory term of education.[81] For adults, libraries offered the opportunity for self-improvement (fig. 4). The Fairbankses of Vermont built the first free library in their state in 1843, and H. H. Richardson's Ames Free

Library (1879), designed for use by the employees of the Ames Tool and Shovel Company of North Easton, Massachusetts, another company town, exemplifies the fine architecture and distinction of these company libraries.[82]

One example of such philanthropic architecture is Hazard Memorial Hall in Peace Dale. The Hall contains a library, reading rooms, lecture hall, and clubroom. Built at a cost of between forty and fifty thousand dollars, it dominates a site in the center of town beside the millstream. Together with the factories, school, and meetinghouse, it attests to the company's architectural achievement. In style it can be termed "Richardsonian Romanesque," and it was contemporary in appearance with other fine buildings of the period. A steeply hipped roof with eyebrow dormers sits atop three stories of frame on masonry construction. To one side projects a large circular tower containing a reading room. In the center of the main facade, a grand arched entranceway opens into a vestibule, above which rises a timber gable jettied over three tiers of windows. Agent William C. Green, a spokesman for the company, described the facility in 1904:

> The building was erected in 1891 to the memory of Rowland Gibson Hazard. It contains a library, which now holds about 10,000 volumes, a hall seating 600 people, several class rooms, a gymnasium, etc. The building, of stone on wood, is an important part of the village architecture, and was deeded by the sons of Mr. Hazard to trustees to hold in perpetuity for the use of the whole community. The hall is not let to any traveling show or organization and for no entertainments that are not considered by the trustees to be for the better interest of the village.[83]

The building held a strategic position in the overall design of the town and served both a visual and a social function; it provided needed services on a scale most towns of similar size to Peace Dale simply could not afford.

The Hazards accepted a position of responsibility in town affairs and set themselves as examples for their employees to observe. Like benefactors in other company towns, they lived in Peace Dale and made "its material and moral prosperity their concern."[84] At least this was the intention of two Hazard daughters, whose interest in cultural uplift brought them to perform at Hazard Memorial Hall. Agent Green continues his description:

> A few years ago the "Sunday musics" were begun by Miss Hazard and her sister, who simply went into the hall on a Sunday afternoon and played and sang for fifteen or twenty minutes, while a few people from the outside straggled in. From that it has grown to be an informal concert each Sunday afternoon for the season, from Christmas until Easter.[85]

Who benefited most from this form of benevolence, the sisters or the workers, is open to question. It would appear, however, that the "laboring classes" in manufacturing towns accepted a measure of patrimony and may even have elicited it. Moreover, Peace Dale's population was two-thirds immigrant by 1885, which probably encouraged the sisters to further their attempts at cultural assimilation.[86]

Community facilities extended paternal supervision by providing buildings and services in which management could reach out and improve or "uplift" the condition of labor. As with their buildings, industrialists built parks and playgrounds for other than aesthetic reasons. Toward the end of the nineteenth century an interest in physical exercise emerged with the German gymnasium movement, and recreation facilities established near the factories were provided to improve workers' health. Then, in the 1890s, the Chautauqua movement introduced cultural subjects to mass audiences and popularized lectures, dance performances, "musics," and art exhibits, all of which required large areas for group assembly.[87] These, of course, came well after a time when the routine of the factory system had begun to diminish the time for such natural activities. Observers other than the Reverend Mr. Harrison had remarked that the factory system and the factory town had caused social deprivation, if also material reward. Advocating paternal supervision on the order of that practiced in South Manchester, Ludlow, and Peace Dale, the writer of "Village Communities of the Factory, Machine Works, and Mine" stated: "It is outside the factory walls that the workman spends most of his life, and here the interest of the employer more rarely follows. This is an oversight!"[88] Employers should become responsible for the welfare of their workers both inside and outside the factory, and families could not be removed to an isolated settlement and then provided with nothing more than employment and expect to live a rewarding life.

The relationship of buildings to layout and their overall management and maintenance cannot be overstressed in describing the company town. The spatial arrangement and physical appearance of factories, houses, and community facilities distinguished these places from the typical nineteenth-century industrial town and established the means for accommodating manufacture without destroying the environment.

The management and urban design of these New England company towns place them in a special category. Their comprehensive organization and control permitted them to prosper without the destructive results experienced elsewhere. The reasons have been outlined, though two conditions should be underscored. First, these towns maintained long-term operational objectives and were dependent on local resources to operate their factories. And second, each town had resident industrialists, whose family members exercised care and authority through paternalism in both employment and community affairs.

Chapter 4
Housing

Obtaining decent housing in industrial towns of the nineteenth century posed a difficult problem for workers and their families. Good or even adequate lodgings were too few in number to relieve overcrowding or provide a minimum of sanitation, and this ominous situation was only partly mitigated by industrialists concerned with reform. Experimental tenements built in several European and American cities after 1850 by philanthropists and mutual aid societies occupied little more than a few streets in otherwise large and squalid districts. Despite the need and magnitude of the problem, and the frightful consequences described by such keen observers as Edwin Chadwick, Friedrich Engels, and Jacob Riis, little was done to improve housing conditions. The task of providing good housing was accomplished more easily in places where chronic social problems and physical constraints did not exist. Where land was inexpensive and previously undeveloped, and streets and utilities could be provided from the outset, decent workers' housing—often company housing—could be built at a nominal cost without overcrowding. Double-family houses or semidetached row houses as opposed to large apartment blocks formed entire residential layouts. A willingness on the part of industrial developers to experiment with improved shelter in new-town developments was in evidence a century ago.

But most company housing, like most public housing of a later period, acquired a negative image. The torpor of older industrial towns dramatized the scene: "The result in many cases has been . . . depressing rows of hideous barracks . . . looking for all the world like a row of institution children."[1] Yet this image was not universal; and in some cases companies offered houses in a variety of sizes, styles, and colors. But even houses in monotonous rows were preferable to the "patches" of shanties built independently by workers, which frequently substituted for company housing.[2] Manufacturers built and maintained houses because workers either could not or would not assume the obligation themselves. Transiency among single people and the lack of occupational alternatives in single-enterprise towns surely discouraged all but senior employees with families, who were secure in their jobs, from home ownership. To some families houses were sold through company-sponsored building and loan associations. The accusation that manufacturers built houses to form monopolies to exact unreasonable rent appears unfounded, however, since higher rent was paid for lodging in nearby cities.[3] Workers in fact paid less rent in proportion to their income in company towns than they did in almost any city, large or small.[4] Though in some instances rents were deducted from wages, they were frequently subsidized in part by the company as an employment attraction.[5] A reluctance to sell houses once rented stemmed from the management practice of controlling the town site in the event of industrial expansion while protecting unsold property. Though this practice surely deprived some families of the security and pleasure of home ownership, it also served to maintain acceptable building conditions and presentable landscapes over a period of years. The problem of maintenance persists today as administrators of public housing for the poor attempt to extend the life of buildings whose tenants cannot afford upkeep.

In instances company housing obtained architectural distinction in terms of spatial and mechanical improvements in low-cost construction. Changes that took place in nineteenth-century housing affected living habits considerably: indoor plumbing, gas, and electricity improved sanitation, heating, and illumination, making dwellings more adaptable to personal needs. When the first international housing congresses convened to exhibit and critique workers' dwellings, they awarded medals for the best-designed houses and house layouts. Model European dwellings in the industrial villages of Noisiel, France and Essen, Germany, and, on more than one occasion, those of the New England towns of Peace Dale, Ludlow, and Hopedale received such honors.

The nature and extent of the housing problem

The overall impact of industrial environments on workers' housing was both dramatic and graphic. Artists' depictions of uprooted rural workers driven to towns and cities and forced to reside in fetid slums poignantly illustrated the human plight caused by the turmoil of the Industrial Revolution.[6] Few towns could match the pace of population increase with a sufficient supply of houses and services. Thousands of destitute families were left with no place to turn for decent lodging. England, the first industrialized nation, met the problem belatedly. Reformers, including industrialists, politicians, doctors, even architects, seized upon the housing issue and brought it before the public in lectures, editorials, sanitary reports, and guides "for building model cottages for the laboring people."[7] Though the English Poor Laws sought agrarian reforms in the 1830s and 1840s, nothing was done to aid the cities before midcentury, short of investigative measures like Chadwick's Public Health Act of 1848. Not until 1855 did London impose a tenement-house law that protected against hazardous construction.[8] Enforced improvements in housing through legislation came slowly, however, and London's resistance to change was to be repeated in American cities shortly after. It took combined probes into health and housing to overcome local resistance by exposing deplorable conditions. To realize how bad housing conditions were, one need only refer to Engels's famous indictment of capitalism in *The Condition of the Working Class in England in 1844* (1845). The terrifying part of Engels's revelation lay in its factual documentation. Outside London, Birmingham, Manchester, Liverpool, Leeds, and other of the larger cities living conditions were less crowded, though often just as degrading. Robert Owen's early struggle to improve New Lanark in the period 1799 to 1813 involved both health and housing programs.[9] In both cities and villages, room for human and structural betterment existed. And before turning to the industrial village, or company town, a brief review of housing conditions in larger cities will be made.

In Europe, and in England especially, architects became increasingly interested after 1850 in designing improved housing for the working class and poor. The popular uprisings of 1848 led directly to housing reform, and the reverberations were felt in most of the industrialized countries. Demands for improvements and financial inducements, such as offered by Louis Napoleon, encouraged architects to design new housing or improve old.[10] They published pamphlets or guides to illustrate model workers' dwellings. The usual format consisted of an outline of existing conditions followed by plans for amelioration. One architect-author of the 1850s prefaced his drawings with a survey of housing in Saint George's in the East, then one of London's more crowded warrens. Thereabouts, he estimated some 6,328 rooms were occupied by separate families, and he quotes a parish minister who witnessed "three to four families, of different sexes and of various ages, living in one small room. They eat, drink, sleep, wash, dress, and undress therein, without curtain or screen of any kind. Every domestic cleanliness is wanting."[11] He found the atmosphere so foul and the tap water so polluted that the lodgers were forced to purchase drinks at nearby pubs. With these numbing findings in evidence, the author offers several tenement plans to make the crowding more bearable, though he does little to assuage the density problem.

Laws requiring the demolition of housing unable to meet minimum health standards, such as were passed in London in 1855 and then amended infrequently thereafter, were rarely invoked and as laxly enforced by officials then as today. Even in the nineteenth century, authorities realized that no matter how bad housing conditions were the crowding would only worsen if old tenements were razed. Sir Bannister Fletcher, known today for his comparative history of architecture, published in 1871 a small treatise that included a chapter entitled "Improvements Advocated—Not Demolition."[12] Fletcher would have had landlords improve their tenements by adding ells to rear courts, thus updating the structures with a kitchen (enlarged skullery), bath, and drain for each flat. Such conveniences as these could have been appended only to tenements that were not built back-to-back, making them comparable to the model Waterlow and Peabody Trust flats of the 1860s.[13] However, Fletcher's proposal reveals a drawback. The ells he would have built into the rear courts and light wells of existing tenements would, on construction, leave barely two feet between opposing walls. Given an average height per tenement of three stories, very little light and fresh air would have made it down those narrow crevices or chasms between the walls.[14] Therefore, the problem of improving existing housing remained difficult to solve. Selective demolition, together with strictly enforced building bylaws, was obviously the answer, though it was reluctantly adopted.

Greater opportunity for sheltering workers lay outside the city where land costs and population densities were less of a factor. By the 1850s model English villages began appearing as satellites to large industrial cities. Erected at a distance from congested and expensive built-up areas, they lay close enough to draw upon the labor supply. Copley near Halifax (1849–53) and Saltaire near Bradford (1850–63) were self-administered company towns, offering an improved type of housing over that in other industrial villages and cities. To be sure, the industrialists who built them, Eduourd Akroyd and Titus Salt, viewed their philanthropy with a mind to make money. They in turn were followed by other enlightened industrialists, such as Cadbury and Lever, whose villages influenced Ebenezer Howard at the close of the century.[15] Copley and Saltaire received the endorsement of reformer James Hole, a member of the Leeds Model Cottage Association, who explained in 1866 "that a better plan for relieving the crowded seats of population would be the erection of 'model' villages outside our large towns. . . . There the artisan might enjoy the blessed gifts of sunlight and pure aire, open space . . . and a cottage garden."[16] After examining the conditions of the working class in London, Leeds, Manchester, and Birmingham, Hole turned to the model village as the only immediate alternative to furnishing housing at a reasonable cost. In reading his account, *The Homes of the Working Classes*, one senses his dismay over the callousness exhibited by tenement owners.[17] The product of their neglect had earlier caught the attention of novelists like Charles Dickens and Herman Melville and artists like Gustave Doré. If *The Homes of the Working Classes* lacks the poignancy of Dickens's *Hard Times* or Melville's *Redburn*, it nonetheless ranks among the best documentaries written on the housing issue.

Similar housing conditions to those described by Hole in England could be found in some American cities. Not until 1868 did Boston receive a "tenement-house law" whereby minimum standards of ventilation, sanitation, and maintenance could be enforced. An investigation by the Massachusetts Bureau of Labor Statistics in 1869 gave evidence to conditions every bit as bad as those in London. Typical of its findings was a North End tenement in Boston buiit in 1857 and comprising sixty-four rooms which rented for from $1.00 to $1.50 a week. Tenants earned on the average $1.25 a day. The building was assessed at thirty thousand dollars and returned 14¼ percent of the investment in annual rent. (These figures are important to bear in mind.) Bureau investigators discovered:

> At our visit we found eight rooms vacant, and 54 families occupying 56 rooms. . . . From the testimony of the lessee and others, there had been as many as 450 occupants at one time, an average of seven persons to a room, each room being 17 × 15 feet, and 7 feet high, or, say 226 cubic feet to each person. The rooms are smoky, damp, unpainted, and mostly unwhitewashed, and are sitting-room, kitchen, wood-room and living-room, except-

ing at the uppermost floor. A few plants in some of the rooms had died, and no wonder. No room and no entry was ventilated.[18]

The tenements described here were not exceptional, and a reading of state and local investigations of other cities offers some insight to equally deplorable conditions. New York also exhibited crowded and insufferable housing, as cited in the *Report of the Council of Hygiene and Public Health upon the Sanitary Condition of the City* (1865).[19] The council's findings produced the city's first tenement-house law in 1867, a year before Boston's. But earlier evidence that New York was becoming an uncomfortable place for the workingman to live is provided in a small booklet from the 1840s, at a time when much of upper Manhattan paradoxically consisted of farms. In 1848 architect T. Thomas published *The Working-Man's Cottage Architecture*, in which he suggests that New York laborers move to the suburbs to escape being "doomed to perpetual confinement at their place of business."[20] The ferry to suburban Brooklyn took time and money, and no doubt most workers preferred to live near their place of employment on Manhattan's southern end. But crowding eventually forced workers out of the city and into suburban settlements.

For workers whose wages hovered at about a dollar a day, purchasing or building a house seemed unlikely if not impossible without some kind of loan or guaranteed financial arrangement. Thomas's booklet alludes to "The Brooklyn Accumulating Fund Association," founded in 1846. It helped workers "obtain the capital necessary for the purchase of Real Estate, Erection of Buildings, Redemption of Mortgages, and other similar purposes."[21] Building and loan associations like the one in Brooklyn helped families who had money enough to make a down payment, though it did not extend help to the majority of laborers unable to save and build without credit.

The first building and loan society appeared in Frankfort, Pennsylvania (now part of Philadelphia), in 1831 and was named the Oxford

Provident Building Association of Philadelphia County. Member associations to the Provident trust increased in number to more than a thousand by the turn of the century with nearly one million subscribers.[22] By the 1870s the still novel idea of building and loans spurred attention among reformers. Edward Everett Hale's valuable study, *Workingmen's Homes*, mentions building and loan societies with much interest and fascination: he cites Josiah Quincy's "Homestead Clubs" as the earliest of Boston's home-loan savings organizations.[23] According to Hale, Quincy, son of the famous Boston mayor and Harvard College president, formed an organization or bank for each of several proposed building sites. The location of these sites depended upon railroad access and nearness to small towns outside of Boston, which could furnish local services such as water and gas. Homestead Clubs appeared in Dedham, Vineland, and Wollaston Heights, the last of which was developed by the Old Colony Railroad.[24]

Building workers' housing in the suburbs emphasized the need for commuter trains with inexpensive fares. Hale's study advocates cheap trains, making it possible for workers to commute each day to city jobs. The Massachusetts Eastern Railroad Cheap Trains Act of 1872 provided the incentive at state level for other roads to lower rates and to give workers inexpensive intercity passes.[25] Nearer to Boston, suburbs connected with streetcars to open still other tracts of housing built for rent as well as for sale.[26] But, in these, development was more costly and speculation keener.[27] Moreover, intercity trains provided rapid transit, which the streetcar did not. At least, it did not before electrification late in the 1880s.[28] Inside Boston, housing reformer Nathaniel Bowditch helped establish the Boston Co-operative Society in 1871. As a demonstration project, the cooperative purchased the notorious "Crystal Palace" tenement in Lincoln Street and proceeded to rehabilitate it by making two holes for light shafts and painting and papering. The idea of opening up the building to light and ventilation later became the subject of a competition in New York in 1879. On a smaller scale, in 1875, Robert Treat Paine began aiding Boston workers by purchasing cottages costing between $2,000 and $3,500. In 1888 he founded the Workingmen's Building Association in the belief that laborers' families should occupy separate homes and not live in tenements.[29] His subscribers were of "the better class of artisans, such as plumbers, carpenters, masons, engineers, etc."[30] However, the dilemma remained for most workingmen with families. If they worked to escape the rookeries and jerry-built alley tenements in the central city, they faced a choice of paying high rent for larger accommodation in streetcar suburbs or buying a cottage within reach of cheap-train suburbs through a building and loan society.

Housing for workers in industrial towns differed from that of the city and suburb. Company housing was placed near the factories since commuter service did not exist. That is, it did not exist until these places became cities in their own turn. In corporation towns that grew into cities, housing conditions as bad as those found in Boston or New York appeared in a remarkably short time. Large cities, developing over a number of years, historically acquired areas of dilapidated housing. It was expected. But for new towns springing up in the course of a few decades to develop equally serious housing problems seemed inexcusable. Companies that originally furnished houses abandoned their building programs as soon as independent realtors moved in to take over the chore. In Cole's study of Lawrence, *Immigrant City*, the period of model town planning and tenement building lasted only from 1845 to 1850.[31] The "power and land companies" that developed the corporate towns sold lots and leased water to individual enterprises, which then built factories and workers' houses adjacent to their purchased section of the canal levee. But later enterprises built only factories since workers were already in supply and the liability of housing could be sloughed off to speculators who also bought land from the development company. What surprised observers most about the corporate town was the rapacity in which its environment became spoiled and unlivable.[32] Parts of towns hardly more than twenty years old would turn into slums. Houses literally rotted into pieces. In "The Sanitary Condition of Working People, in Their Homes and Employments" the Massachusetts Bureau of Labor discovered in 1874 hundreds of wretched dwellings in the relatively nascent corporate towns of Lowell, Lawrence, Holyoke, and Chicopee, causing one inspector to write prophetically: "For myself, I do not hesitate to avow my belief that, for the dwellings of the laboring classes in cities, provision must be made by public authority."[33] Moreover, the lack of adequate shelter in these towns created higher population densities than their building sites could support. Tenements were jammed one next to the other, with some so close (in Lawrence) that rent collectors could step from the porch landing of one tenement over onto the next.[34] Even where windows were placed on the sides of the buildings, they received no direct sunlight. And very little fresh air could find passage into the rooms. Consequently, the close proximity of the houses caused unsanitary and noxious conditions as well as a fire hazard. Diseases like typhoid and tuberculosis increased markedly in proportion to crowding. Between 1870 and 1910 the rise in population in these towns produced dangerous housing shortages: "In little Holyoke, Massachusetts, a town of 11,000 inhabitants in 1870, one block of High Street housed one hundred and five persons in seventeen upstairs rooms—ten people sometimes in one room—yet it was less than a mile to open woods and farm land."[35] Holyoke's population peaked in 1917 with 62,210; but already in 1885, with a tenantry of 25,000, the town placed third to New York and Hoboken, New Jersey, in housing shortage![36] These statistics concealed untold misery for the immigrant families who packed into houses at the average of eleven members per dwelling in 1880.[37] The worst houses in corporate towns, however, were not those built by the company but those erected by speculators who took over this task in the closing decades of the nineteenth century. Graham Romeyn Taylor's description of the tenement shark and his practices in *Satellite Cities* exposes the effect of speculative building in towns where the company constructed houses in insufficient number. Though Taylor writes about Gary, Indiana, founded in 1906, his description also fits the corporation town in New England of a generation earlier. "Shrewd real-estate speculators at once saw their opportunity in the lack of adequate company housing. . . . The wretched housing conditions which developed . . . were and still are a disgrace to the industrial power which created the town."[38] Similarly shrewd speculators built tenements in places like Holyoke to prey on the needs of workers unable to purchase houses of their own or secure decent company housing.

Model dwellings

In England and in countries of northern Europe model or exemplary housing first appeared as industrial estates. The need for better housing was highly visible, and the call for sanitary reform threatened government action. When housing shortages became acute, the solution seemed to lie in the development of industrial villages as satellites to large and crowded cities. In America circumstances differed: here, model housing was not so much the product of national investigations into workers' housing, or of legislation such as that passed in Belgium, England, and France. Rather, in South Manchester and similar towns, the intent was less reform-minded than practical, and more of an independent recognition of sensible standards in housing.[39]

A type of model dwelling for workers appeared at the outset of the nineteenth century in the cottages of early mill towns in southern New England. In Centerville, Harris, and Fiskville, Rhode Island, situated upon the banks of the Blackstone River extending north from Providence and Pawtucket, modest yet handsome mill cottages can still be seen, though now in the midst of a continuous urban setting. There were no boardinghouses in these villages since the population was composed mostly of resident workers with families. Single people roomed and boarded with families. Cottages for each family conformed to a rural tradition of separate living quarters. Detached houses, as opposed to boardinghouses and tenements, served for still another reason: weaving in the first years of the century had yet to be mechanized and placed inside the factory. The "Rhode Island system" of factory spinning and cottage weaving predated the "Waltham [or factory] system" where spinning and weaving both were performed in the factory after 1814. The Rhode Island system placed weavers in separate quarters or cottages with enough room for working and raising families. Typical cottages were those built in 1812 by the Interlaken Mills of Fiskville (fig. 5). These story-and-a-half cottages measure about twenty-two feet square in plan. The first level consists of three rooms including a common living and kitchen area and two bedrooms (one of which kept a loom). Next to the entrance a stair led to a loft or attic chamber. Clapboard siding battened at the corners and eaves covered the pitched-roof, frame structure. The width of the foundation and height of the wall from the ground to beneath the gable measured about the same to form a visually pleasing ratio in exterior proportion. A few cottages were shingled, and some were built of stone; but conventional framing and siding predominated. These cottages illustrate early company housing, but they were not part of separately administered single-enterprise towns. Instead, they formed villages in existing rural communities. Yet where they remain in groups or rows, there is still an obvious spatial distinction in their layout that distinguishes them from other houses not owned by the mills. These earliest cottages were simple and inexpensive to construct, economically planned with a mini-

bedroom   bedroom

living room

5. A mill cottage of frame construction, Fiskville, R.I., ca. 1812. Two additional rooms were located upstairs. Redrawn from a measured drawing by Frank Chouteau Brown, 1935.

mum of decoration, standardized with respect to exterior appearance and interior appointments, and usually well maintained. Built as low-cost houses, they wasted no space, though they fitted the requirements of their tenants. The companies that owned them painted their exteriors (usually white) and kept them in repair, to judge from present appearances.[40]

Similarly modest though distinctive boardinghouses were built for the mill girls at Lowell in the 1820s. Built on the Waltham system, they provided lodging for single workers and were designed with a different purpose in mind than a family's need. Personal services like board and laundry were handled in rooms separate from living quarters, and a matron employed by the company attended to these and other custodial chores. Boardinghouses later underwent a morphological change about midcentury, being subdivided as multifamily tenements. This happened once the immigrant family took the place of the migrant mill girl or single worker. In conception the boardinghouse furnished a shelter designed for transient workers who came to labor in the factories for a temporary period. On this basis they worked fine.[41] From a twentieth-century vantage, their design appears starkly modern: no superfluous applications of decorative woodwork detracted from their appearance or disguised their function; they were as proudly utilitarian as the factories in which their residents worked. Acknowledging the significance of the early boardinghouse in Lowell, John Coolidge has written: "It was comprehensive in conception, it was efficient in operation, and it conformed to folk custom. It is these very qualities which are the ideal of every designer of housing today."[42] However, the boardinghouse was not a solution for workers with families; nor was the tenement. They provided no sense of attachment. Though some workers spent their lives in them, most came and went. The cottage, on the other hand, presumed a less mobile tenantry. Detached and even semidetached dwellings represented a more permanent living arrangement with greater personal privacy and dignity.

South Manchester and Ludlow contained single- and double-family dwellings in addition to a few boardinghouses. It was the stated purpose of their agents that good housing be furnished to attract a stable work force.[43] Moreover, mechanics, weavers, spinners, reelers, and other skilled workers often married and raised families and expected a cottage in which to live. The early weaver's cottage therefore continued as a popular type. The houses at South Manchester varied from those of Lowell and other corporation towns not only in type but also in site planning. At Lowell houses conformed to rows, whereas at South Manchester they were placed informally in clusters following the contour of the land. No axis formed by a lengthy canal squared off lots for factories and houses; there was no fixed plan or layout except that determined by the existing terrain. The smaller company town also managed to retain this scale of building and continued to erect detached and semidetached houses. South Manchester and Ludlow each possess interesting examples of model cottages cited for distinction by journalists, government investigators, and foreign observers.

Cottages of the Cheney Brothers Manufacturing Company in South Manchester can be grouped into several styles according to size and period. Construction lasted from the founding years of the company until World War I. However, it will be sufficient to choose one type for examination before turning to Ludlow's cottages. In the 1860s the company put up a number of one-and-a-half-story L-shaped units for workers with families. In appearance these exhibited the angular asymmetry or "picturesque" form so popular in domestic architecture during the period (fig. 6). A living room and separate kitchen projected in one wing. The other wing, with two bedrooms, intersected at a right angle to form the ell. Attic space could provide

6. A single-family house along a "favorite walk" in South Manchester, Conn. From *Harper's New Monthly Magazine*, 1872.

another bedroom if necessary, depending on family need. A porch, appended to the intersecting nook, opened into the living room. The outside walls were clapboarded, and the pitched roof was accentuated by a scalloped vergeboard beneath the front gable. Gingerbread shingling sheathed the wall area above the eaves, and a railing of wood balusters enclosed the porch, which was supported by a turned post with radial brackets. In 1872 an observer described some other, less visible features:

> The cottages for the workmen in South Manchester have all been designed with an artistic taste, while considerations of their interior convenience have not been overlooked. They are all fur-

nished with a constant supply of water, drawn from springs upon the domain, and also with gas. Thus two most important conditions for comfort are guaranteed, and in these respects the dwellings . . . compare most favorably with such as are usual in small manufacturing towns in New England. Plenty of water and plenty of light, with abundant ventilation, simple necessities as they are, are sadly wanting in the homes of industry, though it requires so little foresight to provide for these, especially in villages where the supply of them is practically infinite.[44]

He also reflects on the rents set by the company. In comparison to Holyoke, for example, a South Manchester house rented for two dollars, the same weekly rate as a room in a boardinghouse. In South Manchester the company maintained low rents, which stayed about the same from the end of the 1860s until the turn of the century.[45] Similarly designed houses in nearby Willimantic, Connecticut, erected by the Willimantic Linen Company and built about the same time in 1865 for fifteen hundred dollars a unit, provide an estimate for the South Manchester units. The annual return on rent to the Willimantic company was 7½ percent, drawing about a tenth of the workers' income.[46] The same figures may be deduced for South Manchester.

Ludlow Associates rented both single- and double-family cottages to its workers. Thirty units erected in 1878, ten years after the company began operations, number among the best houses constructed in the nineteenth century for factory labor. Appearances help to explain why (fig. 7). Folio-sized, color-tinted plates of five styles of detached and semidetached houses built by the company were reproduced in Carroll D. Wright's *Report on the Factory System of the United States*, which was printed and bound together with the 1880 U.S. census on manufacturers. Wright chose them as exemplary of workers' housing in the United States. In exterior appearance each house pre-

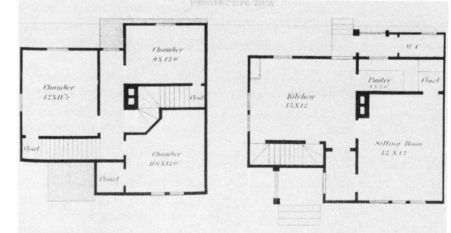

7. A double-family house in Ludlow, Mass., 1878. This is one of five styles of houses rented by the Ludlow Associates and cited as the best workers' housing in the United States by the commissioner of labor. From Wright, *Report on the Factory System of the United States*, 1883.

sents a modest and attractive elevation. What distinguishes them most is the simplicity of their vernacular form; no period ornamentation such as Gothic or Italianate trim decorates them. Instead, they appear rather plain in terms of design. Wide battens at corners, eaves, spandrels, and foundations accented the clean lines that formed the wall planes. Subtle tones of brown or gray rather than white paint covered the walls. Each were frame in construction and two stories in height, and only foundations, fireplaces, and chimney and vent stacks required material other than wood. All five styles provided three upstairs bedrooms and at least two full-sized rooms below, including a kitchen and parlor (and a separate dining room) in the slightly larger detached units. An apartment in a double-family house contained 1,074 square feet of floor area and rented for $1.50 a week or $6.00 a month. Nonemployees were charged higher rent.[47] In illustrating the Ludlow cottages, Wright suggested that the "efforts to secure good homes for their operatives made by the Cheney Brothers, at South Manchester, Connecticut; the Fairbanks Company, at Saint Johnsbury, Vermont; and the Hazards, at Peace Dale, Rhode Island . . . might [also] be described." Thus, the commissioner of labor was given a choice of houses from which to illustrate his report.

The Ludlow houses also received the attention of Budgett Meakin on his tour of New England. He complimented their planning and labeled them "housekeepers' houses,"

that is to say, planned entirely from the point of view of the one woman who has generally to do all the work in them, with rooms wisely arranged, and plenty of stores and cupboards. This most commendable principle is one too often lost sight of, but which is of the utmost value.[48]

The company connected the houses with services such as water, gas, and sewers for indoor plumbing. Water closets were placed either

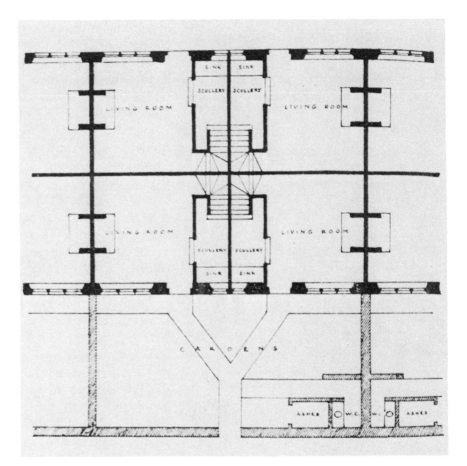

8. Row houses in Copley, Yorkshire, England, 1853. Apartments were constructed back-to-back, a practice later outlawed. From Hole, *The Homes of the Working Classes*, 1866.

on the first floor or in the basement. These conveniences reflected a growing interest in efficiencies and services first called for by Catharine Beecher in her "American Woman's Home" of 1869 and later by E. C. Gardner in *Illustrated Homes* (1875), signaling the beginning of a quiet revolution in domestic shelter completed by the end of the nineteenth century. Years later, Ludlow continued to provide examples of the "superior type" of workers' dwelling.[49]

Industrial villages in England, France, and Germany contained model houses similar in form to those in New England. By comparing examples of workers' housing in New England with those of Europe, it is possible to measure the advantages and advancements in construction and accommodation obtained at home and abroad.

In Akroyd's village of Copley in Yorkshire, England, the dwellings conformed to a row-house arrangement with each apartment having a separate entrance (fig. 8). Each contained three small rooms of considerably less area than provided in houses in New England and on the continent. A two-story, two-bedroom apartment contained only 570 square feet of floor area. While handsome in appearance and substantially built of stone, the arrangement of the cottages was back-to-back as well as attached on side. This resulted in windows offering light and ventilation on one side only. Akroyd abandoned the back-to-back type in his later village of Akroydon built in the 1860s. Copley, Akroydon, Saltaire, Queensbury, West Halifax, and Bessbrook (Northern Ireland), all developed between 1846 and 1863, though early industrial villages, provided houses and community facilities that were far superior to those of Manchester or other industrial cities. In each of these villages rents varied from three to five shillings a week, requiring 15 to 20 percent of a worker's income.[50] Port Sunlight (1887) and Bourneville (1895) came somewhat later and compare more directly to the New England towns.[51] Bourneville, near Birmingham, was the subject of a tour in 1907 during the eighth international housing congress.

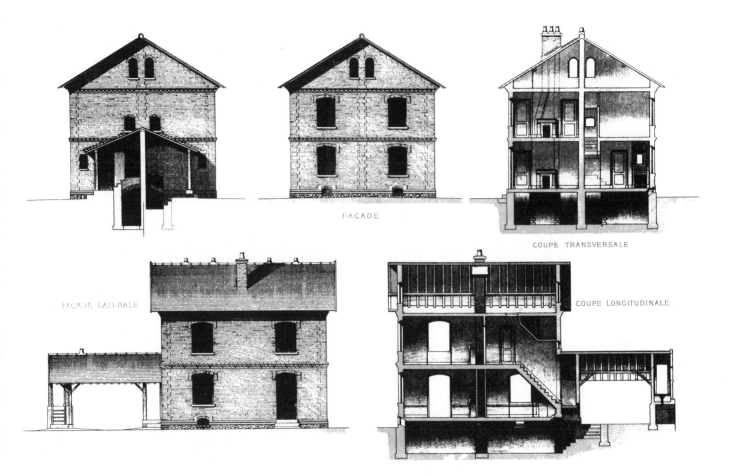

FAÇADE

COUPE TRANSVERSALE

FAÇADE LATÉRALE

COUPE LONGITUDINALE

9. A double-family house in Noisiel, France,
1875. Note the covered passageway between
apartment and privy for the hanging of laundry.
Courtesy of the Bibliothèque nationale.

In France model double-family houses built in 1875 for the Menier Chocolate Company at Noisiel near Paris illustrate a general type of house built by industrialists in northern Europe. On the continent semidetached houses were favored over the British row house. The French introduced double-family dwellings to Europe about the same time they appeared in New England. In Noisiel, best known for the factory designed by Jules Saulnier, double-family houses were built on grids of land 100 feet square (fig. 9). Two-story units faced gable to street with the apartments divided along the axis of the pitched roof, one to each side. On the first floor of each apartment were one bedroom and a kitchen. A one-story annex of laundry-drying space and privy vault attached to the rear of each apartment. The second floor contained the living room and another bedroom, above which was an attic for storage. Total floor area for each apartment amounted to 672 square feet. The houses were built of brick on stone foundations, and the interior walls were plastered. Overall, the outward effect was modest and tidy though prosaic (fig. 10). What is exceptional is that each apartment had its own privy vault provided with containers emptied by the company. Drinking water, however, had to be carried inside from exterior taps. Lighting and heating were furnished by gas from a plant operated by the company, and the most attractive feature was that the apartments rented for the very low sum of 150 francs or what then was the equivalent of $28.95 for a year. This required about a twelfth of the annual wages paid to the head of the family. Each double-family unit cost the company 10,000 francs or $1,930 to build, from which the owner realized only a 3 percent annual return.[52]

The largest single enterprise furnishing workers housing in Europe was located at Essen, Germany, where Friedrich Krupp built his famous armaments. Krupp began erecting houses for his employees in 1861 and had completed 3,659 units by 1892. These houses occupied satellite villages developed within a walking radius of the factories in the central city. Illustrated here is a four-family house in a quadri-

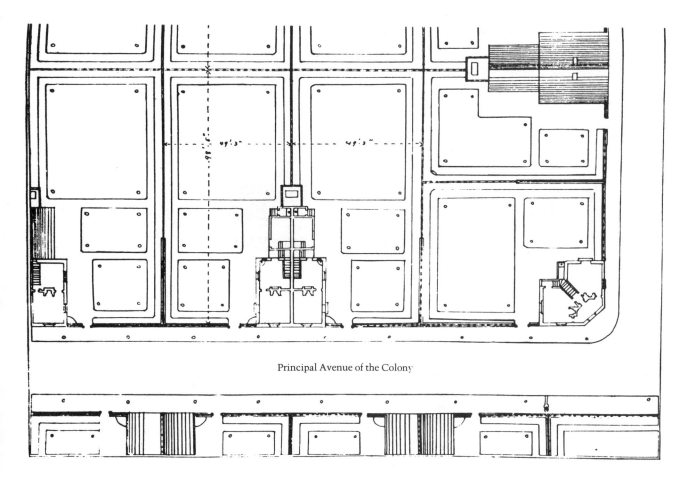

Principal Avenue of the Colony

10. Site plan of double-family houses at Noisiel,
France, 1875. Each family is provided a yard and
garden. From Gould, "The Housing of the Working People," 1895.

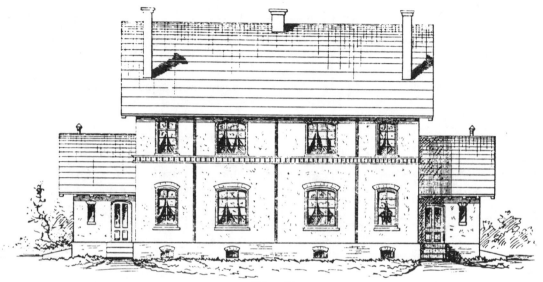

Elevation.

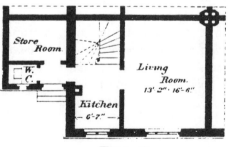

Store Room.

W. C.

Living Room.
13' 2" × 16' 6".

Kitchen.
— 6'-7." —

First Story.

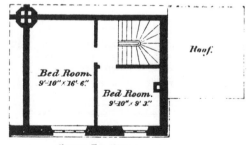

Bed Room.
9'-10" × 16' 6."

Bed Room.
9'-10" × 9' 3."

Hauf.

Second Story.

11. A four-family house in Essen, Germany, 1876. The problem with the houses built by Krupp is evident in the plan. The small apartments and poor ventilation offer small improvement over the row houses at Copley. From Wright, *Report on the Factory System of the United States*, 1883.

partite arrangement (fig. 11) built for Drei Linden in 1876. Other satellite villages included Alfredshof, Altenhof, Cronenberg, Friedrichshof, and Schederhof, all developed between 1860 and 1900. Each apartment offered a living room, kitchen(ette), storeroom, and water closet on the ground floor and two bedrooms above on the second floor. The total floor area was 680 square feet. Though the rooms opened to a window, no through ventilation existed because of the two intersecting dead walls. Load-bearing masonry walls finished in stucco on the exterior supported a tile-covered roof. Investigator E. R. L. Gould reported in the U.S. Bureau of Labor's *Eighth Special Report*, "The Housing of the Working People" (1895), that the apartments were "extremely popular, and when dwellings are vacated applicants are so numerous that, as a rule, only such as have been ten years in the company's employ are considered."[53] Workers paid forty-two dollars a year for the opportunity to rent; and since a foreman in the factories earned forty-five dollars a month, the cost of housing could be managed on about a twelfth of his total income.

In contrast to the workers' housing of Europe, it can be seen that the houses of South Manchester and Ludlow differed in several ways. The New England house furnished about a third more floor area and was built of wood instead of masonry. Of course, in New England, timber for construction was not only plentiful but also conventional. Furthermore, the proportion of space allotted to family functions like dining and cooking varied from one country to another; the British and German house plans afford little kitchen space, though the French provided a large area, probably to include dining. The French also placed living rooms upstairs in the fashion of town houses. Though the French and British cottages provided privy vaults, they required an outside entrance. The New England houses usually placed water closets on the inside instead of using the less convenient attached shed and vault. However, each of these housing developments was well advanced for its time even in having waste disposal;

most small settlements in Europe and America waited until after the turn of the century before furnishing sewerage. At a time when most towns refused to provide such services through taxation, company towns forged ahead and expended the capital for these improvements. All the houses provided a modicum of services in plumbing, heating, and lighting, but sanitary precautions through adequate ventilation were possible only in instances where detached or semidetached dwellings were erected.[54] One final item of distinction was rent. In no place was rent more than 15 percent of the head of household's yearly income. Though attention has been given only to houses constructed in single-enterprise villages, it must be obvious that living conditions in some industrial towns—including the model company town in New England—resulted from raised rather than lowered housing standards.

International housing congresses and exhibits

Attempts to improve workers' housing during the second half of the nineteenth century brought together representatives from different industrial nations to discuss their mutual problem. Officials at these gatherings were mostly government appointees to labor commissions, though exhibitors and guests came largely from the ranks of industrialists, not a few of whom built company towns. The purpose of these gatherings was to share ideas at an international forum on how best to improve housing.

The first international housing congress met in Paris on the occasion of the 1889 Paris Exposition. The year marked the one-hundredth anniversary of the popular revolution, and the life of the worker was made a central theme. Exhibits of model workers' housing were displayed at the fair, while delegates presented lectures and consulted with one another about their building programs. Eventually the exhibits were judged and the best awarded medals. The company housing at Noisiel received a gold medal on this occasion. Model houses had been displayed at other trade fairs, first in London in 1851 and then in Paris in 1867, but never had there been a concerted interest in workers' housing with several exhibits. Though the exposition was international in scope with America participating, the housing congresses were always held in Europe: following the first meeting in Paris was a second in Marseilles in 1892, a third in Bordeaux in 1895, a fourth in Brussels in 1897, a fifth again in Paris in 1900, a sixth in Düsseldorf in 1902, a seventh in Liège in 1905, an eighth in London in 1907, and a ninth in Vienna in 1910. The tenth was postponed because of war. American exhibitors of workers' housing did receive recognition, however, and representatives from the U.S. Bureau of Labor delivered papers transcribed in the reports of these European congresses. What is important is that housing had become an issue as a direct result of industrialization and family displacement. Instances of model housing, however isolated, were recognized and presented to the public at international forums. But because of the attention given to experiments and exhibits of the German *Werkbund* after 1907 and the numerous housing projects constructed throughout Europe following World War I, little has been said regarding these earlier events. Perhaps it was the small-town or suburban location of these earlier experiments that has caused them to go unnoticed.

The agenda of the first international housing congress outlines steps taken to ameliorate housing conditions and suggests several areas for exploration: (1) "Character and origin of efforts to improve workmen's dwellings," (2) "Types of construction and rent," and (3) "Results." The results could allegedly be seen in the material and moral rewards gathered by industry and labor. The French Society for Low-Cost Housing (Société française des habitations à bon marché) sought among its several goals "to make known" as well as "to encourage in all France the construction, by individuals, employers, or local societies, of healthy and cheap houses."[55] Aside from workers' housing at Noisiel, Guise, and Verviers, mention was made of the Société mulhousienne des cités ouvrières (Mulhouse Workingmen's Dwellings Company), Mulhouse, France. The company was founded in 1853 by philanthropist Jean Dollfus. Dollfus, like Quincy and Paine in Boston, formed a building and loan association so that the workers of Mulhouse could purchase a home on easy terms. He hired an architect, Emile Muller, to design model houses (fig. 12) constructed by the association. Of particular interest was their utilitarian design. A collection of these was later published in E. Muller and E. Cacheux, *Habitations ouvrières en tous pays* (1879). As with other countries, France provided examples of workers' houses built by industrialists as well as by philanthropists.

At the fairgrounds the American entries in section 11 of the "Social Economy" department submitted diagrams and statistics on profit sharing by the Peace Dale Manufacturing Company and the N. O. Nelson Company of Saint Louis.[56] Peace Dale took home a silver medal for its exhibit. The only other participants from America were all from New York. Plans for workingmen's dwellings were offered by Edward R. Seligman of Columbia College, the Tenement House Building Company of New York City, and the Improved Dwellings Company of Brooklyn. Of these, only the Tenement House Building Company placed with a silver medal.[57]

Although America did not host a housing congress, it encouraged the display of model housing at the World's Columbian Exposition in Chicago in 1893. In the German Pavilion at Chicago, Krupp set up a papier-mâché model of one of its Essen villages; and, across the midway, the U.S. Pavilion of Labor and Industry sheltered several full-scale model houses erected especially for the occasion. Mention of these is given by Miss Annesley Kenealy, who judged them under the category of "Hygiene and Sanitation." She cites a "model workingman's house" built on behalf of the Philadelphia County Wom-

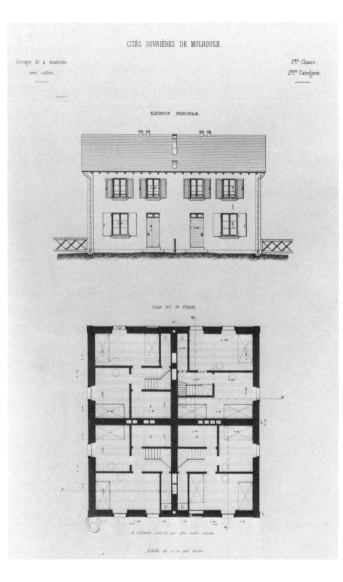

12. A four-family house in Mulhouse, France, 1864. The industrialist and philanthropist Jean Dollfus began his Cités Ouvrières in 1853 and sold rather than rented the apartments. Courtesy of the Bibliothèque nationale.

en's Committee and then discusses another cottage erected by the Improved Dwellings Company of New York. What impressed her most was the contrast the two presented and the "evolution in thought and human need" shown.[58] Somewhat less imposing were plans of workers' housing provided by the various state bureaus of labor and boards of health: in drawings provided by the Pennsylvania State Board of Health, Miss Kenealy made note of the attention given to planting flower beds designed in plan with the dwellings as a beautification measure. Her description of landscaping recalls the work begun by industrialists in model company towns who initiated programs of grounds improvement and encouraged employees to participate. The category embracing the housing exhibit emphasizes the importance of sanitary reform as a social issue. Boards of health and labor struggled hand in hand to present the public with solutions to the housing problem.

Returning to Paris in 1900, American exhibitors of model houses made a sweep of the prizes by taking gold, silver, and bronze medals for their displays. The Paris Exposition of 1900 hosted the largest exhibition ever given of workers' dwellings.[59] The presentation consisted of photographs of the houses mounted on cards attached to display stands along the walls of the Palace of Social Economy. In the center of the space were placed models. All countries shared the same pavilion, though they were divided according to nation. Nine of ten entries from the United States won prizes. In the division of model houses, three company towns placed first, second, and third: Ludlow Associates Manufacturing Company won a gold medal for the houses described earlier; Draper Company at Hopedale won a silver medal for the houses that will be discussed in chapter 7; and the Apollo Iron and Steel Company at Vandergrift, Pennsylvania, took bronze. Vandergrift had been developed in 1895 from plans drawn by Olmsted Associates. In the center of the pavilion lay models of tenements, composing another division of housing. One scaled-down model, measuring four by five feet, won a grand prize for the Tenement House Committee of the Charity Organization Society of New York City. It was an exhibit sponsored by Alfred T. White, whose model tenements first appeared in Brooklyn in 1877.[60]

In expositions that followed until the outbreak of World War I, an increasing number of companies and workers' housing associations entered competition to display their model dwellings. Houses built in company towns constituted a large part of those that won medals and were cited for their advancements. At the Internationalen Wohnungskongress at Vienna in 1910 no less than fifteen industrial housing developments exhibited model houses, with Ludlow, Hopedale, and Peace Dale leading the group.[61] A new division titled "Workmen's Cities" directly focused attention on buildings in company towns. The period just before the war signaled the height of international interest in workers' housing. When the expositions and congresses reconvened in the twenties, interest soon dissipated. Large-scale rebuilding campaigns in Europe and America during and after the war began to furnish workers with decent housing. The need to capture public attention with illustrations of housing conditions had been met.

The construction of company houses ended in New England about the time of World War I. They were no longer built for several reasons. The example of Pullman had stigmatized company housing, and the advent of the automobile lessened the need for workers to reside near the factory. Building and loans began extending mortgage credit to those whom regular banks traditionally refused. Even so, among New England heads of household who were tenants as opposed to homeowners, the number increased from 56 to 65 percent between 1850 and 1930.[62] Building and loan associations (which, incidentally, hosted their first congress at the Columbian Exposition) had begun to propagandize the idea of home ownership for workers as a right of citizenship. Their slogan proclaimed that "The American Home [is] the Safeguard of American Liberties."[63] The availability of mortgages, an overall increase in rental housing provided by developers, arrival of mass transit, and higher wages paid to labor in terms of real income no longer necessitated company housing. However, there had once been a need for such housing, and the model company towns of New England built and exhibited dwellings that largely improved the living conditions of their inhabitants.

Having provided an overview of several New England towns and having emphasized their distinctive traits, resulting from industrial development, paternalism, and housing, we can now evaluate Hopedale and place it within a historical and environmental context.

Part Two
Hopedale, Massachusetts:
A Model Company Town
Chapter 5
The Morphology of Hopedale

Hopedale, Massachusetts, is located about thirty miles southwest of downtown Boston. State Highway 16 offers the most direct route, passing over hill and dale from Wellesley through South Natick, Holliston, and Milford. Two miles beyond Milford lie the outskirts of Hopedale, and a right turn onto Adin Street provides a pleasant entrance to the center of town. Large old homes and a school, partially screened from view by hedgerows and trees, disclose the prosperity of several generations of one family. Near the intersection of Adin and Hopedale streets, the town hall looms into view. This fine edifice of granite and limestone occupies the top of a small hill overlooking the town. From there, turning northward beyond the church and library, the factories, offices, and houses of the company appear below. If one were visiting the town by automobile or—at an earlier time—by carriage, this route would be preferred. However, a different route would be taken for those coming to Hopedale to seek employment in the late nineteenth or early twentieth century.

After boarding a train of the Boston and Albany Railroad in Boston's South Station, a prospective employee would head due west toward Worcester but transfer at the North Grafton Station a few miles before reaching that city. Now far removed from the boisterous port, only the sounds of wheels on the single track of the Grafton and Upton Railroad interrupt the solitude of the oak and hickory forest as the train descends along the Blackstone River valley some fifteen miles above its destination. Near the end of the line, the forest parts to reveal a small and placid lake with factories in the background. There is no station, and the train stops only momentarily at the factory yard. The worker steps off to enter the town through the company's gates.

In this way, a retired machinist named Charles F. Merrill recalled arriving at Hopedale by train on April 19, 1910. He first resided in a boardinghouse before moving into a unit in Bancroft Park: "The times were complacent and untroubled," and "our recreation was simple and inexpensive."[1] Although the new houses were heated by coal furnaces, the company gave away "shop wood" to fire the kitchen stoves before gas lines were connected. Even then food was not cheap, with eggs costing twenty-two cents a dozen and milk ten cents a quart. At Christmas the company organized parties held at the town hall, and the Dutcher house blazed with "candles in every window." After years of service rendered to the company, the call to work remained most vivid in his memory: "I first heard the shop bell ring curfew on the evening of my arrival so long ago. I heard it open the gates of day next morning at six. I heard it call people to work at seven, and again at one. I have heard it perform this routine thousands of times in almost half a century, and its sounds fall as pleasantly on my ear as it did when I first heard it."[2] The halcyon times remembered by Merrill were shared by other employees whose families remain in Hopedale.

For one hundred years, between 1856 and 1956, Hopedale operated as a company town with virtually all property held in ownership by a single enterprise. In 1956 proceedings were begun to dispose of company-owned services and utilities, and the last company houses were sold at auction. From then until 1967 the original enterprise struggled with economic difficulties before finally merging to become a division of a large corporation. Although most company towns have been incorporated into larger cities or have disappeared altogether, a few remain as urban reminders of an earlier age. Hopedale exists today relatively unchanged from the beginning of the century to reveal the environmental and architectural achievement of its single-enterprise development.

A communitarian failure

Beginning in March 1856, the E. D. and G. Draper Company assumed control of Hopedale Community, a small religious settlement that for fourteen years had vacillated between a quest for social harmony and a desire for capital success. After much bickering among members and many economic setbacks, the community's spiritual leader, the Reverend Adin Ballou (1803–90), declared the settlement insolvent. His decision to discontinue became final with a vote by the shareholders to sell their collective property to Ebenezer and George Draper, who would transform Hopedale into a company town. Years later Ballou recounted: "At the time of the dissolution of the joint-stock proprietorship . . . nearly the entire bulk of our real estate possessions, including lands, mill-sites, streets, shops, barns, and other buildings, was transferred by legal conveyance to the firm of E. D. & G. Draper, for their sole use, behoof, and disposal forever."[3] The only buildings and land parcels kept from sale were three houses (sold individually), the chapel and town square, and the cemetery. The last of these was conveyed to the Draper Company by the community's trustees in 1873. In 1973, 86 percent of all undeveloped land still remained in company hands, and residents continued to think of Hopedale as a single-enterprise town.[4]

The Draper Company took possession of what to outward appearances could have been mistaken for a small farming village, since the landscape was mostly open and rural. But a closer look would have revealed a small manufactory with a group of workers' dwellings to one side instead of barns and farmhouses. The surrounding land had once been farmed, but the yield was poor; and the Hopedale Community had turned to industry for support. For a time, the site provided for both. Ballou located his community at the upper end of a valley. Though a portion of the valley was acceptable for cultivation, its principal asset was the Mill River, a tributary of the Blackstone, which offered a source of waterpower for industrial use. The floor of the valley extended four miles in length and one and a quarter miles in width along a north-to-south axis. Above it to the east and west lay a range of hills, the highest of which rose five hundred feet, separating Hopedale Community from the neighboring towns of Mendon and Milford. These hills acted as a barrier against encroachment by these neighbors. Ballou probably had this isolation in mind when selecting the site. The only connecting route then existing was Mendon Road (now State Highway 16). East of Milford the road led up through Wellesley and then on to Boston; west of Mendon it continued for several miles before reaching the Blackstone valley and turning south toward Rhode Island. But even Mendon Road did not encroach. Instead, it crossed the valley about one-half mile's distance south of the settlement. The relative isolation resulting from this location permitted Ballou and his followers a certain amount of freedom in the layout of their settlement.

Understandably, Ballou was more concerned with the social organization of his community than with its site layout. He did employ Fourier's idea of separating working and residential areas in phalansteries.[5] He designated industrial lots and house lots and decided what land was to be farmed. However, he sketched no ideal plan, no grand scheme, to show how these areas should be apportioned. A rough drawing of several streets and a meetinghouse square is all that survives from the 1840s. The first carefully drawn map was not made and recorded until 1855.[6] Although the community developed without a master plan as such, it did receive some forethought. A "Main Street" (later named Hopedale Street) was laid to connect with Mendon Road; and tying into it were several minor streets to mark off a residential section bordered on the south by a square. These early improvements were made in the period after 1849, mostly from the occasional labor of the Hopedale Industrial Army. The army was recruited from the membership "to promote the cheerful prosecution of public improvement"[7] or, in other words, to lay out streets, walks, and public grounds. Its members assembled at the end of workdays and on holidays. Consequently, their contribution was small. One of two community papers, the *Diamond*, however, reflected proudly upon the improvements that had been made by 1851: "Ten years ago there was no such place as Hopedale in existence. Where now are regular streets, fine gardens, flourishing fruit trees, and neat cottages, was then a rough, half cultivated piece of land belonging to a run-down farm."[8] At that date, twenty-eight houses had been constructed, "mostly small and neat," and the population numbered between 150 and 175, counting thirty-six families.[9] Though the settlement had begun to take root, it grew slowly and rather modestly in regard to physical improvement.

In 1842 Ebenezer Draper and his wife, Anna, enlisted as members of Hopedale Community after having listened to Ballou preach the gospel of Christian socialism. Draper brought with him the skill and capital needed to set up and run a machine shop for manufacturing textile machinery. He learned this skill from his father, Ira Draper of Weston, Massachusetts, who began patenting devices for textile machinery in 1816. In 1853 his brother George moved to Hopedale after having become a copartner in the machinery business the year before. A certain portion of the shop and its equipment represented the Drapers' share in the community.

As Hopedale grew, its prosperity depended more and more on the operation of the textile machinery business. Success rested mainly on the brothers' manufacture of a revolving temple, a device for looms that keeps cloth stretched an even width during weaving. To this device were added others as they expanded their line. But running the machinery business took the labor of only seventeen workmen in 1855.[10] Though the income from the Drapers' operation supported other businesses and paid dividend on the joint stock,[11] it alone could not shoulder the financial burden of less productive activities. At the end of each year no surplus capital remained for reinvesting in the business and enabling expansion. Even during the best of years the community barely managed to scrape by, and only then because the Drapers' business found a receptive market. Eventually, the liabilities overreached the dividends, and the enterprise faltered under the strain of paying wage and salary to farmers, ministers, machinists, and teachers, and caring for all their dependents. Having operated for several years in a deficit and with a national depression at hand, the leaders of the community with Ballou at the helm reluctantly decided to abandon ship. Some members left, seeking admission into other utopian settlements, while others stayed behind and went to work for the Drapers.[12] Ballou remained in Hopedale, having been asked by the Drapers to continue his ministry, which he did until retirement in 1876. Reorganized solely for the purpose of manufacturing textile machinery, the settlement developed along a different pattern as a new era of building commenced.

An industrial success

New England experienced a boom in textile mill construction during the 1850s after nearly a half-century of investment in cloth making. Even though Congress had gradually reduced the tariffs on foreign commodities—and cloth in particular—the home market remained profitable, and literally hundreds of small towns throughout New England had invested in mill construction.[13] Early factories were small and their machinery primitive. The largest built their own textile equipment. Consequently, output varied from place to place, depending on the productive capacity of a factory and the efficiency of its machinery. Despite the relatively high cost of labor, it was the vigorous competition among mills before and after 1850 that focused attention on textile equipment.[14] Among the earliest manufacturers to specialize in textile machinery were the Whitins of Whitinsville, Massachusetts, another company town near Hopedale, who had begun making textile machinery in 1831. After expansion in 1847, the Whitins earned recognition as specialists throughout New England.[15] The Drapers had a similar objective and were first to specialize in the manufacture of machinery parts. One item in their line was the spindle. A spindle is a device that holds a bobbin of thread. The faster a spindle could turn (with the least vibration), the faster thread could be spun. Hence, increased production and higher profits were enjoyed by the mill with the best spindles and other machinery. A small item like a spindle could also be modified to fit different makes of spinning frames. The effect of such specialization made textile machinery more efficient and adaptable. In time the Drapers expanded their line to include spoolers, spinning rings, let-off motions, thread guides, eveners, and all form of machinery screws, designed to improve the textile manufacturing process.[16] For these innovations there was a market as long as textile production remained highly competitive. Cloth makers spent anywhere from two-thirds to three-quarters of the sum of building a factory in outfitting it with machinery.[17] To remain competitive, they periodically renovated. Rather than scrap old equipment and purchase all new, they adapted newer parts like improved spindles. In providing this service, the Drapers, the Whitins, the Masons, Saco-Pettee, Fales and Jenks, and other machinery manufacturers found a large and lucrative market.

With the outbreak of civil war business improved markedly. Not only were the Drapers able to expand their line of products,[18] but they were also able to purchase patent rights from competitors.[19] Massachusetts manufacturing statistics of 1865 indicate the company's steady rise in wealth: the value of machinery made increased considerably over that previously recorded in 1855, amounting to $67,539. What is more, capital for investment increased over six times to $32,154.[20] During the intervening ten years the labor force doubled to thirty-eight hands, not counting superintendents, foremen, foundrymen, and stablemen. The company conducted a large livery business since no rail service existed in Hopedale until 1889. Every manufactured item had to be hauled by team and wagon to neighboring Milford, there to connect with the Boston and Albany or Old Colony lines. So out of the way was Hopedale that the Draper company catalogs used to carry elaborate directions on how to reach the town. The lack of rail service may have upset schedules and caused some inconvenience, but it had little effect on production and sales. William F. Draper, George Draper's eldest son, remembered that "From 1865 to 1873 the business was very profitable, twenty per cent [increase per year] being less than the average."[21]

In 1868 Ebenezer Draper retired and sold his share in the company. Apparently George Draper owned more of the business by this date than his brother and had been managing "most of the business by agreement."[22] Ebenezer left Hopedale and reinvested his money in another business, which was located in Boston and engaged in manufacturing fireproof safes.[23] William F. Draper took his uncle's place, and the firm name was changed to George Draper and Son.

Production increased steadily and orders arrived faster than they could be filled.[24] The Drapers happily contemplated a situation similar to that experienced by the Fairbanks brothers of Vermont, of having more orders than stock on hand to fill them during peak periods of business. By 1875 the company employed approximately two hundred men, sold $504,750 worth of machinery, and operated with a capital of $284,000.[25] Despite the national depressions of 1873–77 and 1893–95, the Drapers were hardly affected. The reason may well have been that textile mills used periods of slowdown for retooling. In 1881 the company reported a total employment of 350 persons.[26] During the thirty-year interval following 1886, corresponding to Hopedale's greatest period of urban development, employment mounted from five hundred (in 1886) to seven hundred (in 1896) to twelve hundred (in 1906) to over seventeen hundred (by 1916). During the same interval annual sales increased from $1,200,000 to nearly $7,500,000 with the single largest profit-making item being the Northrop Loom.[27] This invention, on which the Drapers expended $350,000 in experimentation between the years 1887 to 1894, rewarded them with millions. Thanks to the ingenuity of a company designer named James Northrop, the Drapers were able to revolutionize the weaving industry: the advancement over "common looms" lay in a device that automatically changed bobbins of thread, "enabling a weaver to operate twenty looms rather than two. Mills that refused or were hesitant to install the new machinery were soon out of business, and for decades Draper could not keep up with demand."[28] Between 1894 and 1903 the company sold 78,599 Northrop Looms to 210 different textile mills in the United States,[29] and of the more than 400,000 common looms operating at the turn of the century, the majority would be replaced by the Drapers prior to World War I.[30] In 1906 approximately twenty thousand looms were being produced each year at an average wholesale price of $140, and this number does not include those made overseas under license.[31] With the rapid growth of the textile industry in the South, the company expanded its fortune: practically all the looms purchased in the states of South Carolina, North Carolina, and Georgia came from the Drapers (fig. 13).[32]

Although New England textile mills continued to purchase machinery from the Drapers during this period of expansion, the market had turned decidedly to the South. Textile manufacture in the South began at least as early as 1846 when William Gregg erected a mill at Graniteville, South Carolina;[33] however, the Civil War delayed industrialization. Not until after Reconstruction did the South begin attracting a market of its own, largely through the support of New England manufacturers. From the 1880s onward southern mills went up in rapid succession, capturing a third of the cotton textile manufacturing market by 1900.[34] Though the Drapers doubled the size of their Hopedale plant between 1886 and 1896 and again between 1896 and 1906, a decision to further expand meant locating elsewhere. In 1906 a warehouse with offices for sales and services was built in Atlanta, Georgia. Additional outlets opened at Spartanburg, South

Hauling Northrop Looms across S.C.

Jan 21st 1896

13. Transporting a Northrop Loom in South Carolina, 1896. Courtesy of the Merrimack Valley Textile Museum.

Carolina, and Greensboro and Biltmore, North Carolina. At Spartanburg another warehouse was constructed in 1929, and in 1935 additional facilities for service and manufacturing went up in East Spartanburg. But the Drapers built no company towns in the South, or elsewhere in New England, though some facilities were placed in Milford, Massachusetts, and Pawtucket, Rhode Island, before World War I. As early as the 1890s the company had purchased tracts of forest in New England to ensure a supply of materials for wooden products like bobbins and shuttles. Vast reserves of timber were maintained at Beebe River, New Hampshire, as well as at Tupper Lake, New York.[35] Until recently, the Draper Division of Rockwell International continued to make textile equipment and to maintain a respectable market in the manufacture of automatic looms, producing an average of seven thousand units during the 1970s, exported largely to developing countries like Hong Kong, Taiwan, Thailand, and Malaysia.[36] Under new management the business rebounded during the late sixties and early seventies, but the Hopedale plant failed to provide an adequate profit margin and closed for good in 1980.

The profits received from the sale of looms and other textile machinery were plowed back into Hopedale. Valuation on real estate in 1886 amounted to $506,548, counting 191 houses owned outright or in part by the company. By 1916, these figures had changed substantially: the value of real estate climbed to $1,906,000 and the number of dwellings to 462, of which the majority were owned outright by the company.[37] The population increased proportionally from 926 in 1886 to 2,663 in 1916.[38] Technological improvements to streamline operations changed the appearance of Hopedale's factories; old buildings were either razed to make way for new or expanded for additional use so as not to be recognized from their original appearance. Even though a few houses were built after World War II, no significant developments have been made since 1916. For years the company maintained Hopedale's attractive environment, though as buildings age they inevitably fall into disrepair, and since 1916 the enterprise and the town built around it have gradually declined.

Shaping a model company town

Hopedale's principal streets, service facilities, utilities, factories, and houses neared completion in 1916. Development had preceded this, during two periods of building expansion, 1856–86 and 1886–1916. The first period saw the genesis of a company town, and the second witnessed the making of a model community. Development ended with an economic recession and loss of employment during World War I. Although Hopedale continued to manufacture textile machinery and even added to its population, its topography with the exception of some additional houses and a new school remains as it did in 1916. Maps drawn for 1856, 1886, and 1916 depict the site at the beginning and end of its two periods of physical development and serve as a reference for describing expansion. The visual impact produced by physiognomic features like factories and houses can be gauged by perspective views and photographs made during the building campaigns.

By urban standards Hopedale is small; its present population of 3,905, twelve hundred more than in 1916, resides in an area of five and one-half square miles. In view of its size and industry, Hopedale's physical growth can be easily studied and profiled.

In 1916 the Draper Company (then at the height of its corporate strength and prestige) furnished the textile industry in the United States with most of its spinning and weaving machinery.[39] Not only did it occupy a position of leadership among manufacturers, but it also obtained leadership among single-enterprise towns in the quality of the environment built around the factories. From the beginnings made by the Hopedale Community, the Drapers commissioned fine buildings and fashioned new streets and walks, planted trees and gardens, and provided parkland for aesthetic as well as for practical reasons. Well-designed houses and community facilities improved the living conditions of workingmen and their families while lending attractiveness to the site. And, to a large extent, this company town managed to convey its image of a good living and working environment.

1856–1886

After the Draper Company took possession of Hopedale in 1856 (fig. 14), it first enlarged the factories to improve the productive capability of the industrial site that had been partially laid out by the earlier community. Water Street along the Mill River was extended south and Union Street (parallel to Peace Street) was brought across to tie in, laying the way for industrial expansion. Near the upper end of Water Street sat the two factory buildings (fig. 15), one of which

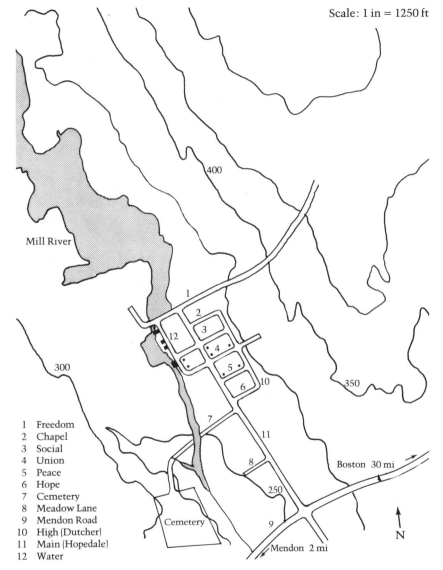

Scale: 1 in = 1250 ft

Mill River

400

300

350

250

Boston 30 mi

Mendon 2 mi

Cemetery

N

14. Map of Hopedale as it would have appeared in 1856 when the Draper Company acquired the site. Only those buildings known to exist are indicated. The industrial area lies west of Water Street.

1 Freedom
2 Chapel
3 Social
4 Union
5 Peace
6 Hope
7 Cemetery
8 Meadow Lane
9 Mendon Road
10 High (Dutcher)
11 Main (Hopedale)
12 Water

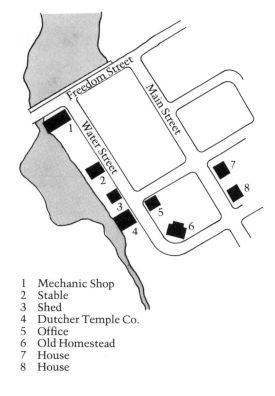

15. Map of the industrial site at Hopedale as it would have appeared in 1858.

1 Mechanic Shop
2 Stable
3 Shed
4 Dutcher Temple Co.
5 Office
6 Old Homestead
7 House
8 House

was already outfitted with a waterwheel to operate a trip-hammer and lathe. It was this building, completed in 1843, that was known as the "mechanic shop" and that first housed the Drapers' enterprise as well as other small businesses and also served for a time as a school (fig. 16).[40] The second building went up three years later in 1846, providing more space and relieving the crowded quarters of the older shop. Named the "cabinet shop" and measuring thirty by forty feet in plan, this second building was also of frame construction though two stories in height. In 1855 a state census on manufacturing recorded the proceeds from these two shops as fifteen thousand dollars in the value of machinery made; operating capital was listed as five thousand dollars.[41] In addition to the shops, several outbuildings, including stables and sheds, also located on Water Street, composed a part of the industrial site. The shops and attendant buildings formed a nucleus around which the company town developed.

Symbolically, factories represent the heart of an industrial town. For a single-enterprise town, they comprise the visual, social, and economic centers of activity. This was the situation in Hopedale, and, during the first period of expansion, the building of factories consumed most of the Drapers' interest and financial investment.

The morphology of the industrial site through the expansion of factories affected the rest of the town as well. New streets were laid and houses for employees were built. Further change was to be seen in the improvement of a dam and reservoir north of the shops.

In 1856 the Drapers persuaded Warren W. Dutcher, inventor of an improved temple, to move to Hopedale and manage a division of the company.

Absorbing a competitor expanded the business while retaining market control. Though the brothers purchased the inventor's patent and operation, they permitted him to manufacture under his own name. Carried as W. W. Dutcher Temple Company, the temple division continued to monopolize the trade. Sales were made through the

16. "Mechanic shop" of the Draper Manufacturing Company, 1843. Known today as the "Little Red Shop," it has been moved from its original site on the southwest corner of Freedom and Water streets and now houses a collection of Draper textile machinery. Courtesy of Scott Wedeking.

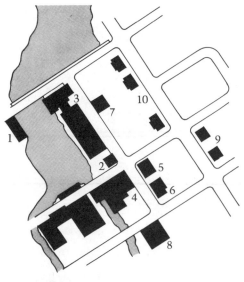

17. Map of the industrial site at Hopedale as it would have appeared in 1875, following expansion.

1 Mechanic Shop
2 Shed
3 Hopedale Machine Co.
4 Dutcher Temple Co.
5 Office
6 Lumber Store
7 Lumber Store
8 Machine Shop
9 Houses
10 Houses

E. D. and G. Draper Company. Dutcher moved into the old cabinet shop before constructing a three-story building beside it in 1860 (also frame and thirty by forty feet) and a new brick factory in 1868. The new factory contained a boiler and enginehouse to supplement water-power and provided three floors of work space.[42] The small mechanic shop was renamed the Hopedale Machine Company in 1868 and transferred to the west side of the river to make room for additional construction. Joseph B. Bancroft, George Draper's brother-in-law, superintended this new division after having worked in the shops since 1847.[43] Again, sales were handled by the Draper Company. For a time Massachusetts required different manufacturing processes even in one enterprise to keep separate records for purposes of inventory and tax. Therefore, the company operated under several trade names before being renamed as simply the Draper Company in 1897, though principal ownership and all partnerships had always resided in the family (see Appendix A).

The overall organization and layout of the industrial site continued to change as the company extended its line of machinery. George Draper acquired a monopoly on spindles after purchasing the inventions of J. Herbert Sawyer of Lowell in 1871 and F. J. Rabeth of Pawtucket in 1878.[44] As with Dutcher, Draper brought Sawyer to Hopedale to set up and run his own department. In 1874 D. A. Sanborn's National Insurance Diagram Bureau made a survey of the Draper factories that describes the layout and type of construction in detail. The number of buildings had multiplied from two to twenty, providing space for three machine shops, two foundries, two finishing mills, one pattern shop, plus sheds for coal, lumber, and other stores, one livery stable, and an office building. Power for operating the mills increased from an original forty-horsepower waterwheel on a thirteen-foot fall beneath the upper privilege to two hundred horsepower produced by a combination of water turbines and steam engines. The turbines (encased wheels) were located at a second dam on the lower

18. "New machine shop" of the Draper Manufacturing Company, 1882, as viewed from the
south with the Mill River in the background.
Courtesy of the Merrimack Valley Textile
Museum.

19. The industrial complex of the Draper Manufacturing Company, 1882, as viewed from the
west with the foundry in the foreground, the old
mechanic shop at far left, and the new machine
shop at right. Courtesy of the Merrimack Valley
Textile Museum.

privilege, which lay parallel to the shops. The company's dependence upon waterpower[45] produced a linear industrial site that extended along the upper and lower privileges. Further separation of factories was produced by the company's departmentalization. In plan (fig. 17) this separation was most noticeable in the insurance diagram of 1874. Castings, spindles, machinery screws, and so on were manufactured at the northern end of the industrial site, and temples were made at the southern end. Gradually, with the introduction of steam engines and further site development, new buildings began filling in the open spaces.

After 1865 Hopedale manifested its economic prosperity through the construction of additional factories, a new office building, and houses for the management and their employees. Hopedale Street was carried north along a winding ledge parallel to the river, and the basin of the upper privilege (the reservoir north of Freedom Street above the shops) was enlarged through dredging and dam improvement.

The factories stood out as the most prominent buildings. Their size and visual impact in relation to the rest of the town enlarged the company's self-image and pride in productive achievement. Built of masonry and designed with architectural appointments in the Italianate and Second Empire styles, they represented substantial additions to the landscape. A new factory 122 feet long and 50 feet wide was added to the existing complex at the northern end of the industrial site in 1882. A mechanical engineer, W. E. Allen, designed the three-story brick structure and its functional mansard belvedere, which contained a water tank (figs. 18,19).[46] The factory also contained a sprinkler system that was manufactured and sold by the company.[47] This, incidentally, was a novel safety feature for the time. Three other buildings of similar size were constructed during the 1880s at the southern end of the site. But the finest addition to the company was a new office building completed in 1880. On this occasion the Drapers employed an architect named Fred Swassey, who later would receive other commissions. The office building required less structural engineering but more finesse regarding style. Although it no longer exists, a photograph (fig. 20) and description survive:

> The new two-story brick office of George Draper and Sons at Hopedale, is being rapidly built, and will be an ornamental and substantial building, 46 feet square and 46 feet high. It is built of quality pressed brick, with black brick trimmings, and a granite base-course and window sills. A pediment in front extends 10 × 19½ feet, and the entrance is by hammered stone steps. The building is of the Venetian style, with five mullian [sic] windows in front. The gable is to be slated with the best black slate, relieved by two belts of colored slate. The portico has a handsome iron crest railing.[48]

This news account also mentions that the building cost eight thousand dollars and was finished inside with oak and with frescoes or plaster trim.

Other evidence of Hopedale's prosperity could be found in the houses of the managing officers. George Draper built a large though modestly designed residence near the intersection of "Draper" and Hopedale streets. Both house and street were completed by 1868.[49] Diagonally across Hopedale Street and north one block, Bancroft erected his new home about the same time on a site now occupied by the library; and, behind the chapel and town square, Dutcher's fine house went up. The first two have since been razed, but Dutcher's handsome Italianate-style residence remains in good condition to this day (fig. 21). Though spaciously proportioned, their houses did not appear pretentious for the architecture of the time or for men of their means. Dutcher's estate— including house, grounds, and outbuildings—was assessed at $14,300.[50] Furthermore, these homes of

20. Office building of the Draper Manufacturing
Company, 1880. Courtesy of the Merrimack
Valley Textile Museum.

21. Warren W. Dutcher house, Hopedale, ca. 1868. Dutcher was one of the first inventors whose patents were acquired by the Draper Company, and his house is similar to the one constructed by George Draper.

management were located near to the shops among the dwellings of their employees. No attempt was made to segregate residential layout. Draper's sons, who began their careers working in the shops, even rented company houses until they were able to build homes of their own.[51]

As housing conditions improved for the Drapers, Dutchers, and Bancrofts, lodging for the work force also took a turn for the better. Double-family houses were erected along Social, Union, and Cemetery streets between 1865 and 1875 to accommodate a work force approaching two hundred men. With an increase in the number of workers with families, the population in 1875 registered 645. Depending on a family's size, either a three- or a four-room apartment in a double-family house could be secured. All houses in Hopedale, from large to small, including the homes of company officers, were frame construction and modest in design. Though a degree of variety existed even in the style of the double-family houses, the overall appearance of the dwellings bestowed the town with a kind of homogeneity. No structures looked especially pretentious or humble, or stood out so as to interrupt the visual serenity that enhanced the landscape.

The completion of Adin Street and the subsequent development of large residential estates became the focus of attention during the 1870s and 1880s (fig. 22). Along this street, which leads southeast from Hopedale Street to merge with Mendon Road, rose the homes of second-generation Drapers, Dutchers, and their associates and kin. The Drapers owned the most imposing property, and their estates overshadowed all others. The effect of this new development was eventually to segregate the homes of the employers from the homes of the workers. Set apart in distance and insulated by large gardens and lawns (some of ten to twenty acres), the second generation sought a life style quite different from that of their fathers. The street was named for Adin Ballou. However, Ballou himself lived out his years in a modest cottage at the crossing of Hopedale and Union streets. Adin

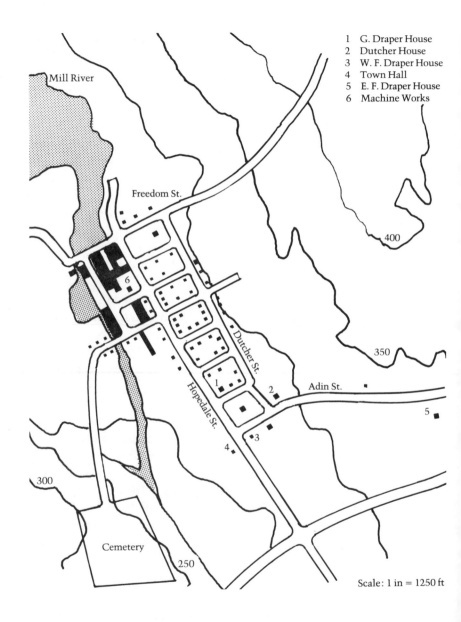

1   G. Draper House
2   Dutcher House
3   W. F. Draper House
4   Town Hall
5   E. F. Draper House
6   Machine Works

Mill River

Freedom St.

Dutcher St.

Hopedale St.

Adin St.

Cemetery

400

350

300

250

Scale: 1 in = 1250 ft

22. Map of Hopedale as it would have appeared in 1886 at the end of George Draper's tenure and the company's first generation of development.

Street displayed a wealth never before seen in Hopedale and provided a grand promenade leading into town from the direction of Milford and Boston. Prior to its construction, visitors entered from the junction of Hopedale Street and Mendon Road or came in the back way along Freedom Street, which took them past the company houses and factories. Adin Street does little to unify the town layout. What it contributes is a splendid vista leading to the center of town lined with trees and elegant homes, adding to the prestige of the Draper family and their company town.

William F. Draper's house, built in 1872 and the first large estate on Adin Street, symbolized the family's turn of fortune (fig. 23). It fell short of reproducing the kind of sophisticated Second Empire style so fashionable at the time in mansions like the Vanderbilt's Château-sur-Mer in Newport, Rhode Island. Instead of stone and marble, it was constructed of wood and slate. Nevertheless, it did manage to provide the "General" with an impressive feature, if by no other contrivance than a tall mansard-roofed belvedere from which he could look down more than thirty feet to the grounds below. (William F. returned from the Civil War, having been mustered out a brevet brigadier general.) He and his wife had made do for a while living in a company house, but after several years of partnership with his father and ensuing prosperity he wanted more substantial quarters. The new house was added to from time to time, which contributed to its awkward proportions. Nonetheless, it obtained a commanding presence and, for the investment of sixteen thousand dollars, was admired as a "beautiful residence."[52]

Another large house along Adin Street belonged to William F.'s brother, Eben S. Draper, who became a partner in the company in 1880. Eben, the youngest of George Draper's three sons (the middle brother, George A., became a partner in 1877), eventually became prominent in politics and was elected governor of Massachusetts in 1909. For his family he built a large, rambling frame structure on

23. William F. Draper house, Hopedale, 1872,
razed in 1923 to make way for the Community
House. From the *Boston Herald,* 1887.

stone foundation about 1885 (fig. 24). This house exhibited a rather handsome character with a romantic flare, as seen in its steeply hipped roof, turrets, bartizans, and round arches. George R. Clarke, a Boston architect, designed it and supervised the construction. It can be labeled Shingle Style, a manner of design then emerging in New England as a native response to American building materials and client requirements.[53] The porte cochère and veranda gave the house a free and open composition associated with a country estate now brought into town. These were places designed for social entertaining and family recreation. It is interesting to note that the wives of both brothers were daughters of Civil War generals. Both houses impose a kind of baronial or feudal aspect, whether intended or not. They were also representative of the homes of other second-generation industrialists of the Gilded Age.

In 1886 Hopedale closed a thirty-year period of expansion as a company town and an era of industrial development. During this first period, the company reached out to acquire more land and to bring new departments of manufacture into town. Starting with the six hundred acres purchased from the community in 1856, the Drapers had acquired nearly the whole outlying valley by 1886, totaling 3,547 acres. All this acreage became a separate political entity, Hopedale Township, in 1886.[54] Thereafter, financial and administrative autonomy would help to protect the site and encourage growth. Overseeing development was a single enterprise; all factories, houses, and community facilities were built to serve the company and its work force. As a result of such comprehensive development, Hopedale's landscape emerged in a consistent and rational way (figs. 25,26). Between 1886 and 1916, the Drapers continued their control over every aspect of development that brought the model company town to a state of completion.

24. Eben S. Draper house, Hopedale, 1885. Designed by George R. Clarke, the "Governor's" house was used to welcome visiting dignitaries and survived into the 1920s, when it was replaced by homes of the third generation of the family. Courtesy of the Merrimack Valley Textile Museum.

An 1888 lithograph of a perspective or "bird's-eye view" taken from a westerly direction reveals a landscape conveying both pastoral and industrial features (fig. 27). Interrupting the pastoral view are the stacks of the factories, sending forth curls of black smoke as symbols of productivity. From the mid-1870s steam power began supplementing waterpower in the shops, though most of these stacks were built for foundries.[55] The perspective presents an immutable architectural image, which is helped in measure by clusters of identical houses. Hopedale's company houses, like houses in other towns chiefly built for speculative purposes, were produced for a specified purpose in repetitious style according to the number built at any one time. The company maintained identical houses in group arrangements because of economic considerations. Some repetition is desirable when planning a development of similar-use buildings. Consistency in building design need not appear monotonous and can visually improve a site if the spatial organization is properly handled. Interspersed among the smaller houses were a school, a chapel, and several boardinghouses, producing enough change through architectural style and volume to avoid monotony. Compensating for the orderliness of Hopedale's architecture was the undulation of its surrounding terrain. Lying between the hills and forming the valley lay an irregular landscape that contrasted with the factories and houses. This variety in topography and building can still be experienced when walking through the town. Differences in terrain posed a challenge to the designers employed by the company.

Beginning in 1887, Dutcher Street pushed north from Freedom Street parallel to the upper privilege, providing homes for company employees in middle management positions, such as department heads and supervisors (figs. 28, 29).[56] In 1888 Dennett and Inman streets off Dutcher looped east, establishing more lots for houses. In contrast to the houses built for operatives, some of these were single-

25. Aerial view of Hopedale, ca. 1886, looking
south with office building in foreground and
screw shop at center. Courtesy of the
Merrimack Valley Textile Museum.

26. Aerial view of Hopedale, ca. 1886, looking south along Hopedale Street with the Joseph Bancroft house in the right foreground. Adin Ballou's modest cottage is at center. Courtesy of the Merrimack Valley Textile Museum.

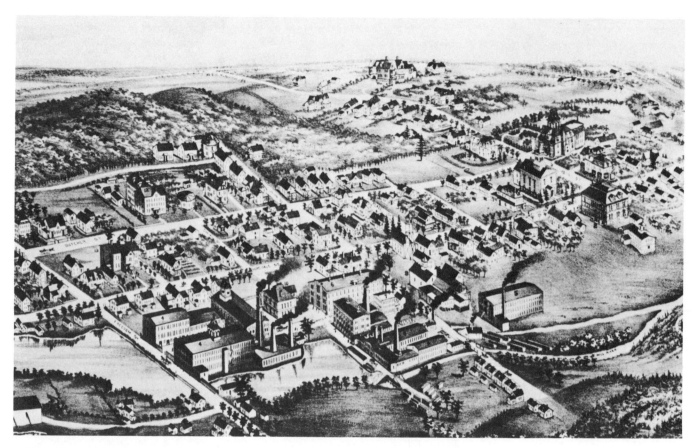

27. View of Hopedale (Boston: O. H. Bailey, 1888). The prominent placement of the factories sending forth curls of smoke captures the essence of this single-enterprise town. Courtesy of the Boston Public Library.

family structures. Now there were four classes of dwellings in Hopedale: (1) homes owned by principals, (2) single-family houses rented by managers (with an option of buying at the end of ten years), (3) double-family houses rented to married workers, and (4) rooms rented in boardinghouses (two in 1888) by single men. Company houses serve as one index for measuring the site quality of a single-enterprise town, and streets and walks provide another. By the mid-1890s the company had built and improved twelve miles of streets and nearly two miles of sidewalks.[57] As if to ensure residential expansion and permanence, streets and sidewalks were singled out for special attention. They presented the image of a well-cared-for town and were often cited by visitors for their outstanding condition.[58] Every so many years, the company surveyed the town for the purpose of street extension. Civil engineers calculated gradients and proposed building sites, and since the streets manifested the company's pride, like manicured fingers on a large industrial hand, no shortcuts were taken in laying fine avenues. Crowned at the center for good drainage, each street was macadamized with crushed stone on a tar and gravel bed. The sides of the streets were lined with granite curbs. Macadam paving worked extremely well with light vehicular traffic. In reference to the streets, an employee recounted:

> The village streets were surfaced with finely crushed stone, which was easy on the horses' feet. In hot, dry weather, they were wet down with a sprinkler cart drawn by a pair of horses, laying the dust and sending up a warm, humid smell as it passed by.[59]

Removing the source of the dust, which needed to be wet down from time to time, and maintaining the roadway occupied a street-cleaning and grounds crew. Presently, most of the streets have been repaved with brick and asphalt and, regrettably, are no longer kept in such excellent condition.

Another pride of the company was its sewage system. By 1892

28. Map of Hopedale as it would have appeared in 1916 at the end of the company's second generation of development and the ultimate completion of its urban plan. Note the Bancroft Park and Lake Point developments to the left and north of the plant.

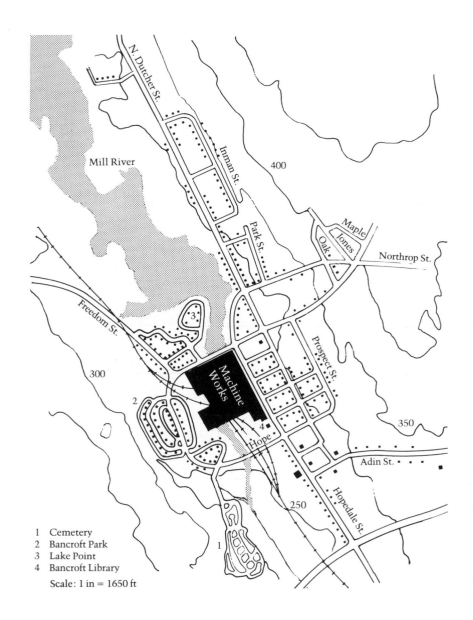

Mill River

N. Dutcher St.

Inman St.

400

Park St.

Maple

Jones

Oak

Northrop St.

Freedom St.

3

Prospect St.

Machine Works

300

2

350

4

Hope

Adin St.

250

1

Hopedale St.

1 Cemetery
2 Bancroft Park
3 Lake Point
4 Bancroft Library

Scale: 1 in = 1650 ft

29. View of Hopedale (Boston: Bert Poole, 1899).
Note the Bancroft Park houses in the background in this view from the east. Courtesy of
the Maps Division of the Library of Congress.

a plan drawn by W. C. Wheelock, c.e., indicated that sewers existed to serve houses along Union, Peace, and Hopedale streets and several houses along Dutcher and Freedom streets.[60] A photograph taken during this time shows the laying of pipe along the center line of Union Street (fig. 30). In 1894 services were extended to Adin Street,[61] and by 1897 nearly every house in Hopedale connected with modern conveniences.[62] As early as 1874 gas and water lines had been laid.[63] It must be remembered in the light of these utilities that Hopedale was a town of only 2,018 population by the turn of the century. That a sewer system had been built makes it an exception among small towns.[64]

Sometime between 1886 and 1888 Warren Henry Manning (1860–1938) visited Hopedale to render his services as a landscape architect and planner. He was employed from 1887 until 1896 by the renowned landscape architect, Frederick Law Olmsted of Brookline. Afterward, he practiced independently.[65] In 1889 he was paid $37.53 by the company for having drawn "plans for grading and planting" on the site of the new high school, south of Mendon Road on Hopedale Street.[66] Manning may also have been employed to landscape the grounds of Eben S. Draper's estate since the same architect received both commissions. And the cemetery, which appears landscaped in the 1888 lithograph, was probably his work. If so, it marks the beginning of professional landscaping services in Hopedale. Apparently, he made a thorough use of plants in landscaping the schoolhouse grounds:

> The grounds about the High School house are being graded. In time it is expected there will be about 1,000 plants and shrubs planted, arranged botanically in families. Saturday, Mr. Manning of Olmsted Landscape company, with several of the pupils, located the position of a number of the shrubs.[67]

Manning would continue to perform landscaping and planning services for the company until 1913. Meanwhile, his reputation and

30. Laying a sewer along Union Street, Hopedale, 1889. Courtesy of the Merrimack Valley
Textile Museum.

31. Bancroft Park double-family houses, Hopedale, ca. 1898. Courtesy of the Merrimack
Valley Textile Museum.

32. Bancroft Park housing, Hopedale, ca. 1898.
Note the stone curbing and curved streets and
walks. Courtesy of the Merrimack Valley
Textile Museum.

commissions carried him all over the United States.

It was Manning who persuaded the company to embrace the principles of contour planning to solve topographic problems encountered with street expansion. Another reason for contour planning was to retain the natural beauty of the town site and especially the acres of forest that surrounded the factories. Before his appearance in Hopedale, site plans were drawn by civil engineers, who surveyed street extensions and designed water, gas, and sewer lines. Arthur Holbrook, C.E., was employed by the company in 1858 to make a complete survey of all property; and in the 1870s and 1880s A. H. Wilder and W. C. Wheelock drew most of the plans.[68] Their improvements had been made on relatively flat terrain and did not require imaginative solutions in plan. But the Bancroft Park housing development gave Manning the opportunity to exhibit his talent. Begun in 1896 and completed in 1903, it combines both aesthetic and engineering considerations in the development of land west of the factories (figs. 31, 32).[69] The site occupies a knoll around which the houses were built in an elliptical arrangement facing outward. The first loop was completed and the houses occupied in 1897.[70] Trees removed during construction were replanted, and a berm immediately east of Bancroft Park, between the houses and the factories, was built up screening the two. Although the houses are located near to the factories, the site has been handled in such a way as to avoid any objectionable infringements such as visual disorder or noise. This type of arrangement compares favorably to that usually found in industrial towns, where the houses are lined up on one side of a street or canal with the shops on the other. Rarely did the company place houses facing the factories, though all the while the factories stood at the heart of the bustling enterprise with its ever-expanding nucleus.

In an address to the Second National Conference on City Planning in 1910, Manning obviously had in mind his work at Hopedale when assessing alternatives to the industrial city:

I would say that much of the improvement of city conditions is to come through the construction of manufacturing villages for the lowest priced labor with all essential pipes, stores, schools, playgrounds, reservations, houses, and gardens, and with enough home character to attract different nationalities and to keep the cost within their income limit.[71]

By this date, the garden-city idea of satellite industrial villages placed near large cities was beginning to take hold in America; and places like Hopedale could be looked upon as prototypes.

Mannings's design for Bancroft Park illustrates the new science of environmental design that lay at the foundation of modern town planning. Topographic analysis was essential to design. Manning was probably responsible for procuring the services of Gordon M. Taylor, a Boston civil engineer, who made contour maps for the new residential sites. By 1899 such maps had also been made for properties east of Prospect Street.[72] Other topographic maps indicate grading undertaken on sites north of Freedom Street above the factories.

Another housing development, which was shown in plan as early as 1904, continued the program of site analysis in contour planning into an area known as Lake Point (which can be seen in the lower-left corner of the 1888 perspective, then occupied by a company ice-house). With thirty double-family houses erected in Bancroft Park, thirty additional duplexes soon appeared on Lake Point along Progress, Soward, and Lake streets.

Lake Point represents the work of another landscape architect and town planner, Arthur A. Shurcliff (1872–1952) of Boston. Shurcliff stated the reasoning behind his design for the Lake Point development in an unpublished paper written sometime between 1904 and 1909:

It has been the practice in the past in too many of the mill villages of this country to place operatives' homes in such relation to the backs of a mill stream or mill pond as to place a premium upon disorder and inconvenience. The old-fashioned way of placing such houses was to back them upon the water and to face them upon an interior road. Everyone is familiar with the results of this program,—in a perfectly automatic way rubbish, ash-dumps, henyards, clotheslines, and privies make their appearance along the edge of the water shores which are naturally attractive, become unnaturally ugly and a source of disease. . . . If a marginal road is arranged immediately adjoining the shore line, and houses are made to face the water, automatic protection of the shore results. The dumping of rubbish, and in general the mis-use of the shores, is fended off. If unsightly conditions prevail about the houses, they are confined to the houses and especially to the rear premises. In these districts, disorder and confusion can be combated and corrected, whereas it cannot be coped with on the shores of streams and ponds without the greatest difficulty.[73]

The peripheral road next to the shoreline also permitted others besides the immediate occupants to enjoy the view of the reservoir and what eventually became parkland on the opposite shore.

For the period, his solution (fig. 33) can be deemed a milestone in the site layout of company housing, comparable to the best government war housing of a few years later. It capitalized upon the aesthetic potential of the small peninsular area while making the most economical use of land in building arrangement. The fusion of these two concerns was no accident. Company officials worked with Shurcliff in studying potential sites and layout.[74] This active participation on the part of the company indicates the close relationship between designer and client. After site selection, Shurcliff then studied the terrain through topographic maps before making sketches of the housing layout.[75]

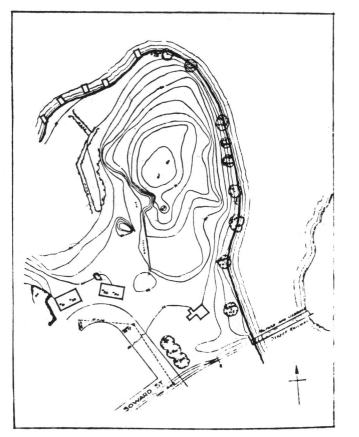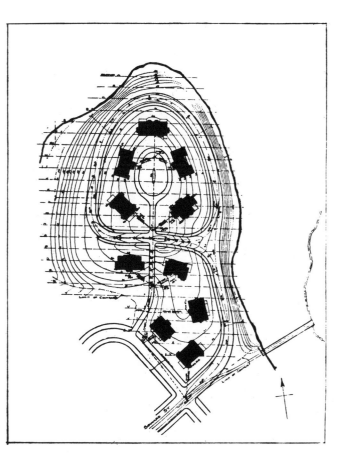

33. Plan of Lake Point housing development, Hopedale, 1904. Arthur A. Shurcliff's drawings indicate contour grading for placement of double-family houses, street, and service road. Courtesy of the Massachusetts Historical Society.

While Shurcliff was engaged in designing the housing site north of the shops, Manning had been retained to design an entirely new development named Prospect Heights, across the town line in Milford yet less than a mile from the shops. Although this development is not located in Hopedale, brief mention of it should be made. Prospect Heights provided additional company houses in cul-de-sac arrangements. Now there was a fifth type in addition to the four types of houses mentioned earlier: multifamily row houses built of brick and placed in clusters with four to six apartments to a block went up instead of additional double-family types. The first of these row houses was completed in 1903, though construction continued on others until 1913.[76] The reasoning for this more economical house type was never carried over into Hopedale, however, where the company continued to build duplexes. Northeast of Freedom and Prospect streets further expansion saw the paving of Northrop Street in 1907 and the erection of additional houses. Shurcliff's services to the company continued as he was responsible for designing Jones, Oak, and Maple streets in 1914, which required developing a site at the junction of Northrop and Freedom streets on difficult terrain. The houses had to be placed on a steep gradient. Nevertheless, he managed to negotiate the problem while keeping the amenity of the wooded site and solving the housing need.

Planners encountered special problems in siting Hopedale's houses. All traffic moved about one locus, the factories; and at a time when employees walked to and from work the distance between home and factory continued to be an important consideration. The company demanded that the houses be located near to the shop and that they be arranged in a density to accommodate employment. Yet the site could not be overbuilt, which would cause congestion, especially in relation to trafficways leading to the factories. At the same time, workers should not be made to walk out of their way purely for the sake of aesthetic considerations. What was needed was a pragmatic solution to industrial housing. This is what Manning and Shurcliff provided. Seeking maximum land use for housing with a minimum amount of street paving and complete separation of operations for living and working, the designers were able to solve the site problem. The company management helped by making the best use of available land and by exercising care after construction through ground and building maintenance.

From the very beginnings the Draper Company turned its attention to site protection. Landscaping would be enhanced by paying careful attention to the upkeep of open spaces. Every effort would be made to police the premises. The company left nothing to chance. Garbage and rubbish were regularly picked up as a company service, and junk was not permitted to accumulate on vacant lots.[77] No fences were put up, which would further divide small yards and interfere with the appearance of open spaces. Not even around the houses of the owning families could fences be built: "Of course there are other property and estates in Hopedale than those owned by the Drapers, but from the property owned by them—that is, in front of and from around the cottages of the employees—all fences are being removed, thus giving the town a much closer resemblance to South Manchester."[78] Also banned were street signs: one employee who came to work in Hopedale in 1910 thought it strange that the company could furnish attractive homes and streets but could not afford street signs. He learned later that this omission was by design.[79] William F. Draper insisted so much on a natural setting with wide vistas that he refused to place distractive numbers or addresses on company houses. Not until after the turn of the century was mail delivered to an individual's home. Before then mail had to be picked up at the post office.[80] The result of site protection enabled Hopedale to maintain as much as possible the naturalness of its environment and to avoid all the ugly man-made obstacles that normally obstruct yards and streets. An argument can be made that the company thwarted efforts to personalize houses and grounds; yet no rules described how houses could be kept or appointed inside, so long as property was not damaged or destroyed.

After the turn of the century and the advent of automobiles, the open landscape of model company towns, like other small towns designed for pedestrians, encountered a formidable enemy. Autos were parked everywhere. Some were driven into front yards, while others straddled sidewalks and occupied streets. At Hopedale (which contained six autos in 1910) all vehicles were treated as storage items, to be displayed only when in use. During the 1890s storage sheds had been constructed along service roads behind houses for family use. However, rather than being aligned in rows immediately behind the houses, they were grouped in one location. These storage sheds, which later became garages, sat apart form the houses and were hidden from street sight. At the Lake Point development these storage sheds occupy spaces entirely removed from the houses in a common arrangement off by themselves and fenced by trees from the view of passersby. (Recently these sheds have been rebuilt in brick exclusively for autos.) Providing an unobtrusive way to store the automobile, the design of such a communal garage arrangement is now readily employed in new towns where pedestrian and vehicular traffic is separated.

Hopedale's second period of growth completed building operations: thereafter, the company depended on improved transportation to carry workers back and forth from other towns. Furthermore, the Drapers had undertaken a program to double factory employment and surely realized that too many additional houses would jeopardize the amenity of the town. There were logistic problems as well, such as deciding upon new sites for building and extending services and utilities. By 1895 over a third of the company's workers resided in Milford,[81] and by 1897 a small electric trolley line connected the two towns.[82] By all accounts, Hopedale had met the challenge of industrial development while maintaining a pleasant as well as a productive environment for its management and work force. The introduction of professional landscaping, planning, and architectural services helped to shape this environment and caused it to be viewed as a model by which to compare other single-enterprise towns.

Chapter 6
Paternalism in Hopedale

Hopedale would never have developed into a model company town had it not been for the personal attachment and benevolent supervision of the Draper family. In reciprocating the Drapers' policies and social overtures, company employees complied with the family's wishes and accepted their station in life. There, as elsewhere, paternalism flourished because of the opportunities and prevailing attitudes of the period, as mentioned in chapter 3. Families with money and positions of authority did not hesitate to shape their destinies, or, for that matter, the destinies of those whom they employed. At the same time, government placed few restrictions on the wealthy while offering little in the way of social security for the poor. Paternalism was more than simply noblesse oblige, it was a style of management that extended beyond personal relations to material objects.

Like the Cheney brothers, Fairbanks brothers, Hubbard brothers, and the Hazards, the Drapers were ambitious in seeking ways to increase productivity and capital return. Yet, keen businessmen that they were, they never exploited their establishments to the detriment of the towns built around them. Their places of business grew, prospered, changed in many ways, but the surrounding environments were not destroyed in the process. Instead, they remained viable and attractive. A corollary can be made between these model manufacturing towns and other company-owned towns, such as those of the extractive industries. Mining towns and oil boomtowns eventually yield their mineral wealth and, in so doing, the life of their environments. On the other hand, the manufacturing town depended upon long-term site development with measures taken to protect the investment. There, wealth was invested instead of extracted. Comparisons can also be drawn between the men who built the model manufacturing towns and those who built the towns of the extractive industries. The Fricks, Goulds, and Rockefellers stood in another league; their fortunes were made in large-scale speculations, and the towns they built were treated as commodities to be bought and sold and eventually discarded. Their towns were rarely distinguished by architecture or social programs for employees, nor were they inhabited by them or their families. Jay Gould probably never set foot in Primero, Colorado, which was built in the 1880s by the Colorado Fuel and Iron Company, though for a time he was the controlling owner of that town and many others like it.[1] In terms of fortunes made and competitive zeal, men like Gould made the Drapers and their kind look diminutive and rather old-fashioned in business practice.

The Drapers and other founders of model company towns may be considered middle-sized in the pecking order of nineteenth-century businessmen, a step up from mechanics and superintendents (and most had graduated from that level). Though not consumed by greed, they never gave anything away; yet it was said about George Draper that "he was not of those who regarded his country as an orange to be squeezed."[2] These men controlled only one town and made it their home. Devoted to one line of business, they staked their reputations on product quality with pride in workmanship as a principal ingredient. In regard to their lineage, none came from particularly humble origins, and all were native-born descendants from seventeenth-century Massachusetts Bay settlers. Religions among them vary, though all were liberal Protestants. In politics all staunchly supported the Republican party and favored protective tariffs. Members of the second generation became state legislators, governors, U.S. congressmen, and even ambassadors. Within two generations, the families in each of the towns advanced from the ranks of artisans and mechanics to become entrepreneurs and public figures. All endorsed some social reform, temperance being favorite. For them, temperance lay at the very heart of maintaining social order and harmony. Abstemious workers were dependable, and they were surely less quarrelsome. Although these company owners and managers imposed rules for temperance and social conduct, they set themselves as examples to follow.

The Drapers

George Draper (1817–87) was a stereotype of the company-town entrepreneur. He transformed Hopedale into a single-enterprise town and laid the foundation for its model image. More so than his brother, he recognized the potential of their business. George was the youngest of three sons of a Weston, Massachusetts, farmer and machinery designer. In 1832, at age fifteen, he went to work as a weaver in a North Uxbridge mill managed by his eldest brother. Two years later he became the superintendent of a cotton sheeting mill in Walpole. But in 1839 he was tossed out of his job "owing to a general depression in manufacturing." He blamed the depression on tariff reduction, which increased competition between New England and European textile manufactures.[3] This brought a turning point in his career. For lack of alternative employment, he went to Lowell and took a job as a spinner with the Massachusetts Manufacturing Company at $1.25 a day. He stayed in Lowell between 1839 and 1843 and probably lived in company housing. In 1843 he left to take a better job as a machinery designer for Edward Harris in Woonsocket, Rhode Island. (The Harris mills in Woonsocket and Harrisville, Rhode Island, and in Ware, Massachusetts, were leading producers of fine woolens.) After working two years in Woonsocket, he received from Harris the position of managing a mill in Ware in 1845 and within a few years superintended the Ware division.[4] A final move and still another turning point arrived in 1853 after a career marked by managerial ability though economic misfortune.

He joined the Hopedale Community in 1853, not because he avowed religious socialism but because he wanted an interest in Ebenezer's (the middle brother's) business with the prospect of becoming the controlling partner. The five thousand dollars brought in hand purchased a copartnership and a position as manager of operations. He could have invested the money in the Harris Company at

Ware. But that would have bought him only a small share in a large company with no hope of becoming a partner. Arriving at Hopedale at age thirty-six, Draper had yet to become his own boss.

The organization of Hopedale Community must have frustrated George Draper because of its impractical business arrangement. Though his brother had met with some success, others barely got by as the social fabric on which the community wove its economy had grown threadbare. Hope rested mainly on the management of a few and the good faith of others, and patience was in short supply all around. When the opportunity arose to buy out the community and start anew, he and his brother took it.

The community's founder, Ballou, never blamed the Drapers for the community's demise, contending that "it was simply a moral failure";[5] yet there existed a sentiment among some members that had the brothers remained steadfast in seeing the venture through difficult times it could have been salvaged.[6] But in the case of Ballou, there may have been special reasons for his silence:

> Most have attributed his [Ballou's] reticence to condemn them as an indication of his kindness. However, Ballou owed a great deal to the Drapers and was apparently aware of this. Ebenezer Draper had contributed heavily to the community. Ballou had taken a trip to the mid-west during the community days at Ebenezer's expense. George Draper personally paid Ballou an annuity and after Draper's death the executors of his will continued to pay this until Ballou's death. . . . Thus it is obvious that Ballou would be reluctant to condemn the family too heartily.[7]

George Draper, on the other hand, tolerated Ballou's religious convictions and obviously respected the minister for reasons of personal character. In his will (he died three years before Ballou), he left him an annual stipend of four hundred dollars.[8] On certain issues the two men shared common beliefs; both avidly supported temperance and abolition. But when war broke out, Ballou urged his followers to remain passive and to avoid the draft, whereas Draper sent his son to war and outfitted other soldiers as well.[9] It should be kept in mind that Ebenezer and not George had been the original convert to Ballou's community; and Ebenezer's retirement in 1868 may have had to do with this earlier alliance. Perhaps by coincidence the year he retired and left was the date of the dissolution of Hopedale Parish, which had lingered on since 1856 as a religious organization.

At the time of the takeover, drastic measures had to be taken to rescue the town and business, but nothing stood in the way of the brothers' restoring the community after rebuilding the town's economy, for the minister remained even if his congregation had largely disbanded. George Draper had no intention of reinstating the old order of things, however. Instead, he did everything possible to remove that which symbolized the earlier enterprise: in 1860 he replaced the original meetinghouse with a Unitarian chapel, and in 1874 he dismantled the old homestead in which the community held its first meetings and charted operations.[10] The only building saved from the earliest times was the mechanic shop, later enshrined as a museum. Moreover, the company town served as a vehicle in accomplishing this end by buoying the family's prestige while erasing evidence of the venture that had preceded it. If ever capitalism triumphed over socialism, Hopedale stood example. Reference to the earlier community was made contemptuously in later years. A guest orator visiting the town in 1887 said of the "Peaceful Christian Brotherhood" that "It was a joint-stock association, sharing capital and profits, and run on common account. The result was a practical bankruptcy, averted only by a change which followed no longer any transcendental line, but turned to the line of hard, practical American business."[11] Though it can be debated that some of the social reforms espoused by the early leaders had carried over into the company town, the population base and physical character had changed drastically since 1856. Ballou had been an idealist who governed by consensus; Draper was a pragmatist who governed by himself. On the issue of war, Draper probably felt he had no choice but to take a stand in favor of involvement. The South posed a threat to his business and profits by having legislated reductions in tariffs. He could blame Clay's Compromise Tariff for his personal misfortune in the 1830s. In a small booklet privately printed and circulated to friends at the end of his career, George Draper said that he had "formed his opinions on the tariff question while a youth at work in a cotton mill, commencing in the year 1832. At that time the whole country was profoundly excited by nullification in South Carolina; and the attention of all intelligent persons was challenged by the acts of South Carolina." Then, "in 1840, after the most exciting canvass I ever have seen, the Democratic party was thoroughly defeated, largely on the issue of a tariff for the protecton of the home market."[12] In the 1870s and 1880s he became intensely interested in this partisan issue and wrote a number of editorials for local and Boston journals. Shortly before his death in 1887, he founded the Home Market Club in Boston to propagandize through its organ, the *Home Market Bulletin*, a policy of "American wages for American Workmen" and "American markets for American people."[13] Among businessmen, especially those in the textile industry, his protectionist views were popular.

Draper was also outspoken on labor: in an article in the *Boston Evening Journal* in 1886, after a year of national labor strikes and riots, he blamed Congress for the plight of Pennsylvania miners of ore. His logic was that foreign competition in steel manufacture resulted in low wages ($302 a year) for miners. He believed that miners should earn the same as machinists, masons, or carpenters, who received two to three times as much. To uplift the situation of workers he firmly believed in education; and, in a letter written in 1881 to a business acquaintance, he tells of his experience in teaching employees to read, write, and figure their bills. Moreover, workers "should be educated to be industrious, frugal, moral, and efficient in their trade or calling."[14] The friends who wrote epitaphs about Draper state that he was "a kind-hearted and benevolent man."[15] This he was, but he was obviously strong-minded and (one gathers) Procrustean in temperament.

After 1868 he had taken Hopedale in hand completely, observing every improvement during the first period of expansion and suggesting patterns of growth as to layout and production. As president of the company and director of operations, he could synchronize Hopedale's business production and employment with housing and recreation facilities, in addition to utilities, water resources, and fuel reserves. Holding a position of central authority, he could plan ahead, keeping priorities in balance by not letting factory expansion and employment get in front of other needs. He consulted with the superintendents who headed the machine shop, temple, and spindle divisions and decided when and where additions were made.[16] At a testimonial to his memory at the Philadelphia Textile School, which he helped to found after the Centennial Exposition of 1876, a former colleague said that his principal contribution to the industry rested with his "energetic exploitation of the product of his establishment, with which he advocated a keen analysis of the results from machines." From the results he obtained ways to continually improve his product. "Men who were brought up in his shops were sought for positions of responsibility and trust in cotton manufacturing."[17] His interest in improvement and perfection found expression outside his shops as well. Draper insisted upon building well-constructed streets, factories, and houses, and thus quality design followed in turn from the product to the town. In another memorial, one writer could not resist using an architectural metaphor in describing his former presence: "He was a strong, simple, massive character. There was granite in his foundations, and on it he erected a plain, substantial and useful life."[18] When he died the shops were closed for a week, and during the burial ceremonies a cortege was formed with "the Hopedale operatives preceding the long train of carriages."[19]

William F. Draper (1842–1910) piloted the company through the second period of expansion. Like his brothers who followed him into partnership, he bought into an already profitable business. He inherited the presidency of the company after his father died, owning the largest interest. Yet, though he may have inherited the position of leadership, he paid in full for his share: when his father bought out his uncle, he sold William F. the former's share at cost plus commission and interest![20] The son took up where his father left off and continued to expand the enterprise and family fortune. In 1887 he brought two more businesses under Draper and Son's management, the Sawyer Spindle Company and the Hopedale Elastic Goods Company.[21] Known as "the General" to his business associates and employees, he undoubtedly enjoyed the vantage from the tower of his Victorian mansion on Adin Street. From there he could look out over several thousand acres of company domain, remembering when the town possessed only two small industrial buildings. The accomplishment was worth reflecting upon.

He attended school in Hopedale and had passed entrance exams for admission to Harvard, but whether out of patriotism, a yearning for adventure, or a lack of interest in study, he volunteered for duty at the outbreak of the Civil War. In correspondence with his family between engagements, he lamented to his mother that he had not taken her advice and attended college: "The very fact that a man has been to College gives him power in certain circles as much as being a Free Mason does in others."[22] He promised to improve his conversational and writing ability, but the social acknowledgment of having a degree —separating him from his father's generation—was also important. Although twice wounded in battles, including those at Roanoke Island, New Bern, Fort Macon, Antietam, and Fredericksburg, he quickly rose through the military ranks as a result of gallantry and leadership. In a letter of fatherly advice, written January 4, 1863, during the Kentucky campaign, George Draper counseled: "Of course a large army cannot be handled like a machine—i.e. successfully—but men in your position & with your ability can do much to make the men bear with patience & comparative cheer." Giving his son additional cheer was the promise of five hundred dollars for his twenty-first birthday and five hundred dollars a year until age twenty-five, as well as a position in the company upon his return at the conclusion of the war.[23] Both his father's example and the responsibility thrust on him by service must have accustomed him to leadership and prepared him for management.

Even more than his father, he took building matters in hand, commissioning architects to design factories, community facilities, and workers' housing, including the hiring of landscape architects for planning and planting. Making a point of visiting Europe every two years, he brought home new ideas regarding architecture and landscaping,[24] and it was he who instituted the program of giving prizes to workmen in return for their embowering the town with trees and plants (about which more will be said later). His second wife, Susan Preston Draper, daughter of Confederate general William Preston of Kentucky, probably encouraged the beautification campaigns since their estate as well as the town grounds was impeccably kept. In later life he took an active part in politics, receiving a nomination for governor in 1888. The Republican party, however, decided to let Oliver Ames of North Easton serve another term. In 1892 William F. was elected a representative to Congress and in 1898 was appointed ambassador to Italy under President McKinley. There, he and his wife lived among the Roman aristocracy at the sumptuous Piombino Palace near the Quirinal.[25] Serving first in the army and then in the factories kept him from getting a college education but not from acquiring a few languages and the ability to move about in noble circles like a rich American in a Henry James novel.

In 1901 he testified before the Industrial Commission in Washington about "the relations and conditions of capital and labor." The questioning he received focused largely upon the Draper Company and the manufacture of textile machinery in general. After describing Hopedale and the different machinery made by the company, he was asked about employment:

Q. Have you many people in your present employment who have been with your company or firm for many years?

A. We have a great many. The proportion is not as large as it would ordinarily be, owing to the great number of new men that we have taken on, but our old hands of 20 or 25 years ago are substantially all there—those who are living.

The inference drawn was that emigration from Hopedale was small and that working conditions were attractive enough to make people stay. In the case of Hopedale, isolation was not a reason for its holding power. Other employment existed nearby in Boston, Worcester, and a dozen smaller towns. Draper was then asked about labor relations:

Q. Have you ever had a labor difficulty?

A. We have never had a general labor difficulty. I do not think we have had a labor difficulty at any time which embraced one-twentieth of the hands employed, and waiving a difficulty between one of our contractors and his men, I do not think we have ever had a labor difficulty that included over 20 men.

When further asked about organized labor, Draper responded by saying that the company did not interfere if workers chose to organize and that some were members of unions and some were not. But "organization does not come to our attention in any way to trouble us."[26] The year the testimony was given, 1901, Charles Buxton Going had cited Hopedale for the "mutual regard" that was practiced in labor and management relations.[27]

When William F. returned to Hopedale in 1904, however, circumstances had changed; and he found his brothers maneuvering to oust him, which they succeeded in doing in 1906.[28] Previously, both he and his father had kept the family in line, though after 1906 there appeared interfamily rivalries from time to time. At least a half-dozen family members—brothers, sons, nephews, and in-laws—vied for offices in the company. The General withdrew from the tribulations of management and moved to Washington, a more inviting and perhaps more cordial place for a man of public affairs, and there he resided until his death four years later.

Eben S. Draper (1858–1914), the governor, directed the company after William F.'s departure. A graduate of the Massachusetts Institute of Technology, he excelled in technical and economic subjects; and, like his brother, he acquired an interest in politics. As a staunch Republican and businessman he was an ardent conservative, and during two terms as governor he rescinded twenty-one bills, vetoing such liberal initiatives as the eight-hour workday. In addition to his interests in Hopedale, he was a director of the Boston and Albany Railroad, National Shawmut Bank of Boston, Milford National Bank, Queen City Cotton Company, and Old Colony Trust Company; and president of the Manville Company.[29] Though he had all the ambition of his older brother, he apparently lacked his rapport in labor relations. When the company suffered its first strike in 1913, he was president; and it was toward him that the Industrial Workers of the World (IWW) vented its anger.[30] Throughout the turmoil, which lasted six months, he remained inflexible in his relations with the strikers.

To gain an indication of the Drapers' wealth and dominance in Hopedale, it is worth noting the valuation on personal property (as separate from realty) owned by the second generation, namely, William F., George A., Eben S., and their two sisters, Mmes Colburn and Osgood:

Personal valuation	1886	1896	1902
Drapers	$ 74,410*	$1,026,150	$2,557,196
Town of Hopedale	189,081	1,370,925	2,808,616

If the personal property of the Dutchers and Bancrofts were added to the 1902 figure—another $251,420—the sum would amount to 96 percent of the total town valuation.[31] Who shared the remainder? The other employees and their families, of course. Despite their marginal share of the Draper Company's wealth, Hopedale was developed primarily with their welfare in mind.

The workers

In view of the desperate plight of many working families who often searched in vain for a decent place to live, it comes as no surprise that Hopedale was once esteemed an "Abode of Comfort, Peace, and Happiness."[32] Those who worked in Hopedale were physically better off than those who lived in corporate towns and other industrial cities. Unsanitary conditions did not exist, and the mortality rate was low. What workers left behind in larger towns and cities was a certain amount of independence with the freedom to change jobs without necessarily changing their place of residence, to purchase food and dry goods in a variety of locations, and to worship in a church of their choice (in a place large enough to support several denominations). Surely some workers longed for such independence, but others with families sought the security offered by the Drapers. Nothing assured nineteenth-century workers of getting another job if unemployed, getting medical help if injured, or finding decent lodging at a reasonable rent. However, among workers in Hopedale there appears to have been less apprehension about these.

*Excluding George Draper's personal property

The Messrs. Draper leave no stone unturned in their endeavors to make the lives of their employees a happy lot. Good and remunerative wages are paid, and the employment is steady and reliable. A faithful and skilled workman is assured of a life situation, and thus he can have no apprehensions with regard to his latter days.[33]

This was the view of the *Boston Herald* in 1887 in a special article devoted to the town. The *Herald* had no particular reason for giving a favorable opinion. To the contrary, George Draper had opposed the tariff views of its editors the year before and had labeled the journal as overly liberal. Then why did it feature Hopedale? The *Herald* had maintained a keen interest during this period in labor strikes and working conditions. Although no direct comparisons were made with other industrial towns, it found Hopedale unusually successful; and the fact was newsworthy.

To test the assertion that a model company town like Hopedale provided a better environment than other industrial towns, a comparison between it and other places of the number of workers who stayed beyond a decade would seem appropriate. But company towns had built-in drawbacks regarding limitations in employment and housing. How could they possibly compare favorably? Moreover, they provide no cross-section of society. In Hopedale only seven different occupations were listed by census between 1870 and 1900, and four of these counted as job titles within the machine shops. Indeed, the principal reason for creating a model town was to retain labor. A high rate of population turnover could be expected. Yet confirming the testimony of William F. Draper to the Industrial Commission is evidence that Hopedale did not experience a high turnover in population. Workers who came with families often stayed. Draper's statement that the old hands of twenty to twenty-five years for the most part were still employed cannot be supported, however. Among heads of household residing in Hopedale in 1870, only 49 percent remained in 1880; and only 29 percent were still around in 1900.[34] These percentages of population recidivism are neither low nor high for towns of similar size. The degree of similarity in recidivism between towns, large and small, agricultural and industrial, has led Stephan Thernstrom to conclude that this reflection of population mobility was attributable more to societal patterns at large than to particular types or locations of settlement. Hence, Hopedale in the decade 1870 to 1880 had exactly the same degree of recidivism as nearby Waltham, home of the American Manufacturing Company and later the Waltham Watch Company, a small industrial town with a mixed economy.[35] But a change occurred between 1880 and 1890 as the number of heads of household who stayed increased to 65 percent; and between 1886 and 1896 only 211 people were dropped from the tax roles, indicating a retention rate of nearly 80 percent.[36] Though Hopedale may have been a good place to live in the 1870s, it was even better after 1886.

The increase in population retention toward the end of the century pertains to families, however, and not to single men. About a fifth of the families took in boarders, and remaining individuals lived in company boardinghouses. The overall percentage of single men either residing with families or living in boardinghouses was quite small, though, amounting to less than 10 percent of the total population. Only one boardinghouse was maintained prior to 1880, though three existed by 1900. Amos and Sally Whipple were the boardinghouse keepers for the company in both 1870 and 1880 (Appendix B), and only one of their twenty-one boarders from 1870 remained in town after 1880; only three of thirty-five in 1880 stayed until 1900.[37] Family men often settled, but single men drifted away.

Predominantly New Englanders, together with English, Scots, Canadians, and not a few Irish, composed the labor force before the turn of the century, after which time other nationalities were hired in number (see Appendix C for a composite of population, nativity, and housing). It was worth a news item in 1887 when two Italians were given jobs, though by 1900, seventy-eight were employed, all "day laborers."[38] Occasionally the Irish got into the news, such as when machinist Mather Quinn died and when "Ginger" Brown wore a shamrock in his hat all day on Saint Patrick's Day in 1883 and his shopmates wanted to know whether he was a "Tip" or "Fardown."[39] Another news account of 1883 mentions the coming and going of a well-liked employee named J. M. David:

> J. M. David, who has been employed in the temple shop since last fall, left town on Monday. He was a man who had won the respect of all his fellow employees, who showed their regard for him by presenting him on Saturday with a fine meerschaum pipe, with a silver plate thereon, on which was engraved, "Presented by his shopmates; March 24."[40]

Though the company trained men, it preferred hiring skilled artisans, which is one reason a number of British were employed, among them James Northrop, designer and foreman, who invented the automatic loom mentioned earlier. In documenting effects of British immigration, Rowland Berthoff has observed that "the 'assimilation' or 'Americanization' of the British was relatively easy," and they were obviously attractive to employers. "With folkways and habits of thought acceptable to Americans, they enjoyed a unique advantage over most newcomers."[41] As operations expanded and as orders for machinery pressed for higher production quotas, other foreign groups received jobs and were rented company houses:

> With a great deal of benevolent foresight the Drapers make no distinction between the foreign workers and the native product in the matter of housing. The homes of the Armenians and the Italians and the Poles are every whit as comfortable and attractive as those of the Yankees.

Even as the Draper Company has changed so must Hopedale change, and yet the hope and prayer is that these changes will not mar the beauty and quiet of New England's model town.[42]

By the time these words had been written in the 1920s, the company had assimilated entirely the various nationalities in both employment and housing. But in 1900 all the Italians, single men, boarded together in one establishment. This was the exception, however, because from 1870 onward the double-family houses were integrated.[43]

Unlike the textile mills, which employed women and children, the Draper Company hired only men and employed them in machinist, designer, and foundryman positions. After the Civil War the pay for machinists increased from an average daily wage of $1.75 to $2.75 in 1885 and to $3.00 in 1900.[44] In 1887 the average pay for a machinist in Hopedale was $2.75, less money than could be earned in Boston or other large cities. Furthermore, workers had little opportunity for advancement within the company. Chances were that a worker who came to Hopedale as a machinist remained one. Machinists, iron molders, toolmakers, and patternmakers kept their occupations and even passed them along to their sons. Occasionally, some would become foremen or overseers within their division, but none broke into the ranks of management. The sons of the Drapers, Dutchers, and Bancrofts filled the openings in salaried positions.[45] Most of the workers who stayed were like Winburn Dennett, born in Maine in 1825, who came to Hopedale as a patternmaker before 1870 and was still working in that occupation in 1900; whose son, Mortimer O., was born in Hopedale in 1872 and was listed as a patternmaker in 1900; and whose son, Mortimer, was born in Hopedale in 1896 and became a patternmaker before serving as town clerk.[46] In other respects, workers and their families faced limitations common to most company towns. There was little choice of where to go or what to buy.

Since the Draper Company owned and managed nearly all the property in town, such matters as edification and personal provisions fell under their purview. Though some workers and their families might have preferred attending services at an Anglican or Catholic church, only one religious building existed in Hopedale (before the old high school was turned over to the Sacred Heart Church in the 1920s). A Greek Revival–style meetinghouse was constructed of wood in 1860 on company property. Although funded by subscription, all but $1,423 of its $6,000 cost was paid by the Drapers.[47] Ballou, a Universalist, presided over the congregation until his retirement, and the old chapel remained until 1898 when the new Unitarian Memorial Chapel replaced it. The existing building, costing sixty thousand dollars and constructed of Milford granite in the Victorian Gothic style, was financed exclusively by George A. and Eben S. Draper and dedicated to their parents.[48] A number of the native-born families are recorded on the church roles, and it was there that their children were baptized. But many other families, including the immigrants, probably abstained from attending the company chapel or sought worship in neighboring towns.

The company owned no commercial buildings, though it rented some commercial space in the town hall. Instead of maintaining a company store, it sold a parcel of land to Henry L. Patrick, the son of a resident farmer, who built a grocery and dry goods store on Hopedale Street in 1886. The brick building that still remains was constructed by a local contractor, Albertus C. Hussey.[49] Patrick obtained a monopoly on trade by virtue of being the only independent businessman; those who refused to buy from him either made the trek to Milford or relied on traveling vendors. However, these limitations drew no adverse attention or publicity. Whether the company discouraged freedom of choice cannot be proven, but neither was it encouraged.

Nevertheless, Hopedale offered its workers job security, free medical aid, and low rents as inducements for staying. Children could receive an education in schools built by the company and outfitted with modern equipment. The Drapers placed special emphasis on education, as indicated in the annual school reports.[50] They were proud of the fact that twice as much money per student was spent for education in Hopedale as in neighboring Milford.[51] Another distinction in Hopedale was its progressive stand on working hours. In 1856 the workday was set at ten hours, whereas other Massachusetts mills operated eleven hours a day, six days a week.[52] In a letter to the Special Commission on the Hours of Labor in 1886, a Hopedale worker, George Gay, wrote "that since the adoption of the ten hour rule mechanics enjoy many more of the comforts of life than formerly." Before, for example, laborers were "too tired to read useful books."[53] In 1887 the workweek was cut to fifty-five hours, a measure the state did not enforce until after the turn of the century. Edward C. Kirkland in *Industry Comes of Age* mentions that Frank Cheney of South Manchester was "one of the most enlightened of employers who pioneered in reducing hours";[54] but the Drapers could have been cited as well. Furthermore, workers managed to save a portion of their earnings. Of the heads of household in 1870 who remained until 1900, all indicated an increase in personal wealth exclusive of real estate, and two-thirds showed a fivefold increase or more. Yet, to cite two extremes: Peter Moore, who in 1851 emigrated from Ireland and by 1870 found employment in Hopedale, managed between then and 1900 to increase his personal wealth from $100 to $1,200; by contrast, William F. Draper, whose personal wealth in 1870 was listed as $13,000 claimed by 1900 a sum of $724,660![55] In Hopedale it was not axiomatic that the poor remain poor, but the wealthy became wealthier.

One of the attributes of a model company town lay in its labor relations and the management's ability to arbitrate differences. Disabled workers and widows with children were given pensions and free lodging by the company, and those who worked until retiring could expect financial and medical assistance in their old age. During times of economic setback, work in the factories was prorated, thereby enabling a slowdown as opposed to a layoff.[56] Thus Hopedale offered its workers and their families a degree of social security. Because of these measures and the Drapers' paternal interest in the welfare and improvement of the community, it had escaped strikes during the nineteenth century. But harmony finally ended. The IWW proved to be a formidable adversary to the Draper Company and effectively called a strike for May 31, 1913, which endured four months. Apparently, the same men who organized the strike at Lawrence the year before were active in Hopedale. Though the issue was wages, a political target was also involved. Eben S. Draper, governor of Massachusetts, represented big business and its dominance over labor. In the end the company won out, refusing to grant a pay hike. Procedures returned to normal, though the image of a model company town had been tarnished.[57] The labor differences that had plagued other industrial towns at last caught up with Hopedale.[58]

The landscape

Hopedale's image as shaped by the paternalism of the Drapers was both symbolic and substantive. It extended beyond conditions of employment to embrace the landscape as well. In October 1886, the Draper Company established a "village improvement society" in Hopedale after a long period of interest in conservation and landscaping. It attracted support from employees and social clubs[59] and eventually developed into a program for awarding prizes for grounds upkeep. It further influenced the planning of a one-thousand-acre park.

Improvement began when "three dozen maple shade trees were delivered to Geo. Draper & Sons . . . which they will have set out on Dutcher street." But the first large task confronting Hopedale's village improvement society required enlarging and designing the layout of the cemetery, which, incidentally, was the starting place of many societies.[60] Planting trees, landscaping grounds, and dredging the Mill River had always been part of the building program as new streets and walks were laid and new factories constructed. Even the earlier community recorded at times "procuring and setting Fruit and Forest trees by the side of the walks."[61] However, in the 1880s Hopedale experienced a fever of continuing activity brought about through considerable attention to landscaping. With the founding of an improvement society, these activities went beyond beautification campaigns to create recreational facilities, to protect waterways, and to bring company workmen as well as administrators to a mutual respect for their environment. It worked, and for years everyone participated in making Hopedale "a Massachusetts garden spot."[62]

Although the Drapers sponsored the village improvement society and paid for a large share of the landscaping, there were independent initiatives as well, for it was reported in May 1887 that "The nursery agents are making their spring delivery of trees and shrubs, and almost everyone in the village seems imbued with the spirit of setting out trees, gauging from the quantity sold here." From one end of Hopedale Street to the other, new trees were set out and old ones were trimmed; tenants planted gardens in yards, and "in many windows a rich array of flowers" could be seen. One lady resident on Hopedale Street hung flower baskets from her porch, of which "the contents are a marvel of beauty" with sprays of periwinkles nine feet in length.[63] Beyond efforts to beautify, recreation, in the form of organized outdoor activities during the eighties, precipitated much of the new landscape interest. Crowds turned out to sit in the churchyard and watch dramas like *Dolly's Delusion*, though sports activities were responsible for drawing the largest numbers during the summers. A boat race on the Mill River above the upper dam during the 1885 Fourth of July celebration turned into a weekly event, repeated throughout the warmer months (fig. 34). At first the reward for winning was a refreshing dip in the river after a hot Saturday morning of working in the shops. Later, however, George Draper gave away prizes amounting to six dollars,[64] which set a precedent for things to come. Then in 1888 a baseball field was made level for the Hopedale Nine.[65] By this date many small towns and companies supported baseball teams, which drew enthusiastic spectators who attended picnics beforehand and dances afterward. These sporting events focused attention on the need for parks.

Before providing a park, Hopedale maintained sidewalks along its principal avenues and kept the grass cut on the public square, though there were no gardens or sports fields maintained especially for recreation. Exercise in the 1880s consisted of evening walks for those who managed the energy after a long day's work. Hopedale's workers, like people in other small towns, strolled at dusk or on Sundays along a prominent street where one could chat with friends or attend to errands. The alternative was to stroll through the cemetery, where courting could also take place; and because this was a popular activity in cemeteries during the nineteenth century, Hopedale's village improvement society probably selected it as a starting point. It formerly had been a graveyard with markers simply placed at random, but after 1886 it received careful attention regarding planning and planting. In addition to the quietude and attractiveness of a landscaped cemetery was the need for a different kind of space, where brass bands could play and drill troops could parade. In 1888 Hopedale possessed both, and the "Zouaves," or drill troops, became a popular spectacle on holidays in their brightly colored uniforms (likely a fe-

34. Draper employees boating on Hopedale Pond
during a Field Day at Hopedale, ca. 1900.
Courtesy of the Merrimack Valley Textile
Museum.

tish of General Draper's).[66] Due largely to the interest aroused by these varied activities of the eighties, Hopedale obtained a park system that was unique for a town of its size. Yet, before discussing the design of the park system, it would be well to look again at the Draper Company's ground maintenance program.

Because of the company's dependence on water as a source of power to operate its machinery, precautionary measures became mandatory in securing and protecting the supply. The upper privilege north of Freedom Street formed a reservoir backed up by the dam located adjacent to the Hopedale Machine Company. Land inundated by the reservoir turned to marsh and flooded inlets to more than thirteen feet above the riverbed. Apart from providing good places for fishing and for bird watching, the riverbanks and backwaters were unused. So long as land surrounding the waters of the upper privilege remained protected and the level and quantity of water needed for operation existed in plentiful supply, no special attention was paid to land conservation. However, when Dutcher Street was carried northward in 1887 parallel to the Mill River and houses were constructed between the two,[67] the danger of site erosion became evident and measures had to be taken to protect the reservoir area. Of course the Draper Company owned all but a small portion of the land surrounding the river and was sole developer of streets and houses. Nevertheless, heedless construction could have endangered the site, both by polluting the waterway and by tearing down the natural embankments that kept the reservoir contained. Uprooting trees and grading house lots could have destroyed the usefulness of the river and, what would have been worse, could have caused accidental seepage into the town below. This the Drapers did not permit; and experience in developing the lower privilege probably served as a lesson in conserving their industrial site. Notice, in the 1888 perspective view and in an 1887 engraving showing the factories from the west bank (fig. 35), the retention of trees along the river's edge. Roots from trees and

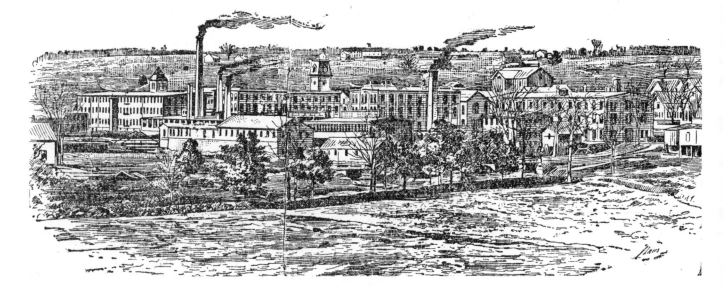

35. Works of the Hopedale Manufacturing
Company as viewed from the west. Note the
trees planted along the Mill River. From the
Boston Herald, 1887.

undergrowth along the banks held the soil in place, and rock embankments further reinforced the shoreline in critical areas around the dams and near the wheelhouses and factories.

Although the conservation of water sites mattered in a very practical way, the company maintained its land for other purposes as well. Future expansion of the enterprise required setting aside areas for later development, thus protecting existing building investment. A reason for single-enterprise ownership was to be able to plan ahead and to make the utmost use of resources at hand. Houses were not sold in the event of having to repurchase them; and, by the same token, houses once built and grounds once landscaped were not to be replaced for lack of care. Since 1856 the management had exercised control over development and had paid some attention to maintenance, but in 1894 things changed. That year George Draper and Sons instituted a participatory plan encouraging workers to take part in grounds maintenance by yard tending, which included the planting of trees and shrubs and the cultivation of flower gardens.[68]

> It is not enough that a wealthy company should build picturesque and homelike dwellings: those who occupy them must have both taste, thrift, and energy to accomplish the results that are in evidence in Hopedale. The way in which a house is lived in is as vital to its appearance as is the way in which one wears his clothing to the appearance of the garments themselves.[69]

Village improvement had brought workers into a cooperative arrangement with management for upkeep.

The improvement society taught planting and plant-tending procedures. Anyone could mow grass, but gardening came as something new, and an interest in these and other aspects of horticulture derived strength during the 1890s through the Hopedale Chautauqua circle.[70] Drawing on a broad base of employee participation permitted the company to capitalize on industrial relations by giving workers responsibility in the image making of the enterprise. Exploiting this new work role, the company derived certain advantages never before obtained: (1) employees could be used in maintenance as well as in production; (2) as a health-promoting measure, the company could illustrate the benefits of outdoor activities; and (3) community spirit and town pride could be manifested in no better way. Implementing this program of worker participation in ground maintenance required guidelines and rewards. So the company provided a consulting gardener who could make suggestions and teach planting practices; yet, at the same time, individual creativity was encouraged through a program of awarding prizes. "We have a system of prizes for care of grounds that results most favorably. The lawns are always green and well cut and many of the tenants introduce elaborate landscape gardening treatment."[71] In 1896 the Hopedale Machine Company, the Dutcher Temple Company, and George Draper and Sons each contributed ninety-five dollars in prizes, as had been the policy for several years. Machinist Charles Bagley won the $10.00 first prize from the Hopedale Machine Company on this occasion, and others received four second prizes of $7.50 and eleven third prizes of $5.00.[72] Competition was not limited to operatives but was open to the management as well, for some years later a first prize went to a supervisor residing on Dutcher Street. The yard maintenance undertaken in Hopedale generated so much enthusiasm that by 1908 over four hundred dollars a year was given in prizes.[73] This practice, emulated by other companies, was largely responsible for placing the Draper Company before the public in several magazines and booklets.[74] Ground maintenance supervised by the company therefore contributed to village improvement and gave even more impetus to the creation of a park system.

The idea of providing a park separate from industrial and residential areas had been voiced at least as early as 1888, when the management proposed to "purchase of Mr. Ballou about five acres of land for town park or take any action in relation to the same."[75] In the meantime, work proceeded on the baseball field or "playground" on land north of Freedom Street between Dutcher and Prospect. The land wanted from Ballou lay at the heart of the residential area near the intersection of Union and Hopedale streets and would serve as a public garden. But Ballou, the only private landholder in this section of town, refused to sell, and the company was unable to purchase his homestead until after he died. Temporarily thwarted in this direction, the company decided to look elsewhere and to accept professional help in selecting a site.

Manning, who was then employed in landscaping the new high school, apparently agreed to assume responsibility for designing the park and participated in discussions of site selection, for in 1890 a committee was appointed to study the park problem after acquiring his services:

> Mr. Manning submitted a report dated Oct. 30, 1891, in which he recommended the taking of about 40 acres of land in the section between Freedom and Adin streets, and about 20 acres of land in the vicinity of the pond. The recommendation as to the first taking was illustrated by a map, the area including portions of the present estates of F. J. and G. M. Dutcher, Mrs. C. H. Colburn, George A. Draper, E. D. Bancroft, and George Otis Draper.[76]

The property proposed by Manning skirted the east side of the central residential area adjacent to Prospect Street at the base of the hill separating Hopedale from Milford. One objective of the designer's was to secure a greenbelt between the two towns. The Drapers, however, decided against moving in this direction since the land encroached on their personal estates. In effect, this eastern zone was deemed a park already, though a decidedly private one. Manning also suggested using land that lay between the playground and the reservoir or pond. Water is a principal ingredient in recreational activities. Moreover, the summer boat races continued to focus attention or at least stir interest in this part of the town. Furthermore, the shoreline offered a variety in terrain and design potential. Access, however, was limited to a couple of points at the southern end of the reservoir because of the ruggedness of the site and the abundant undergrowth. During the winter months when its surface froze, the reservoir was abandoned except for cutting and storing ice. Some skating undoubtedly took place, and since 1914 the company has made it a practice to flood the ice nearest to the dam, creating a smooth surface for playing hockey (fig. 36).[77]

Because the "recommendation as to the land near the pond was not so definite in character," progress toward finalizing a park plan proceeded slowly until 1898.[78] By now Manning had conceived a much larger plan incorporating not just the area at the base of the reservoir but the entire shoreline of the upper privilege, an area of nearly two hundred acres. Engineer Gordon M. Taylor surveyed the site, and Manning drew up the plans, for which he received $454. A Park Commission, consisting of Frank J. Dutcher, Charles F. Roper, and George Otis Draper, accepted the extensive proposal and appropriated fourteen thousand dollars in 1899 to carry out the plan. Because such a large sum would be paid by propertyholders from taxes collected by the town, even though practically all the land was owned by the Drapers and their company, a vote was needed to authorize the go-ahead. Of the thirty-seven votes cast thirty-three favored the plan, and work proceeded.[79]

The achievement that followed was unique: no other company town or, for that matter, small industrial town had conceived such an extensive park system. Within a period of ten years Hopedale's parkland swelled to more than a thousand acres, almost a third of the total acreage of the town. But more significant than the size was the design or landscaping. Manning drew upon training he received from

36. Skating on Hopedale Pond, Hopedale, 1972.
The placid winter setting is much the same as it
was in the nineteenth century.

Olmsted before establishing his own practice as a result of the park project. The Hopedale commission provided him the opportunity on a small scale to do what Olmsted and Eliot did in Boston with the Muddy River development, which emerged as the nation's first regional park system in 1892.[80] Although there is obvious difference in scale, the idea and application were no less advanced for the date. Landscaping Hopedale's park system entailed combining several properties, surveying and planning, and ground reclamation through draining, filling, and replanting. First, "an extensive system of sub-draining, with catchbasins, etc. was put under the charge of Solon M. Allis, the entire work being done with accurate leveling methods, and a plan preserved by which to trace any possible error in working."[81] Allis received $2,766 for performing what can be categorized as draining the land, but this was simply a starting point. Next came excavation and cleaning, which required the removal of obstructions like ledges and boulders. Then grading and manuring prepared the site for replanting varieties of trees and shrubs. Manning stipulated the use of different kinds of trees, including maple, ash, birch, hickory, pine (hemlock), tulip, Carolina poplar, black alder, willow, and Japanese barberry. Though designing the park demanded a tremendous effort entailing many changes in the original landscape, the foremost requirement was to retain as much as possible the natural character of the site, avoiding the appearance of formal gardening:

> The committee in charge has always set itself one determined object—to keep the pond and the park as natural as possible, to refuse any touch of artificiality except in that portion where closeness to the houses forced certain yieldings to a cultivated aspect.[82]

They succeeded in keeping the natural beauty of the site while having extended its use.

Through careful landscaping, the visual potential of the site, with its rock outcroppings and myriad plants and trees, was fully brought out. Each year until 1914 Manning made an addition or an improvement of some type, and the park commissioners continued to support him in carrying out his plans by annually appropriating twenty-five hundred dollars. What is more, they hired a park supervisor or gardener who at times employed up to forty men in grading and planting.[83] The most attractive aspect of the park was designed in 1907 and consisted of a ribbon of trails that wound in and around the irregular shoreline for more than a mile in length (fig. 37). At the southern end of the park, near the boat marina, a beach had been prepared for swimmers in 1899, and in 1904 a bathhouse was erected: Chapman and Frazer designed it for the modest sum of fifty dollars, though it only cost $1,050 to build.[84] The investment was well worthwhile, for men, women, and children took advantage of it during the summer months. Apparently, one of the duties of superintendent Walter F. Durgin was to keep a count of those who used it: "During the season [1905] there were 3,100 baths taken by males, 222 by females."[85] The poor showing for females can be accounted for by the fact that a matron had to be on hand to supervise them; and then for years they maintained separate swimming schedules from the men, which must have been discouraging. Across from the bathhouse, improvements continued on the playfield. A football field was incorporated in the plan, and two tennis courts were laid. At the entrance to the grounds grew flowers and a hedgerow, while at the gate stood an unusual little monument designed in the shape of a textile spindle and cast in bronze. It made a superb hitching post, though probably intended for something else. The principal attraction of the playground, however, consisted of a bandstand with locker room below; erected at a cost of $828 and designed by Chapman and Frazer, it exists today as one of those attractive appointments to every town park of an earlier time.[86] One can almost visualize the brass band playing and Zouaves parading after the Hopedale Nine had won a doubleheader over Milford.

37. Map of Hopedale Park as laid out by Warren Henry Manning between 1898 and 1913. Note the ribbon of trails designed to follow the edge of Hopedale Pond. From *Sixteenth Annual Report of the Park Commissioners of the Town of Hopedale, Mass.*, 1914.

The big event of the year, which took place on the playground, was the annual Field Day, started in 1899. On a mid-August date each year, the shops closed and the whole town turned out to participate in sports events that included bag races, pole vaulting, high jumping, broad jumping, bicycling, canoeing, and something called a tub race.[87] A fascinating record of these events has been kept in photographs, which candidly portray the workers enjoying themselves.[88]

Two observations can be made in evaluating Hopedale's village improvement and park system. One is that comprehensive design of this extent required the participation of interested workers and an enlightened management that was able to make far-reaching decisions and to expend large sums of money for improvement. The other is strictly visual: the drive for beautification and conservation came in response to an interest in natural and even romantic landscapes, which enchanted New Englanders and others throughout this period.[89] That industrialists took part in this development seems to lessen the idea that all were intent on denuding the environment for the sake of business.

The architecture

Hopedale's public buildings gave visual impact to the paternalism cultivated by the company. A town hall, library, school, chapel, and gymnasium stand testament to the pride and wealth invested in the town. The town hall and library, in particular, helped to convey the town's model image; and because of their architecture, they will be described in some detail.

In 1885 George Draper commissioned architect Fred Swassey of Milford to design a building that could be used for manifold purposes, to include spaces for town meetings, record keeping, and social activities. It also required space for small businesses, such as a drugstore and barbershop. Most important, the building had to communicate the image of the town and enterprise (fig. 38). An agreement was made on June 24, 1885, and by August 26 the architect had prepared drawings of the new building for exhibit. The contract for construction was awarded to the Milford Granite Company.[90] Hopedale's buildings were built chiefly of wood, excepting the brick-veneered factories and office building. The new public edifice, however, called for a more durable and expensive material. So, like the foundations of George Draper, it was built of granite. Though commissioned in 1885, the building was not finished until October 25, 1887, when it was formally dedicated: on that occasion the factories again fell silent to honor George Draper, who missed seeing his gift consecrated. But others were on hand to praise the town and its most recent accession. The dedicatory addresses followed an opening prayer and consisted of a half-dozen orations interrupted every so often by the playing of the Hopedale brass band. Gov. John Hall spoke as one of the guests, as he had for a similar occasion in North Easton in 1881 to dedicate the Oakes Ames Memorial Hall, highlighting the day's fanfare.[91] The whole town turned out in celebration, joining in the pomp and pageantry and enjoying a respite from work.[92]

The town hall occupies a site south of the factories at the lower end of Hopedale Street near the intersection of Adin Street and across from the square. For it to be seen at the end of a tree-lined vista from atop Adin Street meant that the site could not be centered at the intersection, because the roadway curved and William F. Draper's house would have blocked the view. The chapel across the street sits well back from the intersection and does not interfere with the view. Unfortunately, the town hall was placed too near the street and did not leave adequate space for a proper approach. The site declines sharply to the west of Hopedale Street, leaving no alternative placement. Even so, the town hall assumes an imposing position, as envisioned by the architect and his client.

The building measures seventy-five feet in width and sixty-nine

38. Town Hall, Hopedale, 1887; Fred Swassey,
architect. It symbolizes the philanthropy of the
Draper family. Courtesy of the Merrimack Valley Textile Museum.

feet in depth and is approximately fifty feet high at the top of its hipped roof. Built at a cost of forty thousand dollars, it comprises two main floors plus a basement and attic, over twenty thousand square feet, a lot of space for the money even then. Above the foundations, the basement contained space for a market, a lockup, rooms for holding caucuses, and mechanical equipment. On the first floor, two rooms for small commercial rentals open separately onto the street, and an arched vestibule leads to a library with rooms for a stack, hall, lavatories, and two clubrooms also used for reading. Just inside the vestibule, a stair provides access to the second and attic floors. An auditorium with a seating capacity of 350 and a stage measuring twenty-four by fifty-two feet occupies a large portion of the second floor, and at each side of the stage are dressing rooms for theatrical performers like the Hopedale Players, who gave a series of "entertainments" for the benefit of the company employees.[93] Across from the auditorium were offices used by the selectmen and town officers, though "every now and then the Selectmen [held] their sessions in the offices of the Draper Company" since all were associated with the business.[94] Above the town offices and auditorium is still another hall, which extends from one end of the building to the other, providing a large area open to the roof for social events like company parties and dances. Regarding architectural style, the building followed contemporary fashion, emulative of the work of H. H. Richardson. It looks like a provincial Richardsonian, being more or less handled in the Romanesque style with a few Renaissance appointments. The proportions are awkward: the plan is overly square, which makes the structure appear very massive, with little exterior detail to relieve the expanses of granite to sides and rear. The pavilion front seems shallow and narrow in proportion to the width of the facade. But the heavy coping above the gable, the fenestration, cornice modillions, and the carving around the entrance vestibule, especially the colonettes, impost blocks, and molding beneath the archivolt, are handsomely rendered. The Milford granite walls were trimmed with Longmeadow brownstone, and the interior was finished in California redwood.[95] The town hall still commands attention as Hopedale's finest landmark, though it presently needs maintenance after years of service. The shop fronts have been renovated, which detracts from the original design and ornamental appointments. Also gone is the iron cresting atop the roof. Nonetheless, it remains a dignified building.

The other community facility that merits description is the Bancroft Memorial Library (fig. 39). Although Hopedale possessed a library as early as the 1840s, the books had been kept in a private dwelling or a church. When the town hall was erected, the library received generous space on the main floor in rooms designed expressly for its purpose; however, a separate depository given entirely to reading awaited Joseph B. Bancroft's forty-thousand-dollar donation of 1898. The new building was a memorial to his wife. Taste had changed by then, and revival architecture called for careful renderings, which were obtained more by copying a historic model than by creative design. Architect Hugh Walker of Boston designed the library after the Gothic chapel of Merton College, Oxford. Like the town hall, it was built of pink Milford granite, though trimmed in white ashlar. The central pavilion front opened onto the circulation floor and control desk, behind and on each side of which were shelving and reading areas. Solid oak enhanced the interior with carved moldings and paneled wainscot. The library occupies a site on the northwest corner of Hope and Hopedale streets north of the town hall. No landscaping distinguishes the building, but a large white marble drinking fountain graces the south side in the form of a bathing sibyl. This sculptural addition was carved by Waldo Story and shipped from Rome in 1904 as a gift from the ambassador's wife, Susan Preston Draper.[96] Inside, the library presently exhibits the colorful jackets of children's books and exciting novels, but at the time of construction it contained mostly self-improvement manuals

39. Bancroft Memorial Library, Hopedale, 1898;
Hugh Walker, architect. The sibyl was sculpted
by Waldo Story. Courtesy of the Merrimack
Valley Textile Museum.

or mechanic's guides, history, and English literature among its several thousand volumes. The library committee, composed of company officials, appointed the librarian and selected accessions. Privilege to borrow was given to all employees and town residents, and no fee was charged.[97] Although other small towns could also boast of handsome buildings, in Hopedale a singular and harmonious relationship existed between its architecture and town layout.

As a result of planning, entailing controlled site development through paternal management, Hopedale achieved its goal. Singular supervision in development enabled the Draper Company to settle its workers in a healthy and visually attractive landscape while participating in a competitive industry during heated and uncertain times.

The Draper Company made an announcement concerning its housing in November 1904:

> We are informed that the Superior Jury of the St. Louis Exposition have [*sic*] awarded us a gold medal for exhibit in Class 136, referring to the housing of the workmen. Visitors to Hopedale have frequently commented on the superior houses furnished by our company for its help. We believe in making our town as attractive as possible as a matter of good business policy, since we are anxious to retain the services of high class labor.[1]

In addition to receiving a gold medal for their housing exhibit at the Louisiana Purchase Exposition, the company previously had earned a silver medal at the Paris Exposition of 1900. Other gold medals would be awarded at Liège in 1905 and Milan in 1906.[2] That Hopedale received these international awards is revealing, because the Drapers never sought public attention for their town or crusaded for housing reform. They did not build model houses to rectify existing conditions among their workers. Rather, theirs was simply a business proposition; good homes attract good workers and keep them healthy and content. This sensible and pragmatic attitude toward housing was not the result of a redirection in policy or new initiative but had been active since operations began.

The first company houses built by the Drapers were placed along the northern end of Hopedale Street in 1857. From that date forward the number increased through periodic building campaigns taken between 1868 and 1874, throughout the 1880s, and again between 1896 and 1915. Aside from three boardinghouses, constructed primarily for single men, and a dozen or so single-family houses for managers located mostly along Dutcher Street, all were double-family in type. Each apartment occupied half of a symmetrical dwelling partitioned in the center by a wall. Placed into that wall was a common chase for

Chapter 7
Company Housing in Hopedale

vents and pipes, servicing both apartments while insulating against noise.

Double-family houses had several advantages over single-family houses or multifamily tenements. Offering greater exterior volume than a detached house, they avoided appearing too small, though they reduced per unit construction costs and development area. As opposed to larger tenements, they conformed to an existing residential scale consistent with houses established by the earlier community. They also represented a smaller replacement liability if seriously damaged or destroyed by fire, and they appealed to families more than row houses or elevated flats because each unit had cross-room ventilation and three-quarter exposure to sunlight while providing a yard to the front, side, and rear. Another advantage over larger tenements was that they could be built in limited number as the need arose. On occasion the Drapers let contracts for building only one house at a time: "The framing of *the* double-tenement house of the Hopedale Machine Company will be commenced this week" (August 30, 1882).[3] Moreover, the time required for constructing one double-family house rarely exceeded one week from start to finish, minimizing delays in time for occupancy and making an easy job for small contractors like Chapman and Winn or Albertus C. Hussey and Son of Milford, who built most of the earlier units.[4] On the other hand, it took Mead, Mason, and Company two months in 1887 to complete a three-story, sixteen-room boardinghouse at the corner of Dutcher and Prospect streets.[5]

If living in a company house subjected tenants to some form of social stigma, it was not because of the living arrangement at Hopedale. Double-family houses had existed from the very beginning, for the earlier community joined families in partitioned structures built in the 1840s.[6] The type continued as a sensible way to build, given the need for economy in both construction time and materials. The Drapers also considered population density and the amount of land available for development, and laying out single-family houses as an alternative posed drawbacks. Detached houses spread development over a greater area, entailing a larger investment in site preparation, whereas a tighter arrangement of houses avoided this problem and left more open area for landscaping. It seems reasonable that considerations of housing density per development area went beyond questions of land economy and available space to the question of time and distance between factory and home. Without overcrowding, workers needed to be housed near the factories to permit them to walk between home and work or return at noon for a hot meal, yet be able to enjoy a yard and a degree of privacy.

Maintenance was also a consideration in building double-family houses: two families shared the same structure and premise, which undoubtedly caused them to recognize upkeep as a mutual obligation. Had the company built "two-family" houses, where different families occupy floors in a vertical arrangement, this responsibility would have been lessened by reason of disposition; for these popular house types, put up by suburban developers in two- or three-story (triple-decker) arrangements all over New England and elsewhere from the 1880s onward, shortchanged those families located on upper levels. Once families moved to a second- or third-floor apartment, they often disregarded the yard and exterior upkeep. The British, who from the eighteenth century built row houses for industrial workers, tried wherever possible to provide each family a pen or garden to either the front or the rear.[7] Ground-floor living satisfied a social need, especially among tenants with children only recently dislodged from rural moorings. Among company towns, the double-family house persisted as a favorite type, constructed both at home and abroad in large number after 1850.[8] Its acceptance, however, depended on land availability and cost. Rarely were double-family houses built by companies in crowded industrial cities except for the highest-paid artisans. Neither were they built where companies intended to sell after a period of rental, in which case single-family houses offered greater attraction.[9]

Although company houses could be easily identified and appeared much the same from one town to the next, rarely were they identical. Even where pattern books provided the source for plans and elevations, subtle changes usually were made. Hopedale's houses were designed chiefly by Boston architects and constructed by Milford contractors, though on occasion a Worcester firm would receive a commission. Rather than forming their own construction company, the Drapers paid for outside services, though they maintained a special interest in building design and quality of construction.[10] Both William F. and Eben S. Draper visited model housing estates at home and abroad and were apprised of the best contemporary designs. In 1907 Eben traveled to England as a representative to the eighth international housing congress, held that year in London. At that time he visited the company housing at Port Sunlight and Bourneville.[11] However, his visits abroad seemed to confirm his earlier preferences and decisions:

> Governor Draper having meanwhile made several visits to similar communities abroad, and, while cognizant of the development there taking place, has nevertheless maintained for Hopedale the same general scheme of development—with certain detail modifications—that had been initiated in 1897, considering that the ideas then inaugurated were more adaptable and workable under conditions of American life.[12]

The "same general scheme" referred to the Bancroft Park houses imaginatively arranged on an attractive site. Furthermore, the Drapers paid handsome prices for "good and substantial" buildings. Between 1857 and 1915 twelve styles of double-family houses, each differing slightly in size, room arrangement, construction, and rent, were put up by the company. Variations in style result from different periods of construction since the Drapers accepted advancements in design and commissioned different architects at different periods, though certain houses were sometimes repeated at a later date. Two houses will be illustrated here because they represent considerable differences not only in design but also in technical advancements.

The "seven sisters" compose a row of double-family houses lining the western extension of Freedom Street, where they were moved in 1907. Before then, they had sat facing Union Street west of the factories and were referred to as "Union row."[13] But as the industrial site expanded they got in the way of manufacturing and had to be removed. Carpenters Chapman and Winn contracted the houses for approximately fifteen hundred dollars each and built them according to an architect's designs, probably drawn by Swassey.[14] Actually, there were two rows along Union Street, the north side or 1874 row and the south side erected much later in 1889—an instance in which similarly designed houses followed at a later date. When moved to their present location, the houses of the two rows were alternated so as to sit one next to the other. Distinguishing the two is a minor feature in the treatment of the roof, which in the later units continues beyond the eave over the porch (fig. 40). Porches on the 1874 row were added in 1887 when the company "put them in thorough repair, adding blinds [shutters], etc. and grading around them."[15] In cost and appearance these houses represent very modest endeavors. Renting for less than other double-families built in Hopedale, they were reduced a dollar a month in 1883 to five dollars.[16] Twenty years later they rented for only $8.80.[17] Exterior dimensions of the 1874 group measure forty by twenty-seven feet in plan, making apartments of twenty by twenty-seven feet per floor: each contains two floors in a story-and-a-half arrangement; the height from the top of the foundation to the apex of the roof is twenty feet, leaving plenty of head height per floor. Dimensioned lumber was used in framing conventional stud walls, and a rafter roof was collared above the chamber level. The

40. Double-family houses along Freedom Street, Hopedale, ca. 1907. The earliest units were constructed in 1874 on Union Street but relocated when the plant expanded. They were variously known as "Union row" and the "seven sisters." Courtesy of the Merrimack Valley Textile Museum.

underpinning rests on a stone foundation containing a basement for storage. Exterior finish consists of clapboards battened at the corners and under the eaves. Inside, three rooms occupy the lower floor— parlor, dining room, and kitchen—and two bedrooms and a bath make the upper (fig. 41). Apartments this size (1,080 square feet) were best suited to families of three, and five including an infant sleeping in the parents' bedroom was maximum. A gable centered on the rear pitch of the wood-shingled roof provided each apartment with light at the head of the stair and a means of drafting air through the bedrooms and bath, providing the doors were opened wide. Windows for the upper level (two on each end) do not satisfactorily ventilate the rooms, insomuch as they attempted to conserve heat. Interior walls were plastered and floors were laid in hardwood. Artificial lighting came from gas wall fixtures before the apartments were wired for electricity in 1907. Four small fireplaces and a kitchen stove furnished heat, though at an early date gas stoves had been adapted. It should be remembered that in the mid-1870s coal furnaces had yet to become widely used for domestic purposes, and fuel oil for heating remained a long way off.

If simplicity in plan and elevation seems a virtue today, these houses were certainly ahead of their time (fig. 42), though by nineteenth-century architectural standards they would have appeared devoid of stylistic consideration, much like earlier mill houses, save for an added porch or gable. What can be praised about their design is the emphasis on utility, since nothing was wasted on ornament or supplied if unessential. In contrast to the houses of the Draper family, the "seven sisters" were unpretentious and functional; yet they furnished their occupants with living conditions every bit as safe and sanitary.

The double-family houses of the Bancroft Park development differ from these earlier units in both design and technical improvements. In 1896 architect Robert Allen Cook of Boston supervised the con-

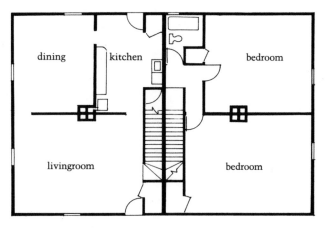

41. Plan of double-family house on Union Street, Hopedale, 1874. The ground floor of one apartment is illustrated on the left; the upper floor of the other is on the right.

dining kitchen bedroom

livingroom bedroom

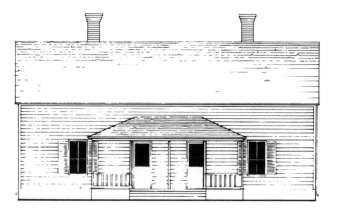

42. Elevation of double-family house on Union Street, Hopedale, 1874.

struction of fourteen houses of a proposed thirty-house site slated for immediate construction.[18] Drawings in addition to those prepared by Cook were solicited from five other local architects: Peabody and Stearns, Edwin J. Lewis, Jr., J. Williams Beal, Chapman and Frazer, and Walter and Kimball. Designs from each met specified requirements as to size and use. All are double-family houses, but variations in plan and exterior treatment separate them into five of eight proposed styles. Each of the Bancroft Park houses built on the inner loop contains approximately the same amount of floor area (fifteen hundred to seventeen hundred square feet) and cost $4,500.[19] Apparently, the Drapers in consultation with the supervising architect and landscape designer decided that an alternate arrangement of styles would enhance the group, avoiding the "Union row" connotation, namely, "seven sisters."[20] The departure from the earlier houses, however, invites the notion that the Drapers considered variety in building style as important to the occupants' sense of identity or individualism. But no statements to that effect suggest such regard, at least on behalf of the company; rather, the newer houses simply followed a continuing policy of making Hopedale attractive to workers. Company houses furnished by the Drapers drew as much public praise before the Bancroft Park development as after, and the 1874 units were probably considered every bit as model for their date as the latter. Nevertheless, considerable advancements had been made during the interim: the Bancroft Park houses contain more floor space and provide better illumination, ventilation, and heating. For example, instead of seven windows for each apartment (as in the case of the 1874 units), there were now twenty-two! More windows came in response to sanitation surveys of workers' housing, which revealed poorly lit and fetid rooms. Though the results of these surveys were available even before the 1870s, changes were slow to be instituted.[21] For one reason, improvements in natural lighting and ventilation awaited the invention of better heating apparatus. Advancing from the open hearth to the Franklin stove to central furnaces with either steam radiators or hot-air outlets amounted to a scientific revolution in heating technology. All depend on radiant or conductive systems, but fuel consumption and effectiveness varied widely. The Bancroft Park dwellings had hot-air central heating that is similar in principle to systems used in homes built today, except that for distribution it relied on gravity flow rather than electric fan. Even so, they were technically advanced for their date and heated with enough efficiency to offset the loss in wall insulation due to added glazing.[22] Plumbing in the newer houses counts for another improvement in that circulating-hot-water piping was made available, whereas the older units provided only a cold-water tap. Both had indoor toilets, sinks, and baths, though only the newer houses connected with a sewer system. The earlier units managed with a cesstank, which served each house prior to the company's expending $550 for laying sewers along Union Street in 1889.[23]

The Bancroft Park houses, designed by Edwin J. Lewis, Jr., of Boston, possessed three rooms on the ground floor—kitchen, dining room, and parlor—plus a pantry and china cabinet, while the upstairs provided three bedrooms, closets, and a bath (fig. 43). Bow-front bays permitted plenty of light to enter parlor and bedroom as well as obtaining variety in room shape. In regard to size and disposition, these apartments could accommodate families numbering from four to a maximum of seven, and the smallest bedrooms measured 9 by 12½ feet. Like the earlier houses, the newer double-families were of frame construction placed on stone foundations enclosing a basement. Roof framing bore evidence of thoughtful design considerations, which help to distinguish the houses from one another while providing space for storage or an added bedroom. The Lewis units display roofs with cross-gables, while others have double-hipped roofs, and still others have gambrels, all of which were well proportioned. Aside from shutters, which became popular domestic appointments during

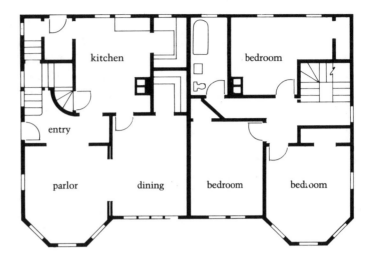

43. Plan of double-family house in Bancroft Park, Hopedale, 1898; Edwin J. Lewis, architect. The ground floor of one apartment is illustrated on the left; the upper floor of the other is on the right.

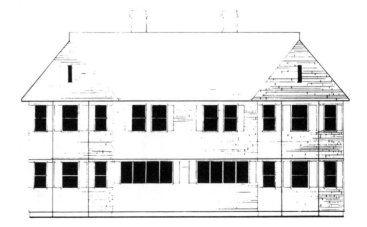

44. Elevation of double-family house in Bancroft Park, Hopedale, 1898; Edwin J. Lewis, Jr., architect.

the Federal period and survived the century, nothing in these houses betokens the historicism so prevalent during the Victorian period, though in regard to contemporary English cottages similarities exist. Specifically, the prominent roofs and banded windows (fig. 44) are not unlike what architects influenced by the Arts-and-Crafts Movement were attempting to create at the turn of the century. H. M. Baillie Scott and Charles F. A. Voysey emphasized the horizontality of roofs and windows and featured the use of prominent cross-gables and projecting bays.[24]

Toward the end of the nineteenth century, however, American architects and architectural critics began calling for a native style. The *American Architect and Building News* and *Architectural Record* carried articles that promoted the cause.[25] In 1896 John Stewardson said that "our smaller houses are developing a style in harmony with the exigencies of the climate and the needs of the people."[26] The houses designed for Hopedale support his observation. Nowhere was this more evident than in the choice of materials and quality of construction. At Bancroft Park exterior siding of cypress shingles covered the walls, which were left unstained to weather. The trim, however, was painted. North Carolina pine was used for interior finish, and the best grade of beech and maple was laid as flooring: "service floors are oiled, the bathroom floors varnished, the remainder are waxed. . . . The plumbing . . . includes an iron kitchen sink, an iron enamel tub and lavatory, and a vitreous [water] closet, with brass water-pipes throughout."[27] As regards design and construction, these houses rank among the best workers' dwellings ever built in the United States.

Affecting all the houses was the company's building maintenance program, which kept up appearances through periodic repairs and improvements. Teams of carpenters, painters, plumbers, paperers, and plasterers made the rounds from house to house: in June 1887, Eldredge and Beattey of Milford received "the contract for papering and painting the Union row houses. . . . The houses will be painted inside and out."[28] Just when the company assembled its own maintenance team is unknown, though by 1901 full-time crews were in operation.[29] Mentioned earlier were the ground crews, which policed streets, parks, vacant yards, and participated in the planting and gardening projects of the village improvement program, but house crews dealt only with building maintenance, and a portion of their time was devoted to painting the houses (interiors and exterior trim) in different though coordinated colors. A description of the maintenance administered by the Draper Company, published by an inquiring journalist, sheds some light on the extent of this endeavor:

> The matter of harmony in house painting is unknown in most of the industrial centers of New England, but not so in Hopedale. Application of the principles of harmony in color is responsible for this little town being truly Yankee in atmosphere.
>
> The Draper Company is a most conscientious landlord. Every property is kept in excellent repair, a corps of carpenters and painters making rounds of each "tenement" at regular intervals. The schedule of caretakers is so arranged that each housewife in Hopedale is sure of having at least one room of her home "done over" once a year. Often she may be so fortunate as to have a complete painting job—inside and outside—done annually.[30]

Like the Cheneys, Hubbards, Hazards, and Fairbankses, the Drapers placed an emphasis on maintenance as a means of sustaining the company's image.

Their business as well as their houses represented a total environmental commitment. Attention to details or appointments in construction and upkeep met the same rigorous inspection that went into manufacturing textile machinery. But when the company divested its housing in the mid-1950s, this care and supervision ceased. The handsome wood-shingle exterior walls weathered to rich brown and trimmed with attractive hues of greens, browns, and yellows were covered with gray asbestos siding to defray costs of repair and painting. Now all the Bancroft Park houses appear soberly dull and alike. Even the roofs have been recovered in a cheaper material of asphalt tile and are further disfigured with television antennas and lead-in wires. Yards once neat and attractive and planted with flowers are now strewn with rubbish and divided into cubicles by cyclone fences.

The rationale behind the Drapers' housing was only indirectly profit-motivated. Though they never intended to lose money, the return on their investment through rent only covered construction costs and paid for maintenance, utilities, and insurance. In 1903 tenants paid fourteen dollars a month[31] in rent for the Bancroft Park houses, which yielded the company a 7½ percent annual return on their original investment. When compared with profit margins recorded for company houses in part I of this study, Hopedale falls into line, though with slightly less moderate rents for its larger units. The Drapers drew a distinction between paternalism and philanthropy: the former helped facilitate a building program, while the latter served to procure needed facilities but was otherwise poor business regarding housing. Illustrating the Drapers' detachment in attitude concerning housing and philanthropy were comments made following Budgett Meakin's visit in 1903. In search of material for his book, *Model Factories and Villages* (1905), Meakin included Hopedale in his itinerary. The Drapers purchased a copy of his study and made the following observation:

> Mr. Meakin came to Hopedale without invitation, and made his investigations independently, taking such photographs as he cared to. He finds many interesting conditions in industries connected with textile manufacture, and refers especially to the Ludlow Mills, . . . Willimantic Linen Company, Cheney Broth-

ers Manufacturing Company, . . . the Whitin Machine Works, the Plymouth Cordage Company, and our own village of Hopedale. We are rather pleased at his reference to our town, as he specifies our conditions as illustrating "America's best."[32]

However much the Drapers appreciated Meakin's praise and endorsement of their housing and other programs, they stopped short of agreeing with the social improvements undertaken by some companies illustrated in his book, saying: "While we are proud of our town and interested in the welfare of our workmen, we are not attempting to compete with the business philanthropy, which often goes to a questionable extreme."[33] Cheney of South Manchester had expressed a similar opinion to the Industrial Commission. The model housing of Hopedale, then, represents not the product of a socially inspired or exceptionally progressive business but rather a sensible approach to a housing problem unique to the nineteenth and early twentieth century.

Chapter 8
Conclusion

Hopedale, together with Ludlow, South Manchester, Peace Dale, and Fairbanks Village, retains much of its former appearance, though it has ceased to operate as a company town. The development of these towns spanned a period of American history known as the "age of enterprise," and their wholesale approach to design, construction, and management is an expression of that early period of industrial investment and organization. As the age drew to a close, however, they diminished with it. The advent of hydroelectric power transmission replaced the need for locating factories near sources of energy, and the availability of inexpensive transportation no longer required the placement of houses nearby. Instead, factories could be located in cities, and workers could commute by streetcar or automobile from outlying suburbs. Decline was accelerated by the withdrawal of paternalism on the part of these companies, and affecting their decisions to relinquish houses and other properties was the passage of federal taxes and antitrust laws.[1] As with other enterprises, company towns felt the burden of government in the twentieth century. A corporation tax was imposed after 1913; and a general reduction in tariffs brought renewed foreign competition. Monopolies not just on businesses but on properties were also investigated.[2] The New England textile industry suffered when chemical companies introduced synthetic fibers, which encroached on cotton, woolen, and silk markets; and textile machine makers participated in their own demise by perfecting items like automatic looms, which operated more efficiently and required fewer repairs. The effect was twofold in that it also put weavers out of work. Depression struck the textile industry earlier than others, in 1924, and then did not ease until the outbreak of World War II, too late for many enterprises that had already succumbed.[3] The thirties saw company towns liquidate their properties; auctioneers sold off entire building sites with houses going at half their former value.[4] When an enterprise in a single-enterprise town ceased operations, the impact was dramatic and devastating.

The model company town offers lessons, however, in urban design and management. It grew in an orderly and economical fashion and was for years an asset to its builder. It further provided efficient and inexpensive housing within an attractive landscape. No building was placed out of walking range, and traffic was mostly pedestrian. Site supervision continued after construction, which ensured the maintenance of houses, factories, and grounds. As a result, Hopedale managed to carry on a large and profitable manufacture while avoiding the corrosive conditions that frequently attended the development of other industrial towns. This environmental commitment lasted as long as the developer exercised control over the site. In the case of the Draper Company, it diminished after 1916 and finally ended in 1967. A decline in business and the divestment of property brought an end to site control not only in Hopedale but also in the other towns, where the process had begun even earlier.[5] Total dependence on a single enterprise became a critical limitation. The company town lacked the flexibility of mixed-economy towns and was unable to attract new business and employment.

The American garden city or satellite city and more recent new towns expand in part upon design principles first applied to company towns. In them, a single enterprise also supervised construction on one large tract of land, laid utilities, and built all the structures. Landscape architects and planners designed industrial layouts and housing sites in contour arrangements, employed such ideas as the superblock, and planted belts of protective parkland. Manning, for example, was hired by Firestone to design Goodyear Heights (1913) and Firestone Park (1916) near Akron, Ohio. Shurcliff later designed Hyde Park Village (1910–15), near Boston, for the American Felt Company.[6] These later commissions located industries near to existing cities for ancillary needs in a satellite relationship. When the government became involved in new-town design, following its war housing, it studied these earlier types and published information about them in the Urbanism Committee report of the late thirties.[7] And, more recently, Henry Churchill, a designer of one of the government's Greenbelts, observed:

> These industrial towns and projects seem to definitely demonstrate the value of unified and strong control of land use. The appearance and integrity of the character of the development is rapidly lost in towns which have reverted to "normal" municipal practices, such as Kingsport, and Longview. Company-owned villages such as Hopedale . . . tend to retain the advantages of their plan.[8]

The Greenbelts and other garden cities did not enjoy the longevity of the company town largely because they reverted too soon to "normal municipal practices." Congressional pressure suspended building (and maintenance) programs. Private homeowners and realtors carved them into smaller parcels and suspended cooperative programs. The result was that some occupants kept up appearances and some did not, while the rapid decline of a few properties discouraged new development when most needed. What the investigators of the Urbanism Committee decried most about the earlier war housing in places like Camden, New Jersey, where neighborhoods fell into ruin for lack of maintenance given to rental units, was precisely what happened in the Greenbelts.[9]

The more recent new towns, those begun in the sixties and seventies, rely again on private developers who exercise authority over design and layout. But there is little reason to believe they will stand up better over a period of time than their prototypes. If they are more flexible to economic change, it is because these towns have little or no employment. For all their emphasis on pedestrian circulation between houses and community centers, they must still contend with the automobile since their residents commute to work. Their appeal is to the family and not the worker and to the well-off and not the poor. Moreover, there is no evidence as yet to indicate whether residents in these towns will be more or less stable in terms of migration than those in other types of single-enterprise developments. They do not appear to be "life-cycle communities."[10] Although new towns are less needed today than in the past, they do serve as experiments demonstrating new approaches to living. Irvine, California, for example, a new town south of Los Angeles, is building condominiums in addition to single-family dwellings. Although the units are sold, the lots are only leased.[11] People go there seeking a mode of living free from custodial responsibilities. Some new towns impose strict regulations on development with the purpose of creating pleasant environments. The population resides in densely spaced clusters of housing (sometimes in mixed ethnic and economic groups), yet within easy access to community spaces. The objective is to reestablish a sense of community, of social reciprocity. These new towns contrast measuredly with company towns in outward appearance, administration, and social makeup. Nonetheless, their principal task of furnishing housing and community facilities in profitable and comprehensively designed towns, small in size though near large cities, remains much the same in effect.

Large-scale developments as seen in new towns can provide the opportunity for successfully combining housing and industry through careful design and planning. But when treated separately, as is so often the case with housing subdivisions, the solutions frequently are poorly conceived, unrelated to bordering areas, and restricted in layout by existing municipal services. Zoning regulations tend to segregate structures according to purpose and size despite their protection to individual homeowners. The challenge of providing attractive and economically arranged sites is considerably greater nowadays. The need to bring planning considerations under one authority, empowered to shape the future and protect the past, is more important than ever before, and the failure to do so is all too evident, especially in small towns because of their size. J. B. Jackson's descriptions of small-town American landscapes reflect a public disregard and misuse of spaces that were once delightful to encounter but now present obstacles to be avoided.[12] The hope is that new towns can adapt to technological change without sacrificing their environments.

Who today would argue that a business enterprise was better suited to govern a town's affairs than elected officials? But if businesses no longer manage the towns they help to develop and support, what obligations, if any, do they have to the environments surrounding them? Attracted by accessible highways, cheap utilities, and low tax rates, new factories are usually consigned to industrial belts away from the centers of towns. Eventually, however, strips of commercial activity appear, and tracts of houses preceded by trailer courts spread around them. Ironically, American businesses, though often organized for large-scale development, leave such peripheral matters to land speculators and small contractors with no long-term interest or investment in the area. What would seem profitable and protective of the enterprise at hand, however, might also appear opportunistic, though no one would accuse those enterprises that build cafeterias, jogging tracks, and handball courts for their employees and provide them with season tickets to cultural and sporting events of paternalism. These concessions to employee happiness and productivity, together with health care and retirement pensions, are negotiated company benefits. Though workers now share greater economic freedom and enjoy better safeguards than in the past, the enterprises near where they live contribute little to a sense of community and even less to the quality of environment.

Since the mid-nineteenth century, low-cost housing has undergone considerable change. Improvements in illumination, ventilation, and heating indicate practical if not always aesthetic advancements in design. Families of five (the average-sized family in Hopedale) gained nearly three hundred square feet of floor space in a twenty-year interval between the mid-1870s and mid-1890s, culminating a trend to larger accommodations realized in most towns except in the houses of the poorest families. The average apartment in a double-family house owned by the Draper Company contained fourteen hundred square feet. Although less area than provided in conventional houses today for middle-income families, it is more than allotted to families of five residing in public housing. What did not change in Hopedale, or for that matter in most other places right up to the present, is the way in which houses were built. Building trades handcrafted houses then as now. Nothing appears to have been prefabricated in the Bancroft Park houses designed in 1896 except doors, windows, fixtures, and a few items of interior trim. Although housing prefabricators were in business in the nineteenth century, they built in limited quantity and rarely in New England.[13] Had companies constructed their own houses instead of hiring outside contractors, construction methods might have been systematized and the product processed much the same way as a textile loom, a bolt of silk, or a bathroom scale. In outward appearance, the company houses built in Hopedale and its cognate towns managed to express sensible and sometimes pleasing designs. Whether or not their simple form and use of indigenous materials constituted a "national style" of architecture, something sought and partly achieved in the late nineteenth century, seems less important in light of other considerations. The case for well-designed houses rested not with stylistic motifs but with the use of rational space suited to domestic requirements. Furthermore, designing low-cost dwellings forced architects to recognize the fundamentals of good housing. In this regard, Hopedale's houses were exemplary.

Comprehensive design entailing maintenance after construction evolved with company towns like Hopedale. A single enterprise controlled construction from beginning to end and was able to coordinate physical expansion with business and employment demand. Factories, houses, community buildings, and parks existed in a manageable number and adequate ratio to provide jobs, shelter, and recreation for workingmen and their families. The desideratum was simply to organize building and space economically and yet attract and sufficiently accommodate a large work force to facilitate business. Some of the design ideas implanted in these towns have been carried forward to the present. Good planning and architecture are timeless, though social and economic motives periodically change. As buildable space diminishes, and as metropolitan regions spread outward to incorporate small towns, attention to urban development will increase. The model company town, for its part, represented a small though seminal achievement in urban design and environmental management.

Appendix A.
Chronology of the
Draper Company,
Hopedale, Massachusetts

1856　Hopedale Machine Company organized, E. D. and G. Draper Company; Joseph Bancroft, superintendent
1856　Warren W. Dutcher temples manufactured in Hopedale
1868　Partnership, George Draper and Son; E. D. Draper retires
1868　William F. Draper taken into partnership
1877　George A. Draper taken into partnership
1880　Eben S. Draper taken into partnership
1880　Hopedale Furnace and Machine Companies consolidated
1886　Hopedale, town incorporation
1887　William F. Draper, Jr., taken into partnership
1888　Hopedale Machine Screw Company chartered
1889　George Otis Draper taken into partnership
1892　Northrop Loom Company chartered
1897　Draper Company absorbs: George Draper and Sons; Hopedale Machine Company; Dutcher Temple Company; Hopedale Machine Screw Company; Northrop Loom Company; Sawyer Spindle Company
1898　Hopedale Elastic Goods Company purchased
1900　Draper Company becomes the largest producer of textile machinery in the United States
1913　Strike of IWW workers
1916　Draper Corporation chartered

Appendix B
Tenants of the Draper Company
Boardinghouses

Name	Age	Job title	Birthplace
1870			
Whipple, Amos	52	boardinghouse keeper	Connecticut
———, Sally	47	boardinghouse matron	Connecticut
Moody, Eben N.	30	carpenter	Maine
———, Pamelia	25	boarder	Massachusetts
Edmonds, George D.	35	machinist	Massachusetts
———, Annie	33	boarder	Rhode Island
Damon, William	40	foundry foreman	Massachusetts
Parker, Lewis	22	machinist	Massachusetts
Wilson, Edwin L.	20	machinist	Connecticut
Gilman, Charles	21	molder	Maine
McClarence, James	25	machinist	Massachusetts
Fuller, Edward	18	machinist	Massachusetts
Gates, Frederick	18	machinist	Nova Scotia
Packer, Willard	30	machinist	Vermont
Duffy, James	30	machinist	England
Chase, William	18	machinist	Rhode Island
Smith, James	22	machinist	New Brunswick
Holt, Henry	21	machinist	Massachusetts
Ward, Frank	18	machinist	Massachusetts
Donahoe, James	20	machinist	Ireland
Howe, Edward P.	21	machinist	Massachusetts
1880			
Whipple, Amos	61	boardinghouse keeper	Connecticut
———, Sally	56	boardinghouse matron	Connecticut
Spofford, A. J.	41	sewing machine agent	Maine
———, Sarah	38	dressmaker	Maine
———, Sarah	15	boarder	Maine
Lewers, Nancy	48	boarder	Connecticut

Name	Age	Job title	Birthplace
O'Connor, Annie	25	servant	Ireland
Howard, Lizza	18	servant	Ireland
Miland, Annie	18	servant	Ireland
Norton, Julia	70	servant	Massachusetts
Coffee, Abbie	17	servant	Massachusetts
Smith, Charlotte	49	servant	Massachusetts
Gallagher, Ida C.	25	servant	New Brunswick
Evans, Charles S.	29	machinist	Rhode Island
Rhodes, Alonzo E.	28	machinist	Maine
Lealand, George E.	20	machinist	Massachusetts
Stone, Adolphous	23	machinist	Canada
Dixon, Walter	17	machinist	Massachusetts
Thurston, Frank	28	machinist	Maine
Brown, James	23	machinist	Massachusetts
Ingraham, Alexander	50	molder	Rhode Island
Pickard, Benjamin J.	24	machinist	Canada
Town, J. E.	59	machinist	Connecticut
———, Isabella	52	boarder	Connecticut
Brennon, Patrick	50	machinist	Ireland
McCaffery, Patrick F.	50	molder	Ireland
McGuire, John	30	molder	Ireland
Finnegan, Joseph	25	molder	Ireland
Woodbury, E.	30	molder	Rhode Island
Chester, L. C.	25	laborer	Massachusetts
Curtis, E. E.	35	molder	Maine
Raftiry, James	25	molder	Connecticut
Capen, E. M.	25	molder	Massachusetts
Stanyard, John N.	50	machinist	Vermont
———, Edward	25	machinist	Vermont

1870

Boardinghouse keeper Whipple
Number of boarders ... 21
Native-born ... 17
(born in New England) ... 17
Foreign-born ... 4

1880

Boardinghouse keeper Whipple
Number of boarders ... 35
Native-born ... 25
(born in New England) ... 25
Foreign-born ... 10

1900

Boardinghouse keeper Andrews
Number of boarders ... 91
Native-born ... 65
(born in New England) ... 42
Foreign-born ... 26

Boardinghouse keeper Fuller
Number of boarders ... 70
Native-born ... 41
(born in New England) ... 27
Foreign-born ... 29

Boardinghouse keeper Guicconi
Number of boarders ... 78
Native-born ... 0
(born in New England) ... 0
Foreign-born ... 78

Appendix C
Population, Housing, Valuation, and
Nativity for Hopedale (1856–1916)

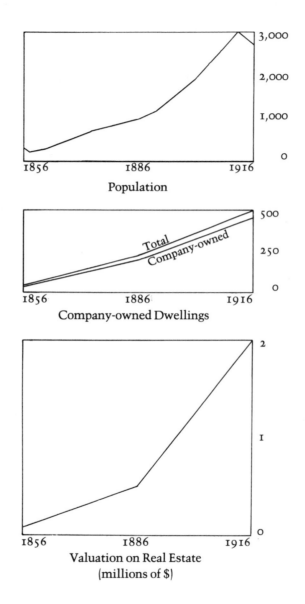

Population

Company-owned Dwellings

Valuation on Real Estate
(millions of $)

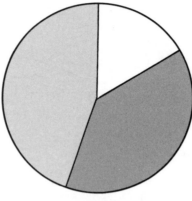

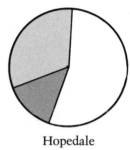

Hopedale

Holyoke
(typical corporate town)

Comparative Nativity
(for 1915)

	Hopedale		Holyoke
Total pop.	2,663		60,741
Native of native-born	1,404		10,153
Native-born	707		27,764
Foreign-born	552		22,824

1 Introduction

1   A brief assessment of the company town and its social structure is provided by J. D. Porteous, *Environment and Behavior: Planning and Everyday Urban Life* (Reading, Mass.: Addison-Wesley, 1977), pp. 330–38. An excellent essay on the architecture and spatial organization of the company town may be found in Leland M. Roth, "Three Industrial Towns by McKim, Mead, and White," *Journal of the Society of Architectural Historians* 38 (December 1979): 317–47.

2   Margaret F. Byington, *Homestead: The Households of a Mill Town*, The Pittsburg Survey, ed. Paul U. Kellogg, vol. 1 (New York: Charities Publication Committee, Russell Sage Foundation, 1910), pp. 1–278.

3   See Charles A. Beard, *Contemporary American History, 1877–1913* (New York: Macmillan, 1924), p. 35; Thomas C. Cochran and William Miller, *The Age of Enterprise* (New York: Macmillan, 1942), pp. 18–20, 63, 71–72; Allan Nevins and Henry Steele Commager, *A Short History of the United States*, 5th ed. (New York: Alfred A. Knopf, 1972), p. 327; Christopher Tunnard, *The City of Man* (New York: Charles Scribner's Sons, 1953), pp. 154–77; and John E. Burchard and Albert Bush-Brown, *The Architecture of America. A Social and Cultural History* (Boston: Little, Brown, 1961), pp. 271–73.

4   Lewis Mumford, *The Culture of Cities* (New York: Harcourt, Brace, and World, 1938), p. 486.

5   Charles Buxton Going, "Village Communities of the Factory, Machine Works, and Mine," *Engineering Magazine* 21 (1901): 66–71.

6   See Richard Wade, *The Urban Frontier* (Cambridge: Harvard University Press, 1959), chaps. 1, 10.

7   Victor Clark, *History of Manufacturers in the United States*, vol. 2 (Washington, D.C.: Carnegie Institution, 1929), p. 3.

8   Tench Coxe, *An Address to an Assembly of the Friends of American Manufacturers, Society for the Encouragement of Manufactures and the Useful Arts* (Philadelphia: Aitken and Son, 1787).

9   See John Borden Armstrong, *Factory under the Elms: A History of Harrisville, N.H.* (Cambridge: MIT Press, 1969); Anthony F. C. Wallace, *Rockdale: The Growth of an American Village in the Early Industrial Revolution* (New York: Alfred A. Knopf, 1978); Constance Noyes Robertson, *Oneida Community: The Breakup, 1876–1881* (Syracuse: Syracuse University Press, 1972); Dolores Hayden, *Seven American Utopias: The Architecture of Communitarian Socialism, 1790–1975* (Cambridge: MIT Press, 1976).

Notes

10   The term "model" is used in the 1878 edition of William Alfred Hinds's *American Communities and Co-operative Colonies* (Chicago: C. H. Kerr, 1908), pp. 146, 220. In France the *ville industrielle modèle* or *les cités ouvrières modèles* came into use after 1850; see Louis-René Villerme, *Sur les cités ouvrières* (Paris: J. B. Bailliere, Libraire de l'Académie nationale de médecine, 1850). For a more recent use of the phrase "model company town," see Jane Jacobs, *The Death and Life of Great American Cities* (New York: Random House, 1961), p. 18.

11   For a recent history of various model industrial villages in Britain, see Gillian Darley, *Villages of Vision* (London: Architectural Press, 1975).

12   Stanley Buder, *Pullman: An Experiment in Industrial Order and Community Planning, 1880–1930* (New York: Oxford University Press, 1967).

13   In addition to Constance M. Green, *Holyoke, Massachusetts: A Case History of the Industrial Revolution in America* (New Haven: Yale University Press, 1939), and John P. Coolidge, *Mill and Mansion: A Study in Architecture and Society in Lowell, Massachusetts, 1820–1865* (New York: Columbia University Press, 1942), see Tamara K. Hareven and Randolph Langenbach, *Amoskeag: Life and Work in an American Factory-City* (New York: Pantheon Books, 1978), and William H. Pierson, Jr., *American Buildings and Their Architects* (Garden City, N.Y.: Doubleday, 1978), 2:28–59.

14   Originally published as *Tomorrow: A Peaceful Path to Real Reform* (1898); Ebenezer Howard, *Garden Cities of Tomorrow*, ed. Frederick J. Osborn (London: Faber and Faber, 1946).

15   See Graham Romeyn Taylor, *Satellite Cities: A Study of Industrial Suburbs* (New York: D. Appleton, 1915).

16   Walter L. Creese, *The Search for Environment: The Garden City, Before and After* (New Haven: Yale University Press, 1966), pp. 110, 191–202.

17   Frederic J. Osborn, *The New Towns* (New York: McGraw-Hill, 1963), chap. 1; idem, "Sir Ebenezer Howard: The Evolution of His Ideas," *Town Planning Review* 21 (October 1950): 222.

18   Grosvenor Atterbury, "Model Towns in America," *Scribner's Magazine* 52 (1912): 20–35.

19   Porteous, *Environment and Behavior*, chap. 5; Robert Sommer, "Man's Proximate Environment," *Journal of Social Issues* 22, no. 4 (1966): 59–68.

20   Hareven and Langenbach, *Amoskeag*, pp. 113–235. Also see William Michelson, *Man and His Urban Environment: A Sociological Approach* (Reading, Mass.: Addison-Wesley, 1970), chap. 3.

21   Several case studies are cited, such as the National Cash Register Company's

works near Dayton; Frederick W. Taylor, *Shop Management* (New York: McGraw-Hill, 1911).

22 Ray Thomas, "Britain's New-Town Demonstration Project," in Gideon Golany, ed., *International Urban Growth Policies: New-Town Contributions* (New York: John Wiley and Sons, 1978), pp. 23–34.

23 Clarence S. Stein, *Toward New Towns for America* (Liverpool: Liverpool University Press, 1951), p. 11.

24 Sam Bass Warner, Jr., *The Urban Wilderness: A History of the American City* (New York: Harper and Row, 1972), chap. 8.

25 The extent to which these towns were different in appearance as seen from both far away and up close is indicated by E. C. Gardner, *Illustrated Homes* (Boston: James R. Osgood, 1875), p. 201; Pierson, *American Buildings*, 2:45–58.

26 David R. Weimer, ed., *City and Country in America* (New York: Appleton-Century-Crofts, 1962), pp. 201–5.

27 John R. Commons, ed., *History of Labor in the United States* (New York: Macmillan, 1918–35), vols. 3, 4.

28 "Hopedale," *Milford Journal*, Dec. 26, 1883.

29 Stephan Thernstrom, *Poverty and Progress: Social Mobility in a Nineteenth-Century City* (Cambridge: Harvard University Press, 1964), chap. 4.

30 See chapter 6.

31 Budgett Meakin, *Model Factories and Villages: Ideal Conditions of Labor and Housing* (London: Fisher and Unwin, 1905), p. 25.

32 Jonathan Baxter Harrison, "A View of the Working Class: Study of a New England Factory Town," in *Democratic Vistas, 1860–1880*, ed. Alan Trachtenberg (New York: George Braziller, 1970), pp. 161, 182.

33 Richard T. Ely, "Pullman: A Social Study," *Harper's Magazine* 70 (1885): 452–66. Also see T. C. Crawford, "The Pullman Company and Its Striking Workmen," *Harper's Weekly* 38 (1894): 686–87.

34 Going, "Village Communities," pp. 70–71.

35 Leifur Magnusson, "Housing by Employers in the United States," *Bulletin of the Bureau of Labor Statistics*, no. 263 (1920), pp. 273–83.

36 Henry-Russell Hitchcock, *The Architecture of H. H. Richardson and His Times* (Cambridge: MIT Press, 1966), chap. 11.

37 In ancient Egypt the pharaohs had built temporary housing for workers' settlements near their pyramids in the second millennium B.C., e.g., Kahun for Hotep Sesostris II. See Paul Lampl, *Cities and Planning in the Ancient Near East* (New York: George Braziller, 1968), p. 26.

38 Article IV of the Constitution proclaims "The right of the people to be secure in their persons, houses, . . ." but does not guarantee fee-simple home ownership. Henry Steele Commager, ed., *Documents of American History* (New York: Appleton-Century-Crofts, 1968), p. 146.

39 Bernard J. Frieden, "Housing and National Goals: Old Policies and New Realities," in *The Metropolitan Enigma*, ed. James Q. Wilson (Garden City, N.Y.: Doubleday, 1970), pp. 170–225.

40 See chapter 4.

41 This study was published posthumously and had been written and left in manuscript since 1876. It did not treat the post-1856 period or the Drapers' contribution to Hopedale. Adin Ballou, *History of the Hopedale Community* (Lowell, Mass.: Thompson and Hill, 1897), p. 1.

42 Ibid., pp. 362–63.

2 Morphology

1 Correspondence between G. W. W. Hanger and Company Agents, Louisiana Purchase Exposition, Department of Labor Letter Press Book, no. 2 (1902), National Archives, Washington, D.C. Hanger, an investigator for the Department of Labor, initiated correspondence with the agents of Hopedale, Peace Dale, Ludlow, and South Manchester to obtain plans and photographs of their towns as well as to verify site conditions, the number of units or dwellings and employees of these exemplary places for the department's display at the Louisiana Purchase Exposition of 1904 in Saint Louis. Eventually, these towns were cited and received medals for their dwellings.

2 John P. Bigelow, *Branches of Industry in Massachusetts, for the Year Ending April 1, 1837* (Boston: Dutton and Wentworth, 1838).

3 Edward Everett, *Address Delivered before the American Institute of the City of New York, October 14, 1831* (New York: Van Norden and Mason, 1831), p. 10.

4 U.S. Bureau of the Census, *Ninth Census, 1870: Report on the Manufacturers of the United States* (Washington, D.C.: Government Printing Office, 1872). For the decade 1860–70, the total profits from cotton goods produced in the six New England states nearly equaled the total value of all manufacturers from Alabama, Mississippi, Louisiana, Texas, Kentucky, Tennessee, and Arkansas (p. 896).

5 *The American System; or, The Effects of High Duties on Imports* (Boston: Nathan Hale's Press, 1828), p. 24.

6 See W. W. Rostow, *The Stages of Economic Growth: A Non-Communist Mani-*

festo (Cambridge: Cambridge University Press, 1967), chaps. 3, 4.

7 Bigelow, *Branches of Industry*, p. 56.

8 J. Leander Bishop, *A History of American Manufactures* (Philadelphia: Edward Young, 1868), 1:415.

9 Allan Pred, "Manufacturing in the American Mercantile City, 1800–1840," in *Cities in American History*, ed. Kenneth T. Jackson and Stanley K. Schultz (New York: Alfred A. Knopf, 1972), p. 117.

10 W. Cooke Taylor, *Factories and the Factory System* (London: Jeremiah How, 1844).

11 John Winter, *Industrial Architecture: A Survey of Factory Building* (London: Studio Vista, 1970), pp. 25–44.

12 Stanley D. Chapman, *The History of Working-Class Housing: A Symposium* (Newton Abbott [England]: David and Charles, 1971), p. 272.

13 Bishop, *History of American Manufactures*, 2:196.

14 Coxe, *Address to Friends of American Manufacturers*, p. 9.

15 Douglass C. North, *Growth and Welfare in the American Past* (Englewood Cliffs, N.J.: Prentice-Hall, 1966), p. 83.

16 William B. Weeden, *Economic and Social History of New England* (New York: Hillary House, 1963), 2:849.

17 U.S. Bureau of the Census, *Tenth Census, 1880: Report on the Manufacturers of the United States* (Washington, D.C.: Government Printing Office, 1883), pp. 542–43.

18 Edward P. Hamilton, "The New England Village Mill," *Old-Time New England* 62 (Fall 1951): 35–36.

19 U.S. Bureau of the Census, *Tenth Census, 1880: Report on Manufacturers*, p. 542.

20 U.S. Bureau of the Census, *Tenth Census of the United States* (Washington, D.C.: Government Printing Office, 1883), 1:209–513, passim.

21 Robert G. Le Blanc, *Location of Manufacturing in the Nineteenth Century*, Geography Publications at Dartmouth, no. 7 (Hanover, N.H., 1969), p. 98.

22 Pred, "Manufacturing in the Mercantile City," p. 123.

23 W. P. Trowbridge, *Reports on the Water-Power of the United States* (Washington, D.C.: Government Printing Office, 1885), pt. 1, p. xi.

24 Ibid., p. xii.

25 Connecting in Boston in 1835 were three railroads, one north to Lowell, one west to Worcester, and one south to Providence; for a sketch of these, see W. M. Whitehill, *Boston: A Topographical History* (Cambridge, Mass., 1967).

26 "Hopedale," *Milford Journal*, June 16, 1880.

27 *Report of the Railroad Commissioner of Rhode Island, 1900* (Providence: E. I. Freeman and Sons, 1901).

28 See chapter 5.

29 *Annual R.R. Report of the State of Connecticut*, no. 41 (Hartford: Case, Lockwood, and Brainerd, 1893).

30 Henry Roland, "Six Examples of Successful Shop Management," *Engineering Magazine* 12 (1896): 271; "Industrial Villages in America," *Garden City* 1 (July 1906): 142.

31 See Carroll D. Wright, in Massachusetts Bureau of Labor Statistics, *Sixteenth Annual Report, 1885, Report on Manufacturers*; Meakin, *Model Factories and Villages*; Roland, "Six Examples."

32 "An Industrial Experiment at South Manchester," *Harper's New Monthly Magazine* 45 (1872): 838.

33 William C. Wyckoff, *Report on the Silk Manufacturing Industry of the United States* (Washington, D.C.: Government Printing Office, 1883), pp. 14, 18.

34 H. H. Manchester, *The Story of Silk and Cheney Silks* (South Manchester, Conn.: Cheney Brothers, 1916), p. 38.

35 L. P. Brockett, *The Silk Industry in America* (New York: George F. Nesbitt, 1876), pp. 35–53.

36 Meakin, *Model Factories and Villages*, p. 24.

37 Ibid., p. 397. Meakin uses the term "parkway" in his description of South Manchester. Like the tidewater towns of colonial America, a broad and lengthy green formed an avenue leading into the town.

38 "Industrial Experiment at South Manchester," p. 843.

39 H. L. Nelson, "The Cheneys' Village at South Manchester, Connecticut," *Harper's Weekly* 34 (1890): 88.

40 Testimony of Frank W. Cheney, in Albert Clarke, ed., *Report of the Industrial Commission* (Washington, D.C.: Government Printing Office, 1901), 14:728–29.

41 *The National Cyclopedia of American Biography* 9 (New York: James T. White, 1907), s.v. "Hazard, Rowland Gibson."

42 *Dictionary of American Biography* (New York: Charles Scribner's Sons, 1932), s.v. "Hazard, Rowland Gibson."

43 Massachusetts, Bureau of Labor Statistics, *Seventeenth Annual Report*, "The Peace Dale Manufacturing Company" (Boston: Wright and Potter, 1886), p. 177.

44 William H. Tolman, "Workmen's Cities in the United States," In *Internationalen Wohnungskongress* (Vienna: Verlag der Zentralstelle für Wohnungsreform in Osterreich, 1911) 9:1075.

45 *The National Cyclopedia of American Biography* 43, s.v. "Hazard, Rowland Gibson."

46 Massachusetts, Bureau of Labor Statistics, *Seventeenth Annual Report* (1886), p. 186.

47 Robert H. Morse, *St. Johnsbury, Vt., and Important Industrial Beginnings, 1830*, Newcomen Society of England, American Branch (Princeton: Princeton University Press, 1945), p. 9.

48 Arthur F. Stone, ed., *St. Johnsbury Illustrated: A Review of the Town's Business, Social, Literary, and Educational Facilities, with Glimpses of Picturesque Surroundings* (Saint Johnsbury, Vt.: Caledonian Press, 1891), p. 79.

49 Ibid., p. 81. "Fairbanks Scales won gold and silver medals: in London in 1851; N.Y. in 1853, Paris in 1867, Vienna in 1873, Santiago, Chile in 1875, Philadelphia in 1876, and Sydney, Australia in 1878. . . . Upon Thaddeus Fairbanks was conferred by Emperor of Austria the Cross of the Order of Francis Josef in 1873."

50 U.S. Bureau of the Census, *Tenth Census*, 1:354.

51 Stone, *St. Johnsbury Illustrated*, p. 70.

52 Edward T. Fairbanks, *The Town of St. Johnsbury, Vt.* (Saint Johnsbury, Vt.: Cowles Press, 1914), p. 417.

53 Massachusetts, Bureau of Labor Statistics, *Thirtieth Annual Report* (1900), p. 226.

54 Alfred A. Noon, ed., *The History of Ludlow, Mass.* (Springfield, Mass.: Springfield Printing and Binding, 1912), p. 226.

55 Massachusetts, Bureau of Labor Statistics, *Thirty-seventh Annual Report* (1906), p. 534.

56 Going, "Village Communities," pp. 70–71.

57 Ibid.

58 See "International Housing Congresses and Exhibits," chapter 4.

59 Warner, *Urban Wilderness*, pp. 104–5.

60 Creese, *Search for Environment*, chaps. 3, 4; Gerald Burke, *Towns in the Making* (New York: St. Martin's Press, 1971), chap. 7.

61 Those who planned these satellite towns include Warren Henry Manning, Arthur A. Shurcliff, Frederick Law Olmsted, Jr., John Nolen, George Miller, Grosvenor Atterbury, Earle Draper, and Arthur Comey.

62 See "Future of Garden Cities in America," *Craftsman* 22 (May 1912): 117–22; D. W. Bartlett, "Industrial Garden City: Torrance, California," *American City* 9 (October 1913): 310–14.

63 Georges Benoît-Lévy, *La Cité-jardin* (Paris: Henri Jouve, 1904), pp. 217–19; see also idem, *Cités jardins d'Amérique* (Paris: Henri Jouve, 1905).

64 Warren H. Manning, "A Step Towards Solving the Industrial Housing Problem,"
    American City, Town and Country ed. 12 (April 1915): 321–25.

65 Arthur C. Comey and Max S. Wehrly, "Planned Communities," in *Supplementary Report of the Urbanism Committee* (Washington, D.C.: Government Printing Office, 1939), pt. 1, p. 110.

66 Warner, *Urban Wilderness*, chap. 4.

67 Mel Scott, *American City Planning since 1890* (Berkeley: University of California Press, 1969), p. 172.

68 Comey and Wehrly, "Planned Communities," p. 165.

69 See Joseph L. Arnold, *The New Deal in the Suburbs: A History of the Greenbelt Town Program, 1935–1954* (Columbus: Ohio State University Press, 1971), chap. 5.

70 Ibid., pp. 92–99. See also Albert Mayer's *Greenbelt Towns Revisited* (Washington, D.C.: National Association of Housing and Development Officials, 1968).

71 Judson King, *The Conversation Fight: From Theodore Roosevelt to the Tennessee Valley Authority* (Washington, D.C.: Public Affairs Press, 1959), pp. 98–114.

72 Ibid.

73 Comey and Wehrly, "Planned Communities," p. 70.

74 See Edward Bellamy, *Looking Backward, 2000–1887* (New York: Random House, 1951).

75 Robert E. Barde, "Arthur E. Morgan, First Chairman of TVA," *Tennessee Historical Quarterly* 30 (Fall 1971): 312.

76 *Chicopee, Georgia, Where Cleanliness Is Next to Godliness* (New York: Doyle, Kitchen, and McCormick, 1930).

77 Earle S. Draper, "Southern Textile Village Planning," *Landscape Architecture* 18 (October 1927): 1–28.

78 Augur's interest in the design of model industrial cities dates to his graduate study at Harvard. See Tracy B. Augur, "Industrial Growth in America and the Garden City" (M.L.A. thesis, Harvard University, 1921).

79 Nolen discusses the planning of industrial towns he designed, including Walpole, Mass.; Kingsport, Tenn.; Kistler, Penn.; and Marimont, Ohio. See John Nolen, *New Towns for Old* (Boston: Marshall Jones, 1927).

80 Founders of the RPAA include Henry Wright, Clarence Stein, Benton MacKaye, Catherine Bauer, Lewis Mumford, et al.; Scott, *American City Planning*, p. 191.

81 Lloyd Rodwin, *The British New Towns Policy* (Cambridge: Harvard University Press, 1956), chap. 4.

82 See Lloyd Rodwin and Lawrence Susskind, "The Next Generation of New

Towns," in James Bailey, ed., *New Towns in America* (New York: Wiley and Sons, 1973), pp. 126–31.

83   J. R. Atkinson, "USA: Private Enterprise Town Building," *Town and Country Planning* 29 (August 1961): 323.

84   Walter F. Wagner, Jr., "A Plea for Planned Communities," *Architectural Record* 154 (December 1973): 85–144.

3   Paternalism

1   Wallace, *Rockdale*, chap. 8.

2   One of the more notorious examples of protectionary management practices involved the issuance of company scrip in place of money. See George Creel, "The Feudal Towns of Texas," *Harper's Weekly* 60 (1915): 77. See also Ole S. Johnson, *The Industrial Store: Its History, Operations, and Economic Significance* (Atlanta: Foote and Davies, 1952), pp. 22–23, 26, 62.

3   In the aftermath of the Pullman strike, social and political analysts soundly condemned paternalism in management practices. The company town received most of the blame and largely deserved the condemnation. The more outspoken critics were Richard T. Ely, *Property and Contract in Their Relation to the Distribution of Wealth* (New York: Macmillan, 1914), vol. 2; Taylor, *Satellite Cities*; Ida M. Tarbell, *New Ideals in Business* (New York: Macmillan, 1916); and Edith Elmer Wood, *The Housing of the Unskilled Wage Earner* (New York: Macmillan, 1919).

4   William Scoresby, *American Factories and Their Female Operatives* (London: Longman, Browne, Gray, Longmans, 1845), pp. 25–27. An excellent social history of Lowell, which discusses the issue of corporate paternalism, may be found in Thomas Dublin, *Women at Work: The Transformation of Work and Community in Lowell, Massachusetts, 1826–1860* (New York: Columbia University Press, 1979).

5   M. C. Birchenough, "Some Diversions of an Industrial Town," *Littell's Living Age* 247 (1905): 603–4.

6   Etienne Clavière and J. P. Brissot, *The Commerce of America with Europe* (New York: T. and J. Swords, 1795), pp. 80–81.

7   By a Merchant [Thomas Tod], *Consolatory Thoughts on American Independence* (Edinburgh: James Donaldson, 1782), p. 19.

8   Ibid., p. 20.

9   U.S. Bureau of the Census, *Tenth Census, 1880: Report on Manufacturers*, p. 576.

See also M. T. Parker, *Lowell: A Study of Industrial Development* (New York: Macmillan, 1940).

10 *Industrial Relations Activities at Cheney Brothers, South Manchester, Connecticut* (New York: National Industrial Conference Board, 1929), chap. 2, "Industrial Relations Division," p. 14.

11 Edward Atkinson, *Cotton Manufactures of the United States* (Washington, D.C.: Government Printing Office, 1883), pp. 8–14; Nelson, "The Cheneys' Village," p. 88.

12 Thernstrom, *Poverty and Progress*, chap. 4, "The Dimensions of Occupational Mobility."

13 Thomas H. West, *The Loom Builders: The Drapers as Pioneer Contributors to the American Way of Life*, The Newcomen Society of England in North America, no. 14 (1952), pp. 31–32.

14 Rowland T. Berthoff, *British Immigrants in Industrial America, 1790–1950* (New York: Russell and Russell, 1953), p. 32.

15 Massachusetts, *Report of the Special Commission on the Hours of Labor, and the Condition and Prospects of the Industrial Classes* (Boston: Wright and Potter, 1866), pp. 43–60, passim.

16 Neither in the *Report of the Special Commission on the Hours of Labor* nor in any statements on employment by the Hazards, Cheneys, Drapers, Hubbards, and Fairbankses was there mention of child employment. By 1880 every New England state prohibited child labor under age ten, and children under fourteen who worked were required to attend school. See Massachusetts, Rhode Island, Connecticut, Maine, New Hampshire, and Vermont Public and General Statutes, 1870–80.

17 Massachusetts, Bureau of Labor Statistics, *Second, Eleventh,* and *Thirteenth Annual Reports* (1871, 1880, 1882); quote from *Eleventh Annual Report* (1880), pp. 65–67.

18 G. W. W. Hanger, "Housing of the Working People in the United States by Employers," *Bulletin of the Bureau of Labor Statistics* 21 (1904): 1103.

19 R. A. Woods, "The Human Touch in Industry," *Munsey's Magazine* 29 (1903): 323.

20 Carroll D. Wright, *The Relation of Political Economy to the Labor Question* (Boston: A. Williams, 1882), p. 30.

21 Ibid., p. 52. For additional information concerning Wright's views on labor and labor statistics, see James Leiby's *Carroll Wright and Labor Reform: The Origin of Labor Statistics* (Cambridge: Harvard University Press, 1960).

22 In promoting schemes to ease management relations with labor, analysts published methods of profit sharing and cooperative ownership. See Nicholas Paine Gilman, "Profit Sharing in the United States," *New England Magazine*, September 1892, pp. 120–28; Frank W. Blackmar, "Two Examples of Successful Profit-Sharing," *The Forum*, March 1895, pp. 57–67; and Ida M. Tarbell, "The Golden Rule in Business," *American Magazine*, March 1915, pp. 37–41. Although Frederick W. Taylor's *Principles of Scientific Management* (1911) enjoyed the widest circulation of this type of book, it followed earlier studies by Gilman, Gibbons, and Shuey on production analysis and employee evaluation.

23 John Gibbons, *Tenure and Toil; or, Rights and Wrongs of Property and Labor* (Philadelphia: J. B. Lippincott, 1888), p. 186.

24 John W. Reps, *The Making of Urban America* (Princeton: Princeton University Press, 1965), pp. 421–24. Further analysis of Pullman was given at the National Gallery Symposium on American Art in 1981. John S. Garner, "Pullman and the Idea of the Model Company Town: Paternalism in Architecture and Urban Design" (University of Delaware, 1981).

25 See J. M. McClelland, Jr., *Longview: The Remarkable Beginnings of a Modern Western City* (Portland, Ore.: Binfords and Mort, 1949). S. Herbert Hare, "The Planning of a New Industrial City," *American City* 29 (November 1923): 501–3.

26 Massachusetts, Bureau of Labor Statistics, *Sixteenth Annual Report* (1885), pp. 10–11.

27 Ibid., p. 4.

28 Buder, *Pullman*, chap. 4.

29 Robert Blauner, *Alienation and Freedom: The Factory Worker and His Industry* (Chicago: University of Chicago Press, 1964). Blauner encountered an unusual degree of complacency when investigating the textile workers of mill towns in North Carolina. See also Hareven and Langenbach, *Amoskeag*.

30 Roland, "Six Examples," p. 285.

31 Ibid.

32 Michael Frisch, *From Town into City: Springfield, Massachusetts, 1840–1880* (Cambridge: Harvard University Press, 1973), p. 36.

33 See chapter 4, "International Housing Congresses and Exhibits."

34 Edwin L. Shuey, *Factory People and Their Employers: How Their Relations Are Made Pleasant and Profitable* (New York: Lentilhon, 1900), p. 194.

35 Ibid., p. 132.

36 Ibid., p. 211.

37 Roland, "Six Examples," p. 285.

38 Birdsley Grant Northrop, "How to Beautify and Build up Our Country Towns" [1869], Frances Loeb Library, Harvard University, Cambridge, Mass.

39 Birdsley Grant Northrop, *Rural Improvement* (New Haven: Tuttle, Morehouse, and Taylor, 1880), p. 45.

40 Ibid., p. 46.

41 Warren Henry Manning, *The History of Village Improvement in the United States* (reprint from *The Craftsman*, February 1904), p. 7.

42 *Caledonian*, May 4, 1841, p. 1.

43 Northrop, *Rural Improvement*, p. 46.

44 Birdsley Grant Northrop, "The Work of Village Improvement Societies," *The Forum* 19 (March 1895): 104.

45 Books written by Hazard include *Essay on Language and Other Papers*, ed. E. P. Peabody (Boston: Phillips, Sampson, 1857); *Our Resources* (New York: Charles Scribner, 1868); *Finance and Hours of Labor* (New York: Charles Scribner, 1868); *Freedom of the Mind in Willing* (New York: D. Appleton, 1864); and *Two Letters, on Causation, and Freedom in Willing, Addressed to John Stuart Mill* (Boston: Lee and Shepard, 1869).

46 "A Model American," *The Critic* 33 (October 1898): 274.

47 Ibid., p. 275.

48 Fairbanks, *Town of St. Johnsbury*, p. 509.

49 "St. Johnsbury, Vt.: A Model New England Town," *Boston Globe*, Sept. 25, 1875, p. 11.

50 Ibid., p. 13.

51 Northrop, *Rural Improvement*, p. 48.

52 "St. Johnsbury, Vt.," *Boston Globe*, p. 11.

53 Massachusetts, Bureau of Labor Statistics, *Fifth Annual Report* (1876), p. 143.

54 "St. Johnsbury, Vt.," *Boston Globe*, p. 11.

55 Northrop, *Rural Improvement*, p. 48.

56 "St. Johnsbury, Vt.," *Boston Globe*, p. 10.

57 Parris Thaxter Farwell, *Village Improvement* (New York: Sturgis and Walton, 1913), p. 6.

58 George B. Tobey, Jr., *A History of Landscape Architecture: The Relationship of People to Environment* (New York: American Elsevier, 1973), chap. 16.

59 Mary Caroline Robbins, "Village Improvement Societies," *Atlantic Monthly* 79 (February 1897): 212.

60 See Marvin Fisher, *Workshops in the Wilderness: The European Response to*

American Industrialization, 1830–1860 (New York: Oxford University Press, 1967).

61 Tarbell, *New Ideals in Business*, p. 146.

62 A. G. Sedgwick, "Village Improvement," *The Nation* 19 (September 1874): 149–50.

63 Andrew Nuquist, Introductory Comments, made at Town Officers' Educational Conference, Local Government series no. 1, Winter 1962.

64 Arthur M. Schlesinger, *The Rise of the City, 1878–1898* (New York: Macmillan, 1933), chap. 3.

65 Henry J. Fletcher, "The Doom of the Small Town," *The Forum* 19 (April 1895): 214.

66 Ibid., p. 218.

67 Ibid., p. 215.

68 See Sherwood Anderson, *Winesburg, Ohio* (New York: Viking Press, 1969).

69 Lewis Mumford, *Sticks and Stones: A Study of American Architecture and Civilization* (New York: Boni and Liveright, 1924), chap. 4.

70 H. W. S. Cleveland, *Landscape Architecture, as Applied to the Wants of the West; . . .* (Chicago: Jansen, McClurg, 1873), p. 17.

71 "It would be well for those having the interest of the village in charge, to adopt an early resolution to accept no gifts, and to allow no work of construction or embellishment, which is not, first of all, appropriate to the modest character of a well-regulated country village," George E. Waring, Jr., *Village Improvement and Farm Villages* (Boston: James R. Osgood, 1877), p. 18.

72 Nathaniel Hillyer Egleston, *Villages and Village Life, with Hints for Their Improvement* (New York: Harper and Brothers, 1878), p. 52.

73 Andrew Jackson Downing, *Landscape Gardening, Adapted to North America* (New York: Wiley and Putnam, 1844), pp. 340–41.

74 Andrew Jackson Downing, "Our Country Villages," in Weimer, *City and Country in America*, p. 165.

75 "St. Johnsbury, Vt.," *Boston Globe*, p. 11.

76 Charles Mulford Robinson, *Modern Civic Art; or, The City Made Beautiful* (New York: G. P. Putnam's Sons, 1903), p. 19.

77 Charles Eliot, *Landscape Architect* (1902; rpt. Freeport, N.Y.: Books for Libraries Press, 1971), "Beautiful Villages" (from the *Youth's Companion*, June 2, 1892), p. 377.

78 No matter how small a company town, it usually contained at least two denomi-

nations, if sometimes only one structure. Evangelical faiths figured more prominently in the South, where management and labor were occasionally brought together. See Liston Pope, *Millhands and Preachers* (New Haven: Yale University Press, 1942).

79 Shuey, *Factory People and Their Employers*, p. 169.

80 See Michael Katz, *The Irony of Early School Reform* (Cambridge: Harvard University Press, 1959).

81 U.S. Bureau of the Census, *Tenth Census, 1880: Report on Manufacturers*, pp. 66–67.

82 *Reports of the Selectmen, Treasurer, and Assessors, of the Town of Easton, Mass.* (Taunton, Mass.: C. A. Hack and Son, 1878). Other philanthropic endeavors carried out by the Ames family are listed in Leverett Saltonstall, "Memoir of the Hon. Frederick Lothrop Ames, A.B.," *The Colonial Society of Massachusetts, Transactions* (Boston: Published by the Society, 1895), p. 261.

83 Hanger, "Housing of the Working People," p. 1268.

84 Massachusetts, Bureau of Labor Statistics, *Seventeenth Annual Report* (1886), p. 186.

85 Hanger, "Housing of the Working People, p. 1268.

86 Massachusetts, Bureau of Labor Statistics, *Seventeenth Annual Report* (1886), p. 178.

87 The Chautauqua movement began in the 1890s as summer educational festivals in Chautauqua, N.Y., and spread throughout the country. Perusing summer and fall issues of the *Chautauqua Magazine*, *The Arena*, the *New England Magazine*, *Atlantic Monthly*, *The Critic*, the *Saturday Review*, the *Overland Monthly*, *The Nation*, *Scribner's Magazine*, *The Forum*, *Munsey's Magazine*, and the *Independent* brings to light the small-town enthusiasm engendered by these turn-of-the-century gatherings.

88 Going, "Village Communities," p. 66.

4 Housing

1 Lawrence Veiller, "Industrial Housing Developments in America," *Architectural Record* 43 (March 1918): 231.

2 Lowell, Lawrence, and Holyoke, to cite three corporation towns, each contained notorious "patches" or shanty districts; see Donald Cole, *Immigrant City: Lawrence, 1845–1921* (Cambridge: Harvard University Press, 1963), chap. 3.

3 Comparative rents between industrial cities and company towns are cited in

Massachusetts, Bureau of Labor Statistics, *Sixteenth Annual Report* (1885), pp. 1–28; and E. R. L. Gould, "The Housing of the Working People," in U.S. Bureau of Labor Statistics, *Eighth Special Report* (1895), pp. 419–36.

4   Tabulated figures exist for working-class family expenditures from U.S. and Massachusetts labor statistics in the period 1885 to 1890. The average rent paid by workers was 18.58 percent of their total income. This was 6 percent higher than was proportionally paid in the company towns studied. Marcus T. Reynolds, *The Housing of the Poor in American Cities* (Baltimore: Guggenheimer, Weil, 1893), pp. 24–25.

5   M. Jules Challamel, ed., *Compte rendu et documents du Congrès international des habitations à bon marché* (Paris: La Société française des habitations à bon marché, 1900), pp. 310–45; see also Hanger, "Housing of the Working People."

6   See sketches of life among the poor in London as illustrated by Gustave Doré, *Les Miserables des pauvres*; a comparison was provided in Lawrence with the photography of Richard A. Hale, an employee of the Essex Company, whose archive is in the collection of the Merrimack Valley Textile Museum, Andover, Mass.

7   Least-known sources on nineteenth-century workers' housing are those written by architects. Though they often sidestep reform issues, they furnish lessons in practical design and construction. See Bruce Allen, *Rudimentary Treatise on Cottage Building; or, Hints for Improving the Dwellings of the Labouring Classes* (London: John Weale, 1854); Bannister Fletcher, *Model Houses for the Industrial Classes* (London: Longmans, Green, 1871); and John Birch, *Examples of Labourers' Cottages, with Plans for Improving the Dwellings of the Poor in Large Towns* (London: Edward Stanford, 1871).

8   Octavia Hill, *Homes of the London Poor* (New York: New York State Charities Aid Association, 1875), p. 8.

9   Robert Owen, *A New View of Society* (London: Caddell and Davies, 1813), p. 7.

10   Leonardo Benevolo, *The Origins of Modern Town Planning* (Cambridge: MIT Press, 1967), p. 119.

11   Allen, *Rudimentary Treatise on Cottage Building*, p. 9.

12   Fletcher, *Model Houses for the Industrial Classes*, chap. 10.

13   Between 1862 and 1865 the Improved Industrial Dwellings Company (Ltd.) began construction on ten blocks of apartment buildings at Finsbury, London. The project was initiated by Alderman Sidney H. Waterlow and later carried his name. Though these model tenements were an improvement over existing types, Fletcher rightly objected to their plans, with their "mute attempts to bring in light through back ells"; ibid., p. 2. In 1862 the Peabody Donation Fund, subscribed by

the American businessman George Peabody, received a sum of £150,000 to begin construction of model tenements. To this amount were added four other bequests after 1866. "The Peabody Trustee's buildings, at Islington, Shadwell, and Spitalfields [London] provide about 404 dwellings, comprising one, two, and three rooms respectively, containing in all 891 rooms, at an average total cost amounting to £97,994 for buildings. The average rent of each dwelling is 3s.11d., and of each room 1s.10d. per week"; Birch, *Examples of Labourers' Cottages*, p. 39. A more recent description of these buildings can be found in John Nelson Tarn, *Working-Class Housing in Nineteenth-Century Britain* (London: Architectural Association, 1971).

14 Providing testimony on the condition of rear courts in Liverpool tenements, a medical officer reported: "Nothing short of a tornado can effectually ventilate these courts; in still weather the atmosphere in them is unchanged and unchangeable"; Seventh Report of the Medical Officer of the Privy Council (1864), cited in James Hole, *The Homes of the Working Classes* (London: Longmans, Green, 1866), p. 13.

15 See Creese, *Search for Environment*, p. 204.

16 Hole, *Homes of the Working Classes*, pp. 63–64.

17 Hole writes: "It is inconceivable how so many men in this country, while accumulating enormous fortunes, can reconcile it to their consciences so utterly to disregard the condition of those who contribute so much to its acquisition"; ibid., p. 69.

18 Massachusetts, Bureau of Labor Statistics, *First Annual Report* (1870), p. 170.

19 John H. Griscom, *The Sanitary Condition of the Laboring Population of New York, with Suggestions for Its Improvement* (New York: Arno Press, 1970).

20 T. Thomas, *The Working-Man's Cottage Architecture, Containing Plans, Elevations, and Details, for the Erection of Cheap, Comfortable, and Neat Cottages* (New York: R. Martin, 1848), p. 4.

21 Ibid.

22 John Nolen, "Organization of Credit for Housing Purposes," in *Internationalen Wohnungskongress* (Vienna: Verlag der Zentralstelle für Wohnungsreform in Osterreich, 1911), 9:464.

23 Edward Everett Hale, *Workingmen's Homes: Essays and Stories* (Boston: James R. Osgood, 1874), pp. 22–23. Also see Cynthia Zaitzevsky, "Housing Boston's Poor: The First Philanthropic Experiments," *Journal of the Society of Architectural Historians* 42 (May 1983): 157–67.

24 Hale, *Workingmen's Homes*, p. 29.

25 Ibid., p. 4.

26 Sam Bass Warner, Jr., *Streetcar Suburbs: The Process of Growth in Boston, 1870–1900* (Cambridge: Harvard and MIT Press, 1962), chaps. 4–5.

27 The *Boston Commercial Bulletin* in the 1880s provides excellent insight into Boston's suburban speculation. Ads for workers' housing in Arlington in 1887 indicate keen competition among developments.

28 Warner, *Streetcar Suburbs*, chap. 2.

29 Gould, "Housing of the Working People," p. 336.

30 Ibid.

31 Cole, *Immigrant City*, chap. 2.

32 Dublin, *Women at Work*, pp. 20, 134–35.

33 Massachusetts, Bureau of Labor Statistics, *Fifth Annual Report* (1874), p. 31.

34 Cole, *Immigrant City*, pp. 70–71.

35 Cochran and Miller, *Age of Enterprise*, p. 264.

36 James Ford et al., *Slums and Housing* (Cambridge: Harvard University Press, 1936), 1:187.

37 Green, *Holyoke, Massachusetts*, chap. 9.

38 Taylor, *Satellite Cities*, p. 197.

39 See Gould, "Housing of the Working People," pp. 98–104, 128–30, 231–38. See also Wright, *Relation of Economy to Labor*, and Meakin, *Model Factories and Villages*.

40 The Interlaken Mills cottages at Fiskville, R.I., merit special attention. See A. N. Fowler, "Rhode Island Mill Towns," *Pencil Points* 17 (May 1936), 271–86. It should also be noted that in England a half-dozen booklets were published carrying designs of laborers' cottages, some strikingly modern. Cf. John Wood, *A Series of Plans for Cottages or Habitations of the Labourer, Either in Husbandry, or the Mechanic Arts* (London: J. Taylor, 1806); and Joseph Gandy, *The Rural Architect; Consisting of Various Designs for Country Buildings* (London: John Harding, 1805), plates 2, 4.

41 Richard P. Horwitz, "Architecture and Culture: The Meaning of the Lowell Boardinghouse," *American Quarterly* 25 (March 1973): 64–82; Dublin, *Women at Work*, chap. 5.

42 Coolidge, *Mill and Mansion*, p. 115.

43 Going, "Village Communities," pp. 70–71.

44 "Industrial Experiment at South Manchester," p. 840.

45 Ibid.

46 Gould, "Housing of the Working People," p. 328.

47 Carroll D. Wright, *Report on the Factory System of the United States* (Washington, D.C.: Government Printing Office, 1883), p. 72.

48 Meakin, *Model Factories and Villages*, pp. 401–2.

49 In 1911 the Ludlow house types, "Weston," "Plymouth," and "Longmeadow," were still being used as models for low-cost housing; "Moderate Cost House," *American City* 4 (April 1911): 156–60. For other technical advancements in nineteenth-century American housing, see Reyner Banham, *The Architecture of the Well-Tempered Environment* (Chicago: University of Chicago Press, 1969), pp. 98–99.

50 Wright, *Report on the Factory System*, pp. 68–69.

51 Creese, *Search for Environment*, chap. 4.

52 Gould, "Housing of the Working People," pp. 351–53.

53 Ibid., p. 385. A thorough account of the Krupp villages can be found in W. F. Willoughby, "Industrial Communities," U.S. Bureau of Labor Statistics Bulletin no. 5 (July 1896).

54 Only in detached and semidetached dwellings is cross-room ventilation obtainable. The interior walls of row houses and quadriplexes interrupt the flow of air.

55 M. Antony Roulliet, ed., *Congrès international des habitations à bon marché* (Paris: G. Rongier, 1889), p. 17.

56 U.S., Congress, House, *Reports of the United States Commissioners to the Universal Exposition of 1889 at Paris*, Ex. Doc. 410, 51st Cong., 1st sess., 1889–90, p. 435. Information about the N. O. Nelson Co. can be found in John S. Garner, "Leclaire, Illinois: A Model Company Town, 1890–1934," *Journal of the Society of Architectural Historians* 30 (October 1971): 219–27.

57 House, *Reports of the Commissioners to the Universal Exposition*, pp. 341, 436.

58 U.S., Congress, House, *Reports of the Committee on Awards of the World's Columbian Commission*, H. Doc. 510, 57th Cong., 1st sess., 1901–2, 2:926.

59 U.S., Congress, Senate, *Report of the Commissioner General for the United States to the International Universal Exposition, Paris, 1900*, S. Doc. 232, 56th Cong., 2d sess., 1900–1, p. 385.

60 Ibid., p. 474.

61 Tolman, "Workmen's Cities," pp. 1074–75.

62 Louis Wirth and Edward Shils, "Urban Living Conditions," *Supplementary Report of the Urbanism Committee*, pt. 2 (Washington, D.C.: Government Printing Office, 1939), p. 167.

63 Nolen, "Organization of Credit," p. 468.

5 The Morphology of Hopedale

1 Charles F. Merrill, "Hopedale as I Found It" (Paper presented to the Hopedale Community Historical Society, Bancroft Memorial Library, Hopedale, Mass., 1957), p. 2.

2 Ibid., p. 4.

3 Ballou, *Hopedale Community*, p. 307.

4 Interview with Mr. Mort Dennett, Town Clerk, Hopedale, Mass., August 1973.

5 Hinds, *American Communities and Co-operative Colonies*, p. 220.

6 A. H. Wilder, Plan of the Hopedale Village Site, recorded April 3, 1855, Worcester, Mass.

7 "The Hopedale Industrial Army: Record of Its By Law, Rules, Regulations, and Proceedings" (handwritten and recorded by A. G. Spalding, 1849), Bancroft Memorial Library, Hopedale, Mass.

8 "Hopedale," *Diamond*, Oct. 15, 1851. The following observations were also made: "There is a village, a chapel, used also for a schoolhouse, a printing office, several shops for mechanical purposes, some of which contain machinery carried by waterpower, besides a few barns and a few other usual out buildings. Connected with this village is a farm containing nearly 500 acres, proportionally divided into pasturage, meadow, and tillage. The soil is not usually below mediocrity, but is at present under a pretty good cultivation, and possesses capabilities as yet but partially drawn out and improved."

9 Ibid.

10 Francis De Witt, *Branches of Industry in Massachusetts* (Boston: William White, 1856), p. 510.

11 "Record Book of the Hopedale Community," no. 2, Bancroft Memorial Library, Hopedale, Mass. (arguments for dispossession written in longhand, January 1856).

12 *Hopedale Reminiscences* (Hopedale, Mass.: Hopedale School Press, 1910), p. 32.

13 Caroline F. Ware, *The Early New England Cotton Manufacture* (New York: Columbia University Press, 1931), chap. 1.

14 Robert Brooke Zevin, *The Growth of Manufacturing in Early Nineteenth-Century New England* (New York: Arno Press, 1975), pp. 10–47.

15 Thomas R. Navin, *The Whitin Machine Works since 1831: A Textile Machinery Company in an Industrial Village* (Cambridge: Harvard University Press, 1950), p. 64.

16 Catalog: *George Draper & Son, Manufacturers of Cotton Machinery and Selling Agents for the Hopedale Machine Co., Dutcher Temple Co., and Sawyer Spindle Co.* (Hopedale, Mass., 1887), p. ix.

17 "Statistics of Cotton Manufacturers in New England, 1866," *New England Cotton Manufacturers' Association*, no. 1, Constitution (Boston: Wright and Potter, 1872), pp. 10–11.

18 George Draper, "Let-off Motions for Looms," *New England Cotton Manufacturers' Association*, no. 8 (Boston: T. W. Ripley, 1870). Draper describes research and testing as a special department of the company's operation.

19 "Draper Company Patents," *Cotton Chats*, February 1905.

20 Oliver Warner, *Branches of Industry in Massachusetts, for the Year Ending May 1, 1865* (Boston: Wright and Potter, 1866), p. 590.

21 William F. Draper, *Recollections of a Varied Career* (Boston: Little, Brown, 1908), p. 218.

22 *Opening Argument of Nathan Sumner Myrick, Esq., Testimony, and Closing Argument of Hon. Selwyn Z. Bowman, before the Legislative Committee on Towns, 1886 . . .* (Boston: Rand, Avery, 1886), p. 36.

23 "E. D. Draper," *Cotton Chats*, September 1901. The older brother reportedly lost his fortune investing in safes, forcing him to accept gratuities from George Draper.

24 "There are, it is said, orders already received sufficient to require a full production for several months to come"; *Milford Journal*, Feb. 19, 1874.

25 Carroll D. Wright (Chief of the Bureau of Statistics of Labor), *The Census of Massachusetts, 1875*, vol. 2, *Manufacturers and Occupations* (Boston: Albert J. Wright, 1877), p. 160.

26 George Draper and Sons, *Improvements in Cotton Machinery* (Hopedale, 1881), p. viii.

27 Statistics for gross value of products made were reported on a ten-year interval in Wright, *Census of Massachusetts*, vol. 2, *Manufacturers*; from 1885, these figures are listed by town.

28 "Worthy Ware for the World's Weavers," *Skyline* 31, no. 2 (1973): 36.

29 *Cotton Chats*, February 1903, p. 104.

30 The Draper Company delighted in keeping statistics of this kind and, of course, in publishing them in *Cotton Chats* and *Textile Texts*: Their figures are taken from abstracts of the Department of Commerce and Labor, bulletin 63, passim.

31 *Cotton Chats*, October 1906, p. 2.

32 Ibid., September 1902, p. 2. The company published a record of all sales in total numbers, the name of the company sold to, and the location.

33 Clark, *History of Manufacturers*, pp. 540–58.

34 Ibid.

35 The Tupper Lake forest reserve contains seventy-five thousand acres; Draper Corporation, Hopedale, Mass., advertising booklet, 1954.

36 "Worthy Ware for the World's Weavers," p. 36.

37 Padraic King, "Hopedale Industrial Paradise of Bay State," *Boston Sunday Post*, June 1929, p. 20.

38 Charles F. Gettemy, *The Decennial Census, 1915: The Commonwealth of Massachusetts* (Boston: Wright and Potter, 1918), p. 110.

39 Interview with Mr. Edmund Deerborn, Draper Division, Hopedale, Mass., September 17, 1973.

40 Ballou, *Hopedale Community*, p. 107.

41 De Witt, *Branches of Industry*, p. 510.

42 Catalog: *George Draper & Son*, p. x.

43 Bancroft became vice-president after George Draper died in 1887 and, eventually, president in 1905. However, he was never a partner.

44 C. J. H. Woodbury, *The Testimonial to the Philadelphia Textile School* (Boston: New England Textile Manufacturers' Association, 1898), p. 11.

45 Waterwheels in Worcester County, Mass., outnumbered steam engines by 801 to 359 in 1875; and, of the 801, 618 were turbines rather than breast, float, flutter, tub, undershot, or overshot wheels. Wright, *Census of Massachusetts*, vol. 2, *Manufacturers*, p. 324.

46 *Milford Journal*, June 14, 1882.

47 Catalog: *George Draper & Son*, p. 191.

48 "Draper and Son's New Office," *Milford Journal*, Aug. 18, 1880.

49 Work on Adin Street commenced in 1868. F. W. Beers, *Map of Milford* (New York: F. W. Beers, 1870).

50 "Assessors' Report," *First Annual Report of the Town Offices of the Town of Hopedale, 1886* (Milford, Mass.: Journal Job Printing House, 1887), p. 33.

51 Draper, *Recollections*, p. 179.

52 "Hopedale," *Milford Journal*, July 26, 1882.

53 The classic work on American domestic architecture of the Victorian period, which discusses the shingle style, is Vincent J. Scully, Jr., *The Shingle Style and the Stick Style: Architectural Theory and Design from Richardson to the Origins of Wright* (New Haven: Yale University Press, 1971), chap. 5.

54 *Opening Argument in Favor of the Incorporation of Hopedale*, p. 187.

55 D. A. Sanborn, *Re-Survey, Milford, Mass.* (New York: D. A. Sanborn's National Insurance Diagram Bureau, April 1874).

56 *State Atlas of Massachusetts* (1898), s.v. "Hopedale, Worcester County."

57 Ibid.

58 *Cotton Chats*, November 1904, p. 3.

59 Merrill, "Hopedale as I Found It," p. 3.

60 W. C. Wheelock, Plan of the Sewers for the Hopedale Machine Company, Hopedale, Mass., April 1892.

61 Ibid.

62 Frank W. Hammett, Plan of Sewers for the Draper Company, Hopedale, Mass., 1897.

63 "Hopedale," *Milford Journal*, Oct. 22, 1874.

64 Even during the post–World War I years, many small industrial towns were fortunate to have a good dry-vault system with removable ash cans. See *American City*, Town and Country ed. 9–14 (1911–16).

65 *The National Cyclopedia of American Biography* (New York: James T. White, 1947), s.v. "Manning, Warren Henry."

66 *Fourth Annual Report of the Town of Hopedale, 1889* (Milford, Mass.: Daily Journal Printing House, 1890), Report of the School Committee, p. 5.

67 "Hopedale," *Milford Journal*, Apr. 30, 1890.

68 A valuable record of Hopedale's physical planning may be found in the Office of Plant Engineering, Draper Division, Rockwell International.

69 "Hopedale," *Milford Journal*, May 25, 1896. The company disclosed that plans were underway for the construction of fourteen new double tenements on the "Union Street extension," as the Bancroft Park development had been originally labeled.

70 Ibid., May 5, 1897.

71 Warren H. Manning, "Villages for Workingmen and Workingmen's Homes," *Proceedings of the Second National Conference on City Planning and the Problems of Congestion*, Rochester, N.Y., May 2–4, 1910 (Cambridge: Cambridge University Press, 1910), p. 103.

72 Gordon M. Taylor, Topographical Plan, Hopedale, Mass., May 24, 1899.

73 Arthur A. Shurcliff, "Text to Accompany Illustrations of Article Describing the Arrangement of Houses on a Peninsula in the Mill-Pond above the Works of the Draper Co. at Hopedale, Massachusetts," Shurcliff Papers, Massachusetts Historical Society, Boston, Mass.

74 Paul R. Smith, "An Instance of Practical and Esthetic Industrial Housing," *American City*, Town and Country ed. 13 (December 1915): 476–77.

75 G. G. Eastman and A. A. Shurcliff (landscape consultant), Plan of Lake Street: West Pond Lot Groups, Hopedale, Mass., 1910.

76 "More Brick Tenements," *Milford Daily News*, July 5, 1913: "Another large building development is being planned for the Draper Co., on their land between Water, Prospect and Main streets, in Milford. The ground, which was partly laid out 12 years ago by Warren H. Manning, one of the leading landscape architects of Boston, is again being studied with a view of division into house lots. The tract includes about 50 acres of land. . . . plans and specifications for these are being prepared from the Office of Peabody & Stearns, State St. Boston. . . . Manning is planning the roads to be built through the tract."

77 *Cotton Chats*, December 1905.

78 *Boston Herald*, Oct. 25, 1887, p. 5.

79 King, "Hopedale Industrial Paradise," p. 20.

80 Ibid.

81 "Hopedale," *Milford Journal*, July 1, 1895.

82 Coach service existed between Hopedale and Milford from the 1860s by private carrier; however, with increased employment in the Draper shops during the 1890s, an electric trolley (one) operated to serve workers living in Milford. The track was laid in 1896, and in 1897 the *Milford Journal* (June 16) reported a collision between two automated vehicles, the trolley and the town steamroller, which caused the reporter to speculate on the dependability of the horse. The trolley went out of operation during the 1930s.

6 Paternalism in Hopedale

1 For the most part, social programs and genuine concern on the part of management for mining families were subliminal. See L. Lewis, "Uplifting 17,000 Employees," *World's Work Magazine* 9 (1905): 5939–50.

2 *Boston Herald*, Oct. 25, 1887, p. 5.

3 "Memorial to George Draper," Pennsylvania Museum and School of Industrial Art, Philadelphia, 1898.

4 "The Late George Draper," *Milford Journal*, June 15, 1887.

5 Lewis G. Wilson, "Hopedale and Its Founder," *New England Magazine* 4 (April 1891): 204.

6 William S. Heywood, a charter member of the Hopedale Community who remained after the dissolution along with Ballou, edited the minister's history of

Hopedale. Heywood may have added a few critical remarks in the closing chapter: "I did at the time greatly deplore the decisive step on their part [the Drapers] by which our associated endeavors were brought to an end. I longed to have them and all my associates prize the cause as I did, see the matter as I saw it, feel as I felt, and be willing and happy to do with their means as I should have done had I been favored as they were—use them for the good of our body and for the continuance and advancement of the work to which we were all sacredly pledged. And I then had, as I have now, no doubt, that if these two brothers had been so minded, the Community would have gone on prospering and to prosper for many years after its career was terminated." Ballou, *Hopedale Community*, p. 351.

7   Barbara Louise Faulkner, "Adin Ballou and the Hopedale Community" (Ph.D. dissertation, Boston University, 1965), p. 298.

8   *Boston Herald*, Oct. 25, 1887, p. 5.

9   Ballou, *Hopedale Community*, p. 253; Woodbury, *Testimonial to the Philadelphia Textile School*, p. 15.

10   Adin Ballou, "The Old House at Hopedale," *Milford Journal*, Dec. 4, 1874.

11   Ibid.; the guest orator was the Honorable John D. Long, former governor of Massachusetts.

12   In addition to writing several letters voicing his opinion in favor of high tariffs, available both at the State House Library, Massachusetts State Capitol, and the Boston Public Library, Draper made a habit during the 1870s and 1880s of passing along his opinions to the *Milford Journal*. From reading his words, it can be gathered that he was not only self-made in finance but also self-assertive in matters of public opinion.

13   Woodbury, *Testimonial to the Philadelphia Textile School*, p. 12.

14   George Draper, "Tariff and Wages," *Boston Evening Journal*, July 9, 1886; idem, *Some Views of the Tariff Question* (Boston: E. L. Osgood, 1886), p. 28.

15   Woodbury, *Testimonial to the Philadelphia Textile School*, p. 14.

16   "Remarks of Mr. Bancroft," *Boston Herald*, Oct. 25, 1887, p. 5.

17   Woodbury, *Testimonial to the Philadelphia Textile School*, p. 6.

18   *Boston Herald*, Oct. 25, 1887, p. 5.

19   "The Late George Draper," *Milford Journal*, June 15, 1887.

20   Draper, *Recollections*, p. 180.

21   Sawyer Spindle Company operated under the same arrangement as the Dutcher Temple Company, with George Draper and Son being principal owners and selling agent. The Hopedale Elastic Goods Company was owned in part by George

Draper's son-in-law, E. H. Osgood, until 1898. Both firm names were discontinued in 1897.

22 Letter of May 1, 1863, William F. Draper Correspondence, Library of Congress, Department of Manuscripts, Washington, D.C.

23 Letter of January 4, 1863, Draper Correspondence.

24 Draper, *Recollections*, p. 206.

25 "Drapers in Rome," *Milford Journal*, Jan. 5, 1898.

26 Testimony of William F. Draper, in Clarke, *Report of the Industrial Commission*, pp. 463, 464.

27 Going, "Village Communities," p. 66.

28 Draper, *Recollections*, pp. 376–77.

29 *The National Cyclopedia of American Biography* (New York: James T. White, 1933), s.v. "Draper, Eben Sumner."

30 A thorough account of the strike and ensuing labor unrest was carried in the *Milford Daily News* and the *Milford Journal* between April 1, 1913, and September 18, 1913.

31 "Assessors' Report," *Sixteenth Annual Report of the Town Offices of the Town of Hopedale, 1901* (Milford, Mass.: G. M. Billings, 1902), p. 45.

32 *Boston Herald*, Oct. 25, 1887.

33 Ibid., p. 5.

34 This information was taken from the manuscript census of the United States from 1870, 1880, and 1900, which provides a listing by name as well as other pertinent facts. "Census of Population for Hopedale in Worcester County, Mass., 1870, 1880, and 1900," enumerated in longhand and maintained in original copy by the National Archive, Washington, D.C.

35 Stephan Thernstrom, *The Other Bostonians: Poverty and Progress in the American Metropolis, 1880–1970* (Cambridge: Harvard University Press, 1973), chap. 9, and tables 9.1 and 9.2, pp. 222, 226.

36 Although the 1890 manuscript census was destroyed, the 1880 enumeration can be supplemented with the Milford and Hopedale tax records. The tax records were published in Assessors' Reports for Hopedale after 1886, indicating tax on head of family and size of family.

37 "Census of Population for Hopedale, 1870, 1880, and 1900."

38 Ibid.

39 "Hopedale," *Milford Journal*, Mar. 21, 1883.

40 Ibid., Mar. 28, 1883.

41 Berthoff, *British Immigrants in Industrial America*, p. 125.

42 King, "Hopedale Industrial Paradise," p. 20.

43 In the manuscript census, each dwelling is numbered; and the double-family houses can be identified by those having two families, thus showing which families lived side by side. Boardinghouses can be similarly identified, "boarders" designated.

44 Massachusetts, Bureau of Labor Statistics, *First Annual Report* (1870), passim.

45 "Census of Population for Hopedale, 1870, 1880, and 1900."

46 Interview with Mort Dennett, Hopedale, Mass., August 1973.

47 Peter Hackett, "Hopedale—The Town" (Bancroft Memorial Library, Hopedale: Paper presented to the Hopedale Community Historical Society, Bancroft Memorial Library, Hopedale, Mass., October 24, 1960), p. 2.

48 Hanger, "Housing of the Working People," p. 1208.

49 *Milford Journal*, Dec. 1, 1886.

50 Hopedale appropriated more money for education than other towns in Massachusetts of comparable size and other larger cities as well. Town of Hopedale, *First Annual Report of the School Committee* (Milford, Mass.: Daily Journal Printing House, 1887), passim.

51 Eugene E. Oakes, *Studies in Massachusetts Town Finance*, Harvard Economic Studies, vol. 57 (Cambridge: Harvard University Press, 1937), p. 24.

52 Not until 1874 did Massachusetts limit the workday to ten hours, and not until 1901 was the workweek reduced to fifty-eight hours, Berthoff, *British Immigrants in Industrial America*, p. 34.

53 Massachusetts, *Report of the Special Commission on the Hours of Labor*, p. 63.

54 Edward C. Kirkland, *Industry Comes of Age: Business, Labor, and Public Policy, 1860–1897*, The Economic History of the United States, vol. 6 (New York: Holt, Rinehart, and Winston, 1961), pp. 342–43.

55 The manuscript census for 1870 cites personal and real estate valuations and in addition to name and nationality gives the date of arrival in America. Assessors' Reports provide valuations after 1886. "Census of Population for Hopedale, 1870"; "Assessors' Report," *Sixteenth Annual Report, Hopedale, 1901*.

56 "Hopedale," *Milford Journal*, Feb. 19, 1874; Dec. 26, 1883.

57 *Milford Daily News*, Sept. 18, 1913.

58 In Massachusetts alone prior to 1880, there were 159 recorded strikes; Lowell was the first to suffer a major strike, when, in 1836, the mill girls paraded in protest of a 12½ percent reduction in wages. Information about strikes before 1880 may be obtained from the Massachusetts Bureau of Labor Statistics, *Second Annual Re-*

port (1871), *Eleventh Annual Report* (1880), and *Thirteenth Annual Report* (1882).

59 "Hopedale," *Milford Journal*, Oct. 13, 1886.

60 Ibid., Nov. 3, 1886.

61 *"The Hopedale Industrial Army,"* Proceedings of April 26, 1851.

62 G. Sherman Johnson, "A Massachusetts Garden Spot," *New England Magazine* 40 (July 1909): 608.

63 "Hopedale," *Milford Journal*, May 4, 1887; May 18, 1881; Sept. 15, 1880.

64 Ibid., July 8, 1885.

65 Ibid., June 20, 1888.

66 Ibid., Nov. 20, 1888.

67 Ibid., Sept. 22, 1886; Jan. 19, 1887.

68 Ibid., Dec. 2, 1896.

69 Johnson, "Massachusetts Garden Spot," p. 608.

70 "Hopedale," *Milford Journal*, Dec. 22, 1897.

71 *Cotton Chats*, December 1905.

72 "Hopedale," *Milford Journal*, Dec. 2, 1896.

73 "Yard Prizes," *Cotton Chats*, December 1908.

74 Refer to chapter 3; see also Edwin Longstreet Shuey, "Outdoor Art and Working-men's Homes," *American Gardening* 19 (1898): 498–500; idem, *Factory People and Their Employers*, p. 169; Roland, "Six Examples," p. 271; Going, "Village Communities," p. 66; Johnson, "Massachusetts Garden Spot," p. 607.

75 *First Annual Report of the Park Commissioners of the Town of Hopedale, Massachusetts* (1899), p. 3.

76 Ibid., p. 4.

77 *Sixteenth Annual Report of the Park Commissioners of the Town of Hopedale, Massachusetts* (1914).

78 *First Annual Report of the Park Commissioners*, p. 4.

79 Ibid.

80 See Albert Fein, *Frederick Law Olmsted and the American Environmental Tradition* (New York: George Braziller, 1972); see also Eliot, *Landscape Architect*.

81 *First Annual Report of the Park Commissioners*, p. 9.

82 James Church Alvord, "What the Neighbors Did in Hopedale," *Country Life in America* 25 (January 1914): 61.

83 Ibid.

84 *Sixth Annual Report of the Park Commissioners of the Town of Hopedale, Massachusetts* (1904), p. 4.

85 *Seventh Annual Report of the Park Commissioners of the Town of Hopedale,*

Massachusetts (1905), p. 5.

86 *Eighth Annual Report of the Park Commissioners of the Town of Hopedale, Massachusetts* (1906), p. 3.

87 "Tub Race, Pole Vault," *Cotton Chats*, November 1908.

88 The Draper Company maintained a photograph album of its activities, including annual Field Day events; Merrimack Valley Textile Museum, North Andover, Mass.

89 See Fein, *Frederick Law Olmsted*, chap. 5.

90 "Hopedale," *Milford Journal*, Aug. 26, 1885.

91 *Oakes Ames, 1804–1873: A Memoir, with an Account of the Dedication of the Oakes Ames Memorial Hall, at North Easton, Mass., Nov. 17, 1881* (Cambridge, Mass.: Riverside Press, 1883): "At the dedication of the (North Easton) Memorial Hall, four to five hundred people traveled from Boston to North Easton by special trains, and such dignitaries as Governor John Long, etc. spoke. The building, designed by H. H. Richardson, is one of the best of its type."

92 *Second Annual Report of the Town of Hopedale, 1887* (Milford, Mass.: Journal Steam Press, 1888), p. 3.

93 *Boston Herald*, Oct. 25, 1887, p. 5.

94 King, "Hopedale Industrial Paradise," p. 20.

95 *Second Annual Report of the Town of Hopedale*, p. 4.

96 *Cotton Chats*, March 1906.

97 Lewis G. Wilson, "Milford and Hopedale," *New England Magazine* 27 (December 1902): 507.

7 Company Housing In Hopedale

1 "Honors from St. Louis," *Cotton Chats*, November 1904.

2 West, "The Loom Builders," pp. 31–32.

3 "Hopedale," *Milford Journal*, Aug. 30, 1882; emphasis added.

4 Ibid., June 14, 1882; Dec. 1, 1886.

5 Ibid., Jan. 5, 1887; Feb. 12, 1887.

6 Ballou, *Hopedale Community*.

7 See Tarn, *Working-Class Housing*.

8 Architectural magazines, which occasionally featured articles about working-class housing, almost always illustrated double-family types. See, e.g., *Architec-*

tural Review (Boston) 4 (1916); of the dozens of examples illustrated, all are double-family.

9   "J. B. and J. M. Cornell Co., Coldspring, New York," *Bulletin of the Bureau of Labor*, no. 21 (1904), p. 1268.

10   "Hopedale," *Milford Journal*, Aug. 18, 1880.

11   *Papers Submitted to the Eighth International Housing Congress* (London: National Housing Reform Council, 1907).

12   Frank Chouteau Brown, "Workmen's Housing at Hopedale, Mass.," *Architectural Review* (Boston) n.s. 4 (April 1916): 64.

13   "Hopedale," *Milford Journal*, Apr. 18, 1883.

14   Ibid., Sept. 22, 1880.

15   Ibid., May 4, 1887.

16   Ibid., Apr. 18, 1883.

17   Robert Leavitt Davison, "The Problem of Low-Cost Housing," *Architectural Review* n.s. 4 (May 1916): 79. Davison illustrates one of the 1874 units and quotes its rent at $2.20 a week.

18   "Hopedale," *Milford Journal*, May 25, 1896.

19   Hanger, "Housing of the Working People," p. 1208.

20   For a discussion of the company row image, see Veiller, "Industrial Housing Developments," p. 231.

21   Investigations into housing conditions were conducted by the Massachusetts Bureau of Labor throughout the 1870s and by individual city sanitary commissions; refer to chapter 4. As early as 1842, Andrew Jackson Downing, in *Rural Cottages and Villas* and later in *The Architecture of Country Houses* (New York: Wiley and Putnam, 1850), prescribed room size and ventilation need; e.g.: " 'Warming and Ventilating': Fresh air—red blood, health and ventilation, amount of fresh air intake is important. Proper room circulation: Exhaust at the ceilings and intake at the floor."

22   See Banham, *Well-Tempered Environment*. Banham discusses the history of improvements in mechanical systems, though some of his revelations may be conservative in date, at least by American standards.

23   "Hopedale," *Milford Journal*, Mar. 6, 1889.

24   Cf. Grane House, Shackleford (1897) by C. F. A. Voysey; H. Briggs and Son housing, Normanton (1904). See David Gebhard, *Charles F. A. Voysey, Architect* (Los Angeles: Hennessey and Ingalls, 1975).

25   In particular, see E. A. Freeman, "An Architectural Masquerade," *American*

Architect and Building News 12 (September 1882): 120–21; J. S. Barney, "Our National Style of Architecture Will Be Established on Truth, Not Tradition," *Architectural Record* 24 (November 1908): 381–86; A. D. F. Hamlin, "Style in American Architecture," *Architectural Record* 1 (March 1892).

26 John Stewardson, "Architecture in America: A Forecast," *American Architect and Building News* 51 (1895): 51–52.

27 Brown, "Workmen's Housing at Hopedale," p. 67.

28 "Hopedale," *Milford Journal*, June 1, 1887.

29 *Cotton Chats*, December 1901.

30 King, "Hopedale Industrial Paradise," p. 20.

31 Hanger, "Housing of the Working People," p. 1208.

32 *Cotton Chats*, August 1905.

33 Ibid.

8 Conclusion

1 A Canadian study found the withdrawal of paternalism was a principal cause of the decline of the company town. "Single-Enterprise Communities in Canada: A Report to the Central Mortgage and Housing Corporation by the Institute of Local Government," mimeographed (Kingston, Ont.: Queen's University, 1953), p. 253.

2 See Robert H. Wiebe, *Businessmen and Reform: A Study of the Progressive Movement* (Cambridge: Harvard University Press, 1962), chap. 7.

3 A chapter could be written on the causes of decline in the textile industry, and fortunately this is provided in R. C. Estall, *New England: A Study in Industrial Adjustment* (New York: Frederick A. Praeger, 1966), chap. 3; specific cases are cited in Douglas G. Woolf, "New Era in New England," *Textile World* 91 (Dec. 1941): 73–77.

4 Samuel T. Freeman and Co., Auctioneers, *Forty-One Desirable Properties in a Very Attractive Village at North Easton, Massachusetts, To Be Sold on the Premises, Thursday, June 19, 1930* (Boston, 1930).

5 In New England the sale of company housing and other properties began voluntarily in the first decades of the twentieth century as demand for home ownership increased. Then, with the appearance of cheap automobiles in the 1920s, workers could purchase a Model T and commute to work. Thus, it no longer was necessary for the company to reserve or furnish housing. The Depression brought the wholesale liquidation of many nonproductive properties. By 1940 most towns, including

South Manchester and Peace Dale, had disposed of their housing. The nature of this process is described in Harriet L. Herring, "Sale of New England Mill Houses," *Textile World* 91 (January 1941): 64–66.

6 Shurcliff to Carl Rust, Chief Landscape Architect, U.S. Housing Corporation, Washington, D.C., August 9, 1919, Shurcliff Papers, Massachusetts Historical Society, Boston, Mass.

7 Comey and Wehrly, "Planned Communities." The original survey in manuscript contains a larger list of towns with detailed information about Peace Dale and other model company towns. Copies are in the Library of Congress, Washington, D.C., and the Frances Loeb Library, Harvard University, Cambridge, Mass.

8 Henry S. Churchill, *The City Is the People* (New York: W. W. Norton, 1962), pp. 76–77.

9 Comey and Wehrly, "Planned Communities," pp. 66–67.

10 William H. Whyte, *The Last Landscape* (Garden City, N.Y.: Doubleday, 1968), p. 256.

11 "New Town Rises Back at the Ranch," *Business Week*, Sept. 23, 1967, p. 182.

12 J. B. Jackson, *Landscapes: Selected Writings of J. B. Jackson*, ed. Ervin H. Zube (Amherst: University of Massachusetts Press, 1970), pp. 107–12, 116–31.

13 Builders of prefabricated housing, such as the Gordon–Van Tine Co., which received its start after the Chicago fire in 1871, provided houses for a number of mill towns but designed no layouts; *Housing Labor: A Book Written by Businessmen for Businessmen and Dealing with Housing as a Means for Getting and Holding Labor* (Davenport, Iowa: Gordon–Van Tine, 1918).

Because so little has been written about company towns in America, especially in regard to urban design, they remain little known and little understood in terms of their development. J. D. Porteous, a geographer, has published a very useful bibliography entitled *The Single-Enterprise Community in North America*, in the Council of City Planning Librarians series, no. 207 (1971). It includes chiefly twentieth-century sources and very few government reports. To find information about early company towns, the best way is to peruse bulletins of the U.S. Bureau of Labor and congressional records and reports, as well as professional journals in engineering, architecture, and city planning. It is hoped that this bibliography will fill some of the gaps.

Entries have been grouped under the following headings: Primary Sources, Secondary Sources, and Hopedale. Consideration was given to providing a bibliography on workers' housing, apart from what is cited, but this would have entailed listing sources on city tenements and philanthropic societies more often than company towns. However, several authors listed under primary sources (also see U.S. Documents) contributed most of what we know about this subject. Carroll D. Wright, G. W. W. Hanger, Leifur Magnusson, E. R. L. Gould, Emile Muller, and Budgett Meakin also illustrated their descriptions. Lists of relatively unknown articles, books, and pamphlets on low-cost housing can be found in the publications of the international housing congresses after 1889.

Bibliography

Primary sources

Allen, Bruce. *Rudimentary Treatise on Cottage Building; or, Hints for Improving the Dwellings of the Labouring Classes.* London: John Weale, 1854.

America's Recreation Center: Hershey, the Chocolate Town. Souvenir commemorating the thirtieth anniversary. Hershey, Penn., 1933.

Armstrong, John Borden. "Harrisville: A New Hampshire Mill Town in the Nineteenth Century." Ph.D. dissertation, Boston University, 1962.

Atterbury, Grosvenor. "Model Towns in America." *Scribner's Magazine* 52 (1912): 20–35.

Augur, Tracy B. "Industrial Growth in America and the Garden City." M.L.A. thesis, Harvard University, 1921.

Bell, Frank H., ed. "Corey Is Ready." *Jemison Magazine* 1 (March 1911): 3.

Benoît-Lévy, Georges. *Cités jardins d'Amérique.* Paris: Henri Jouve, 1905.

Bigelow, John P. *Branches of Industry in Massachusetts, for the Year Ending April 1, 1837.* Boston: Dutton and Wentworth, 1838.

Birch, John. *Examples of Labourers' Cottages, with Plans for Improving the Dwellings of the Poor in Large Towns*. London: Edward Stanford, 1871.

Birchenough, M. C. "Some Diversions of an Industrial Town." *Littell's Living Age* 247 (1905): 602–4.

Blackmar, Frank W. "Two Examples of Successful Profit-Sharing." *The Forum*, March 1895, pp. 57–67.

Challamel, M. Jules, ed. *Compte rendu et documents du congrès international des habitations à bon marché*. Paris: La Société Française des habitations à bon marché, 1900.

Chicopee, Georgia, Where Cleanliness Is Next to Godliness. New York: Doyle, Kitchen, and McCormick, 1930.

Clavière, Etienne, and J. P. Brissot. *The Commerce of America with Europe*. New York: T. and J. Swords, 1795.

Cleveland, H. W. S. *Landscape Architecture, as Applied to the Wants of the West; with an essay on Forest Planting on Great Plains*. Chicago: Jansen, McClurg, 1873.

Collins, D. C. "The Design and Construction of Industrial Buildings." *Engineering Magazine* 33 (1907): 107.

Coolidge, John. "Low Cost Housing: The New England Tradition." *New England Quarterly* 14 (1941): 6–24.

Coxe, Tench. *An Address to an Assembly of the Friends of American Manufacturers, Society for the Encouragement of Manufactures and the Useful Arts*. Philadelphia: Aitken and Son, 1787.

Crawford, T. C. "The Pullman Company and Its Striking Workmen." *Harper's Weekly* 38 (1894): 686–87.

Creel, George. "The Feudal Towns of Texas." *Harper's Weekly* 60 (1915): 77–78.

Davison, Robert Leavitt. "The Problem of Low-Cost Housing." *Architectural Review* (Boston) 9 (May 1916): 79–80.

De Witt, Francis. *Branches of Industry in Massachusetts*. Boston: William White, 1856.

Downing, Andrew Jackson. *The Architecture of Country Houses*. New York: Wiley and Putnam, 1850.

———. *Landscape Gardening, Adapted to North America*. New York: Wiley and Putnam, 1844.

———. "Our Country Villages." In *Rural Essays*, ed. George William Curtis. New York: Leavitt and Allen, 1857.

Draper, Earle S. "Southern Textile Village Planning." *Landscape Architecture* 18 (October 1927): 1–28.

Eads, George W. "N. O. Nelson, Practical Cooperator, and the Great Work He Is Accomplishing for Human Upliftment." *The Arena* 36 (April 1906): 463–80.

Egleston, Nathaniel Hillyer. *Villages and Village Life, with Hints for Their Improvement.* New York: Harper and Brothers, 1878.

Ely, Richard T. "Pullman: A Social Study." *Harper's Magazine* 70 (1885): 452–66.

———. "Pelzer, South Carolina. *Harper's Magazine* 105 (1902): 41–45.

Fairbanks, Edward T. *The Town of St. Johnsbury, Vt.* Saint Johnsbury, Vt.: Cowles Press, 1914.

Farwell, Parris Thaxter. *Village Improvement.* New York: Sturgis and Walton, 1913.

Fletcher, Bannister. *Model Houses for the Industrial Classes.* London: Longmans, Green, 1871.

Fletcher, Henry J. "The Doom of the Small Town." *The Forum* 19 (April 1895): 214–22.

Fowler, A. N. "Rhode Island Mill Towns." *Pencil Points* 17 (May 1936): 271–86.

Freeman, E. A. "An Architectural Masquerade." *American Architect and Building News* 12 (September 1882): 120–21.

Gandy, Joseph. *The Rural Architect; Consisting of Various Designs for Country Buildings.* London: John Harding, 1805.

Gardner, E. C. *Illustrated Homes.* Boston: James R. Osgood, 1875.

Gibbons, John. *Tenure and Toil; or, Rights and Wrongs of Property and Labor.* Philadelphia: J. B. Lippincott, 1888.

Gilman, Nicholas Paine. "Profit Sharing in the United States." *New England Magazine*, September 1892, pp. 120–28.

Going, Charles Buxton. "Village Communities of the Factory, Machine Works, and Mine." *Engineering Magazine* 21 (1901): 66–71.

Grimmer, A. K. "The Development and Operation of a Company-Owned Industrial Town." *Engineering Journal* 17 (1934): 219–23.

Hale, Edward Everett. *How They Lived in Hampden.* Boston: James R. Osgood, 1884.

———. *Workingmen's Homes: Essays and Stories.* Boston: James R. Osgood, 1874.

Hare, S. Herbert. "The Planning of a New Industrial City." *American City* 29 (November 1923): 501–3.

Herring, Harriet L. "Sale of New England Mill Houses." *Textile World* 91 (January 1941): 64–66.

———. "Selling Mill Houses to Employees." *Textile World* 90 (June 1940): 115.

Hinds, William Alfred. *American Communities and Co-operative Colonies.* Chicago: C. H. Kerr, 1908.

Hole, James. *The Homes of the Working Classes.* London: Longmans, Green, 1866.

"Housing: Government Aid or Private Enterprise? A Survey Reported Jointly by the American City and the Architectural Forum." *Architectural Forum* 19 (February 1936): 81–87.

Housing Labor: A Book Written by Businessmen for Businessmen and Dealing with Housing as a Means for Getting and Holding Labor. Davenport, Iowa: Gordon–Van Tine, 1918.

Howe, F. C. "Industrial Villages in America." *Garden City* 1 (July 1906): 142–50.

"An Industrial Experiment at South Manchester." *Harper's New Monthly Magazine* 45 (1872): 838–53.

Industrial Relations Activities at Cheney Brothers, South Manchester, Connecticut. New York: National Industrial Conference Board, 1929.

Larcum, Lucy. *A New England Girlhood.* Boston: James R. Osgood, 1889.

Lewis, L. "Uplifting 17,000 Employees." *World's Work Magazine* 9 (1905): 5939–50.

McCarthy, P. "Morgan Park: A New Type of Industrial Community." *American City* 14 (1916): 150–53.

Manchester, H. H. *The Story of Silk and Cheney Silks.* South Manchester, Conn.: Cheney Brothers, Advertising Dept., 1916.

Manning, Warren Henry. *Handbook for Planning and Planting Small Home Grounds.* Stout Manual Training School, 1899.

———. *The History of Village Improvement in the United States.* Reprint from *The Craftsman,* February 1904.

———. "Villages for Workingmen and Workingmen's Homes." *Proceedings of the Second National Conference on City Planning and the Problems of Congestion,* Rochester, N.Y., May 2–4, 1910. Cambridge: Cambridge University Press, 1910.

May, C. "Indian Hill: An Industrial Village at Worcester, Massachusetts." *Architectural Record* 41 (1917): 20–35.

Mayer, Albert. "A Technique for Planning Complete Communities." *Architectural Forum* 66 (1937): 19–36, 126–46.

Meakin, Budgett. *Model Factories and Villages: Ideal Conditions of Labor and Housing.* London: Fisher and Unwin, 1905.

"A Model American." *The Critic* 33 (October 1898): 274.

Morse, Robert H. *St. Johnsbury, Vt., and Important Industrial Beginnings, 1830.* Newcomen Society of England, American Branch. Princeton: Princeton University Press, 1945.

Muller, Emile, and E. Cacheux. *Habitations ouvrières en tous pays.* Paris: Baudry, 1889.

Nelson, H. L. "The Cheneys' Village at South Manchester, Connecticut." *Harper's Weekly* 34 (1890): 88.

Nolen, John. "Organization of Credit for Housing Purposes." In *Internationalen Wohnungskongress*. Vol. 9. Vienna: Verlag der Zentralstelle für Wohnungsreform in Osterreich, 1911.

Noon, Alfred A., ed. *The History of Ludlow, Mass.* Springfield, Mass.: Springfield Printing and Binding, 1912.

Northrop, Birdsley Grant. "How to Beautify and Build up Our Country Towns" [1869]. Frances Loeb Library, Harvard University, Cambridge, Mass.

———. *Rural Improvement.* New Haven: Tuttle, Morehouse, and Taylor, 1880.

———. "The Work of Village Improvement Societies." *The Forum* 19 (March 1895): 95–104.

Pond, Irving K. "Pullman: America's First Planned Industrial Town." *Illinois Society of Architects Monthly Bulletin* 1 (1934): 7.

Reports of the Selectmen, Treasurer, and Assessors, of the Town of Easton, Mass. Taunton, Mass.: C. A. Hack and Son, 1878.

Reynolds, Marcus T. *The Housing of the Poor in American Cities.* Baltimore: Guggenheimer, Weil, 1893.

Robbins, Mary Caroline. "Village Improvement Societies." *Atlantic Monthly* 79 (February 1897): 212–22.

Roland, Henry. "Six Examples of Successful Shop Management." *Engineering Magazine* 12 (1896): 69–85, 271–85.

Scoresby, William. *American Factories and Their Female Operatives.* London: Longman, Browne, Gray, Longmans, 1845.

Sedgwick, A. G. "Village Improvement." *The Nation* 19 (September 1874): 149–50.

Shuey, Edwin L. *Factory People and Their Employers: How Their Relations Are Made Pleasant and Profitable.* New York: Lentilhon, 1900.

"Single-Enterprise Communities in Canada: A Report to the Central Mortgage and Housing Corporation." Mimeographed. Kingston, Ont.: Queen's University, 1953.

Stewardson, John. "Architecture in America: A Forecast." *American Architect and Building News* 51 (1895): 51–52.

"St. Johnsbury, Vt.: A Model New England Town." *Boston Globe*, Sept. 25, 1875.

Stone, Arthur F., ed. *St. Johnsbury Illustrated: A Review of the Town's Business, Social, Literary, and Educational Facilities, with Glimpses of Picturesque Surroundings.* Saint Johnsbury, Vt.: Caledonian Press, 1891.

Taylor, Graham Romeyn. "Granite City: Gary." *Survey Magazine* 29 (1912): 582–98, 781–87.

Taylor, W. Cooke. *Factories and the Factory System.* London: Jeremiah How, 1844.

Thomas, T. *The Working-Man's Cottage Architecture, Containing Plans, Elevations, and Details, for the Erection of Cheap, Comfortable, and Neat Cottages.* New York: R. Martin, 1848.

[Tod, Thomas]. *Consolatory Thoughts on American Independence.* Edinburgh: James Donaldson, 1782.

"The Town of Kohler, Wisconsin: A Model Industrial Development." *Architecture* 51 (April 1925): 149–54.

A Trip through the Whitin Machine Works, Manufacturers of Textile Machinery. Boston: Walton Advertising and Printing, 1925.

Veiller, Lawrence. "Industrial Housing Developments in America." *Architectural Record* 43 (March 1918): 231–57.

Villerme, Louis René. *Sur les cités ouvrières.* Paris: J. B. Bailliere, Libraire de l'Académie nationale de médecine, 1850.

Waring, George E., Jr. *Village Improvement and Farm Villages.* Boston: James R. Osgood, 1877.

White, Alfred T. *Improved Dwellings for the Laboring Classes: The Need and the Way to Meet It on Strictly Commercial Principles.* New York: G. P. Putnam, 1879.

Wolfe, Albert Benedict. *The Lodging House Problem in Boston.* Boston: Houghton, Mifflin, 1906.

Woods, R. A. "The Human Touch in Industry." *Munsey's Magazine* 29 (1903): 323–24.

Wright, Carroll D. *The Relation of Political Economy to the Labor Question.* Boston: A. Williams, 1882.

MASSACHUSETTS DOCUMENTS

Bureau of Labor Statistics. *First Annual Report* (1870), pp. 164–85; *Third Annual Report* (1872), pp. 437–43; *Fifth Annual Report* (1874), pp. 29–48; *Eleventh Annual Report* (1880), pp. 65–67; *Sixteenth Annual Report* (1885), pp. 1–28; *Seventeenth Annual Report* (1886), pp. 177–86; *Thirtieth Annual Report* (1900), p. 226; *Thirty-seventh Annual Report* (1906), p. 534. Boston: Wright and Potter.

Gettemy, Charles F. *The Decennial Census, 1915: The Commonwealth of Massachusetts.* Boston: Wright and Potter, 1918.

Report of the Special Commission on the Hours of Labor, and the Condition and Prospects of the Industrial Classes. Boston: Wright and Potter, 1866.

Wadlin, Horace G. *The Census of Massachusetts, 1885.* Vol. 2, *Manufacturers.* Boston: Wright and Potter, 1886.

———. *The Census of Massachusetts, 1895.* Vol. 2, *Population and Social Statistics.* Boston: Wright and Potter, 1897.

Warner, Oliver. *Branches of Industry in Massachusetts, for the Year Ending May 1, 1865.* Boston: Wright and Potter, 1866.

Wright, Carroll D. *The Census of Massachusetts, 1875.* Vol. 2, *Manufacturers and Occupations.* Boston: Albert J. Wright, 1877.

U.S. DOCUMENTS

Bureau of the Census. *Ninth Census, 1870: Population.* Vol. 1. Washington, D.C.: Government Printing Office, 1873.

———. *Tenth Census, 1880: Manufacturers.* Washington, D.C.: Government Printing Office, 1883.

———. *Tenth Census, 1880: Population.* Vol. 1. Washington, D.C.: Government Printing Office, 1883.

Clarke, Albert, ed. *Report of the Industrial Commission.* Vol. 14. Washington, D.C.: Government Printing Office, 1901.

Comey, Arthur C., and Max S. Wehrly. "Planned Communities." In *Supplementary Report of the Urbanism Committee,* pt. 1. Washington, D.C.: Government Printing Office, 1939.

Congress. House. *Reports of the Committee on Awards of the World's Columbian Commission.* Vol. 2. H. Doc. 510. 57th Cong., 1st sess., 1901–2.

———. House. *Reports of United States Commissioners to the Universal Exposition of 1889 at Paris.* Ex. Doc. 410. 51st Cong., 1st sess., 1889–90.

———. Senate. *Report of the Commissioner General for the United States to the International Universal Exposition. Paris, 1900.* S. Doc. 232. 56th Cong., 2d sess., 1900–1.

Gould, E. R. L. "The Housing of the Working People." In U.S. Bureau of Labor, *Eighth Special Report of the Commissioner of Labor.* Washington, D.C.: Government Printing Office, 1895.

Hanger, G. W. W. "Housing of the Working People in the United States by Employers." *Bulletin of the Bureau of Labor* 21 (1904): 1103–1248.

Magnusson, Leifur. "Housing by Employers in the United States." *Bulletin of the Bureau of Labor Statistics,* no. 263 (1920), pp. 30–283.

Report of the United States Coal Commission. Washington, D.C.: Government Printing Office, 1925.

Trowbridge, W. P. *Reports on the Water-Power of the United States.* Pt. 1. Washington, D.C.: Government Printing Office, 1885.

Wirth, Louis, and Edward Shils. "Urban Living Conditions." *Supplementary Report of the Urbanism Committee.* Pt. 2. Washington, D.C.: Government Printing Office, 1939.

Wright, Carroll D. *Report on the Factory System of the United States.* Washington, D.C.: Government Printing Office, 1883.

Secondary sources

Allen, James B. *The Company Town in the American West.* Norman: Oklahoma University Press, 1966.

Armstrong, John Borden. *Factory under the Elms: A History of Harrisville, N.H.* Cambridge: MIT Press, 1969.

Arnold, Joseph L. *The New Deal in the Suburbs: A History of the Greenbelt Town Program, 1935–1954.* Columbus: Ohio State University Press, 1971.

Atkinson, J. R. "USA: Private Enterprise Town Building." *Town and Country Planning* 29 (August 1961): 323.

Bailey, James, ed. *New Towns in America.* New York: Wiley and Sons, 1973.

Banham, Reyner. *The Architecture of the Well-Tempered Environment.* Chicago: University of Chicago Press, 1969.

Barde, Robert E. "Arthur E. Morgan, First Chairman of TVA." *Tennessee Historical Quarterly* 30 (Fall 1971): 312–13.

Batchelor, Peter. "The Origin of the Garden City Concept of Design." *Journal of the Society of Architectural Historians* 28 (October 1969): 184–200.

Bauer, Catherine. *Modern Housing.* Boston: Houghton Mifflin, 1934.

Bellamy, Edward. *Looking Backward, 2000–1887.* New York: Random House, 1951.

Benevolo, Leonardo. *The Origins of Modern Town Planning.* Cambridge: MIT Press, 1967.

Berthoff, Rowland T. *British Immigrants in Industrial America, 1790–1950.* New York: Russell and Russell, 1953.

Bishop, J. Leander. *A History of American Manufactures.* 3 vols. Philadelphia: Edward Young, 1868.

Blank, Joseph P. "Good-by to the Company Town." *Reader's Digest* 74 (January 1959): 109–12.

Blauner, Robert. *Alienation and Freedom: The Factory Worker and His Industry.* Chicago: University of Chicago Press, 1964.

Blumin, Stuart. "Mobility and Change in Antebellum Philadelphia." In *Nineteenth Century Cities*, ed. Stephan Thernstrom and Richard Sennett. New Haven: Yale University Press, 1969.

Breckenfeld, Gurney. *Columbia and the New Cities*. New York: George F. Nesbitt, 1971.

Buder, Stanley. *Pullman: An Experiment in Industrial Order and Community Planning, 1880–1930*. New York: Oxford University Press, 1967.

Burchard, John E., and Albert Bush-Brown. *The Architecture of America: A Social and Cultural History*. Boston: Little, Brown, 1961.

Burke, Gerald. *Towns in the Making*. New York: St. Martin's Press, 1971.

Byington, Margaret F. *Homestead: The Households of a Mill Town*. The Pittsburgh Survey, edited by Paul U. Kellogg, vol. 1. New York: Charities Publication Committee, Russell Sage Foundation, 1910.

Chapman, Stanley D. *The History of Working-Class Housing: A Symposium*. Newton Abbott [England]: David and Charles, 1971.

Churchill, Henry S. *The City Is the People*. New York: W. W. Norton, 1962.

Clark, Victor. *History of Manufacturers in the United States*. 3 vols. Washington, D.C.: Carnegie Institution, 1929.

Cochran, Thomas C. "The Social History of the Corporation in the United States." In *The Cultural Approach to History*, edited by Caroline F. Ware. New York: Columbia University Press, 1940.

Cochran, Thomas C., and William Miller. *The Age of Enterprise*. New York: Macmillan, 1942.

Cole, Donald. *Immigrant City: Lawrence, 1845–1921*. Cambridge: Harvard University Press, 1963.

Commons, John R., ed. *History of Labor in the United States*. 4 vols. New York: Macmillan, 1918–35.

Coolidge, John P. *Mill and Mansion: A Study in Architecture and Society in Lowell, Massachusetts, 1820–1865*. New York: Columbia University Press, 1942.

Creese, Walter L. *The Search for Environment: The Garden City, Before and After*. New Haven: Yale University Press, 1966.

———, ed. *The Legacy of Raymond Unwin: A Pattern for Planning*. Cambridge: MIT Press, 1967.

Darley, Gillian. *Villages of Vision*. London: Architectural Press, 1975.

Dublin, Thomas. *Women at Work: The Transformation of Work and Community in Lowell, Massachusetts, 1826–1860*. New York: Columbia University Press, 1979.

Dupont: The Autobiography of an American Enterprise. New York: Charles Scribner's Sons, 1952.

Eliot, Charles. *Landscape Architect.* 1902. Reprint. Freeport, N.Y.: Books for Libraries Press, 1971.

Estall, R. C. *New England: A Study in Industrial Adjustment.* New York: Frederick A. Praeger, 1966.

Fein, Albert. "The American City: The Ideal and the Real." In *The Rise of an American Architecture*, edited by Edgar Kaufmann, Jr. New York: Praeger, 1970.

———. *Frederick Law Olmsted and the American Environmental Tradition.* New York: George Braziller, 1972.

Feiss, Carl. "The Factory and the Town." *Architectural Record* 109 (May 1951): 112.

———. "New Towns for America." *Town and Country Planning* 28 (July 1960): 235–40.

Fisher, Marvin. *Workshops in the Wilderness: The European Response to American Industrialization, 1830–1860.* New York: Oxford University Press, 1967.

Ford, James, et al. *Slums and Housing.* Vol. 1. Cambridge: Harvard University Press, 1936.

Frieden, Bernard J. "Housing and National Goals: Old Policies and New Realities." In *The Metropolitan Enigma*, edited by James Q. Wilson. Garden City, N.Y.: Doubleday, 1970.

Frisch, Michael. *From Town into City: Springfield, Massachusetts, 1840–1880.* Cambridge: Harvard University Press, 1973.

Garner, John S. "Leclaire, Illinois: A Model Company Town, 1890–1934." *Journal of the Society of Architectural Historians* 30 (October 1971): 219–27.

Gebhard, David. *Charles F. A. Voysey, Architect.* Los Angeles: Hennessey and Ingalls, 1975.

Golany, Gideon, ed. *International Urban Growth Policies: New-Town Contributions.* New York: John Wiley and Sons, 1978.

Green, Constance M. *Holyoke, Massachusetts: A Case History of the Industrial Revolution in America.* New Haven: Yale University Press, 1939.

Hall, Edward T. *The Hidden Dimension.* Garden City, N.Y.: Doubleday, 1966.

Handlin, Oscar. *Boston's Immigrants: A Study in Acculturation, 1790–1860.* Cambridge: Harvard University Press, 1941.

Handlin, Oscar, and John Burchard, eds. *The Historian and the City.* Cambridge: MIT Press, 1960.

Hareven, Tamara K., and Randolph Langenbach. *Amoskeag: Life and Work in an*

American Factory-City. New York: Pantheon Books, 1978.

Hayden, Dolores. *Seven American Utopias: The Architecture of Communitarian Socialism, 1790–1975.* Cambridge: MIT Press, 1976.

Herring, Harriet L. *Passing of the Mill Village.* Chapel Hill: University of North Carolina Press, 1949.

Hitchcock, Henry-Russell. *The Architecture of H. H. Richardson and His Times.* Cambridge: MIT Press, 1966.

———. *Architecture of the Nineteenth and Twentieth Centuries.* Baltimore: Penguin Books, 1968.

Horwitz, Richard P. "Architecture and Culture: The Meaning of the Lowell Boardinghouse." *American Quarterly* 25 (March 1973): 64–82.

Howard, Ebenezer. *Garden Cities of Tomorrow.* 1902. Reprint. Edited by Frederic J. Osborn. London: Faber and Faber, 1946.

Johnson, Ole S. *The Industrial Store: Its History, Operations, and Economic Significance.* Atlanta: Foote and Davies, 1952.

King, Judson. *The Conservation Fight: From Theodore Roosevelt to the Tennessee Valley Authority.* Washington, D.C.: Public Affairs Press, 1959.

Kirkland, Edward C. *Industry Comes of Age: Business, Labor, and Public Policy, 1860–1897.* The Economic History of the United States, vol. 6. New York: Holt, Rinehart, and Winston, 1961.

———. *Men, Cities, and Transportation: A Study in New England History, 1820–1900.* 2 vols. Cambridge: Harvard University Press, 1948.

Lanck, W. Jett, and Sydenstricker, Edgar. *Conditions of Labor in American Industries.* New York: Funk and Wagnalls, 1917.

Le Blanc, Robert G. *Location of Manufacturing in the Nineteenth Century.* Geography Publications at Dartmouth, no. 7. Hanover, N.H., 1969.

Leiby, James. *Carroll Wright and Labor Reform: The Origin of Labor Statistics.* Cambridge: Harvard University Press, 1960.

Lewis, Nelson P. *The Planning of the Modern City.* New York: John Wiley and Sons, 1916.

Lynd, Robert S., and Helen M. Lynd. *Middletown: A Study in Contemporary American Culture.* New York: Harcourt, Brace, 1929.

McClelland, J. M., Jr. *Longview: The Remarkable Beginnings of a Modern Western City.* Portland, Ore.: Binfords and Mort, 1949.

Mayer, Albert. *Greenbelt Towns Revisited.* Washington, D.C.: National Association of Housing and Development Officials, 1968.

Michelson, William. *Man and His Urban Environment: A Sociological Approach.*

Reading, Mass.: Addison-Wesley, 1970.

Mumford, Lewis. *The Culture of Cities*. New York: Harcourt, Brace, and World, 1938.

————. *The Letters of Lewis Mumford and Frederic J. Osborn: A Transatlantic Dialogue, 1938–70*. Edited by Michael Hughes. New York: Praeger, 1972.

————. "A New Approach to Workers' Housing." *International Labor Review* 75 (February 1957): 1–7.

————. *Sticks and Stones: A Study of American Architecture and Civilization*. New York: Boni and Liveright, 1924.

Navin, Thomas R. *The Whitin Machine Works since 1831: A Textile Machinery Company in an Industrial Village*. Cambridge: Harvard University Press, 1950.

Nolen, John. *New Towns for Old*. Boston: Marshall Jones, 1927.

Noyes, John Humphrey. *History of American Socialisms*. Philadelphia: J. B. Lippincott, 1870.

Nuquist, Andrew. Introductory Comments. Town Officers' Educational Conference. Local Government series no. 1. Winter 1962.

Oakes, Eugene E. *Studies in Massachusetts Town Finance*. Harvard Economic Studies, vol. 57. Cambridge: Harvard University Press, 1937.

Pearson, Norman. "Elliot Lake: Experiment in Conformity." *Town and Country Planning* 27 (May 1959): 199–203.

Pierson, William H., Jr. *American Buildings and Their Architects*. Vol. 2. Garden City, N.Y.: Doubleday, 1978.

Pope, Liston, *Millhands and Preachers*. New Haven: Yale University Press, 1942.

Porteous, J. D. *The Company Town of Goole: An Essay in Urban Genesis*. Hull [England]: University of Hull Occasional Papers in Geography, 1969.

————. *Environment and Behavior: Planning and Everyday Urban Life*. Reading, Mass.: Addison-Wesley, 1977.

————. "The Nature of the Company Town." *Transactions of the Institute of British Geographers* 51 (1970): 127–42.

Pred, Allan. "Manufacturing in the American Mercantile City, 1800–1840." In *Cities in American History*, edited by Kenneth T. Jackson and Stanley K. Schultz. New York: Alfred A. Knopf, 1972.

Reps, John W. *Cities of the American West*. Princeton: Princeton University Press, 1979.

————. *The Making of Urban America*. Princeton: Princeton University Press, 1965.

Robinson, Charles Mulford. *Modern Civic Art; or, The City Made Beautiful*. New York: G. P. Putnam's Sons, 1903.

Roddy, Edward G. *Mills, Mansions, and Mergers: The Life of William M. Wood*. North

Andover, Mass.: Merrimack Valley Textile Museum, 1982.

Rostow, W. W. *The Stages of Economic Growth: A Non-Communist Manifesto*. Cambridge: Cambridge University Press, 1967.

Roth, Leland M. *A Concise History of American Architecture*. New York: Harper and Row, 1979.

———. "Three Industrial Towns by McKim, Mead, and White." *Journal of the Society of Architectural Historians* 38 (December 1979): 317–47.

Scott, Mel. *American City Planning since 1890*. Berkeley: University of California Press, 1969.

Shlakman, V. *Economic History of a Factory Town: A Study of Chicopee, Mass*. Smith College Studies in History. Northampton, Mass., 1935.

Stein, Clarence S. *Toward New Towns for America*. Liverpool: Liverpool University Press, 1951.

Tann, Jennifer. *The Development of the Factory*. London: Cornmarket Press, 1970.

Tarn, John Nelson. *Working-Class Housing in Nineteenth-Century Britain*. London: Architectural Association, 1971.

Tarbell, Ida M. *The Nationalizing of Business*. New York: Macmillan, 1936.

———. *New Ideals in Business*. New York: Macmillan, 1916.

Taylor, Frederick W. *Shop Management*. New York: McGraw-Hill, 1911.

Taylor, Graham Romeyn. *Satellite Cities: A Study of Industrial Suburbs*. New York: D. Appleton, 1915.

Thernstrom, Stephan. *The Other Bostonians: Poverty and Progress in the American Metropolis, 1880–1970*. Cambridge: Harvard University Press, 1973.

———. *Poverty and Progress: Social Mobility in a Nineteenth-Century City*. Cambridge: Harvard University Press, 1964.

Tobey, George B., Jr. *A History of Landscape Architecture: The Relationship of People to Environment*. New York: American Elsevier, 1973.

Turner, Ralph E. "The Industrial City: Center of Cultural Change." In *The Cultural Approach to History*, edited by Caroline F. Ware. New York: Columbia University Press, 1940.

Wade, Richard. *The Urban Frontier*. Cambridge: Harvard University Press, 1959.

Wallace, Anthony F. C. *Rockdale: The Growth of an American Village in the Early Industrial Revolution*. New York: Alfred A. Knopf, 1978.

Warner, Sam Bass, Jr. *Streetcar Suburbs: The Process of Growth in Boston, 1870–1900*. Cambridge: Harvard and MIT Press, 1962.

———. *The Urban Wilderness: A History of the American City*. Harper and Row, 1972.

Whyte, William H. *The Last Landscape*. Garden City, N.Y.: Doubleday, 1968.

Wiebe, Robert H. *Businessmen and Reform: A Study of the Progressive Movement*. Cambridge: Harvard University Press, 1962.

Wood, Edith Elmer. *The Housing of the Unskilled Wage Earner*. New York: Macmillan, 1919.

Woolf, Douglas G. "New Era in New England." *Textile World* 91 (December 1941): 73–77.

———. "What's Ahead for the Mill Village." *Textile World* 90 (February 1940): 114–15.

Wright, Gwendolyn. *Building the Dream: A Social History of Housing in America*. New York: Pantheon Books, 1981.

Zaitzevsky, Cynthia. "Housing Boston's Poor: The First Philanthropic Experiments." *Journal of the Society of Architectural Historians* 42 (May 1983): 157–67.

Zevin, Robert Brooke. *The Growth of Manufacturing in Early Nineteenth-Century New England*. New York: Arno Press, 1975.

Hopedale

Alvord, James Church. "What the Neighbors Did in Hopedale." *Country Life in America* 25 (January 1914): 61.

Ballou, Adin. *History of the Hopedale Community*. Lowell, Mass.: Thompson and Hill, 1897.

Brown, Frank Chouteau. "Workmen's Housing at Hopedale, Mass." *Architectural Review* (Boston) n.s. 4 (April 1916): 62–68.

Chase, William H. *Five Generations of Loom Builders: A History of the Draper Corporation*. Cambridge, Mass.: Printed for the Draper Corporation, 1950.

Clark, Edie. "Hopedale, Massachusetts." *Yankee Magazine*, April 1982, pp. 56–61.

Cotton Chats, September 1901 to December 1908.

The Diamond, Oct. 15, 1851.

Draper Corporation. Advertising and Public Relations booklet. Hopedale, Mass., 1954.

Draper, Eben S. "What Massachusetts Has Contributed to the Welfare of the American People." In *Biographical History of Massachusetts*, edited by Samuel Atkins Eliot. Boston: Massachusetts Biographical Society, 1911.

Draper, George. "Let-off Motions for Looms." *New England Cotton Manufacturers' Association*, no. 8. Boston: T. W. Ripley, 1870.

———. *Some Views of the Tariff Question: By an Old Business Man, Who Believes in the American Market for the American People*. Boston: E. L. Osgood, 1886.

———. "Tariff and Wages." *Boston Evening Journal*, July 9, 1886.

Draper, George Otis. *Venturing Betimes*. Milford, Mass., 1931.

Draper, William F. *Recollections of a Varied Career*. Boston: Little, Brown, 1908.

Faulkner, Barbara Louise. "Adin Ballou and the Hopedale Community." Ph.D. dissertation, Boston University, 1965.

George Draper & Son, Manufacturers of Cotton Machinery and Selling Agents for the Hopedale Machine Co., Dutcher Temple Co., and Sawyer Spindle Co. Catalog and company history. Hopedale, Mass., 1887.

Hackett, Peter. "Hopedale—The Town." Paper presented to the Hopedale Community Historical Society, Bancroft Memorial Library, Hopedale, Mass., October 24, 1960.

"Happy Hopedale: Abode of Comfort, Peace, and Happiness." *Boston Herald*, Oct. 25, 1887.

"The Hopedale Industrial Army: Record of Its By Law, Rules, Regulations, and Proceedings." Handwritten and recorded by A. G. Spalding, 1849, and H. D. Carter, 1851–54. Bancroft Memorial Library, Hopedale, Mass.

Hopedale Reminiscences. Hopedale, Mass.: Hopedale School Press, 1910.

Hopedale, Town of. "Assessors' Report." *First Annual Report of the Town Offices of the Town of Hopedale, 1886*. Milford, Mass.: Journal Job Printing House, 1887.

———. "Assessors' Report." *Tenth Annual Report of the Town Offices of the Town of Hopedale, 1895*. Milford, Mass.: G. M. Billings, 1896.

———. "Assessors' Report." *Sixteenth Annual Report of the Town Offices of the Town of Hopedale, 1901*. Milford, Mass.: G. M. Billings, 1902.

———. *First Annual Report of the Park Commissioners of the Town of Hopedale, Mass.* 1899.

———. *Fifth Annual Report of the Park Commissioners of the Town of Hopedale, Mass.* 1903.

———. *Sixth Annual Report of the Park Commissioners of the Town of Hopedale, Mass.* 1904.

———. *Sixteenth Annual Report of the Park Commissioners of the Town of Hopedale, Mass.* 1914.

———. *Second Annual Report of the Town of Hopedale, 1887*. Milford, Mass.: Journal Steam Press, 1888.

———. *Fourth Annual Report of the Town of Hopedale, 1889*. Milford, Mass.: Daily Journal Printing House, 1890.

Johnson, G. Sherman. "A Massachusetts Garden Spot." *New England Magazine* 40 (July 1909): 606–14.

King, Padraic. "Hopedale Industrial Paradise of Bay State." *Boston Sunday Post*, June 1929.

Merrill, Charles F. "Hopedale As I Found It." Paper presented to the Hopedale Community Historical Society, Bancroft Memorial Library, Hopedale, Mass., 1957.

"Milford and Hopedale." *New England Magazine* 27 (December 1902): 487–508.

The Milford Journal, 1850–1916: June 7, 1873; Feb. 19, Oct. 22, Dec. 10, 1874; Aug. 11, Aug. 18, Nov. 17, 1875; Mar. 7, 1877; Aug. 7, Dec. 25, 1878; Oct. 8, Oct. 29, Nov. 10, Nov. 12, 1879; Mar. 24, June 16, Aug. 18, Sept. 15, Sept. 22, Oct. 6, 1880; May 18, June 8, July 13, 1881; Feb. 1, May 24, June 14, July 26, Aug. 30, Sept. 6, Oct. 11, 1882; Feb. 18, Mar. 21, Mar. 28, Apr. 18, June 6, June 20, July 18, Dec. 26, 1883; May 7, 1884; Apr. 1, June 24, July 8, July 15, Aug. 5, Aug. 26, Sept. 30, Oct. 7, Dec. 2, 1885; Feb. 10, May 12, Sept. 22, Oct. 6, Oct. 13, Nov. 3, Dec. 1, 1886; Jan. 5, Jan. 19, Feb. 12, Apr. 20, May 4, June 1, June 15, Aug. 17, 1887; Feb. 22, May 2, June 20, Nov. 20, 1888; Mar. 6, July 17, Sept. 25, 1889; Apr. 30, 1890; Feb. 17, 1892; May 25, Oct. 7, Dec. 2, 1896; Feb. 24, May 5, June 16, July 7, Nov. 10, Dec. 22, 1897; Jan. 5, 1898.

Opening Argument of Hon. Joseph Bennett, Testimony, and the Closing Argument of J. H. Benton, Jr., Esq., before the Legislative Committee on Towns for 1886 in Remonstrance against the Incorporation of Hopedale. Boston: Rand, Avery, 1886.

Opening Argument of Nathan Sumner Myrick, Esq., Testimony, and Closing Argument of Hon. Selwyn Z. Bowman, before the Legislative Committee on Towns, 1886, in Favor of the Incorporation of the New Town of Hopedale. Boston: Rand, Avery, 1886.

The Practical Christian, Sept. 10, 1845.

Reasons Why Hopedale Should Be Set Off from Milford. Printed circular, 1886.

"Record Book of the Hopedale Community," no. 2. Handwritten and recorded by Mary A. Walden, Aug. 31, 1853, to Jan. 25, 1856. Bancroft Memorial Library, Hopedale, Mass.

Shurcliff, Arthur A. Business correspondence, 1906–52. Shurcliff Papers. Massachusetts Historical Society, Boston, Mass.

Smith, Paul R. "An Instance of Practical and Esthetic Industrial Housing." *American City*, Town and Country ed. 13 (December 1915): 476–77.

West, Thomas H. *The Loom Builders: The Drapers as Pioneer Contributors to the American Way of Life.* The Newcomen Society of England in North America, no. 14. Princeton: Princeton University Press, 1952.

Wilson, Lewis G. "Hopedale and Its Founder." *New England Magazine* 4 (April 1891): 197–212.

"Worthy Ware for the World's Weavers." *Skyline: Rockwell International* 31, no. 2 (1973): 35–41.

MAPS AND ATLASES

Beers, F. W. *Map of Milford.* New York: F. W. Beers, 1870.

Eastman, G. G., and A. A. Shurcliff. Plan of Lake Street, West Pond Lot Groups, Hopedale, Mass., 1910.

Hammett, Frank W. Plan of Sewers for the Draper Company, Hopedale, Mass., 1897.

Holbrook, A. Plan of Hopedale Properties of E. D. Draper, Hopedale, Mass., 1858.

Manning, W. H. Map of Roads and Trails, Hopedale Park, Hopedale, Mass., 1913.

Sanborn, D. A. *Re-survey, Milford, Mass.* New York: D. A. Sanborn's National Insurance Diagram Bureau, April 1874.

State Atlas of Massachusetts. "Hopedale, Worcester County." 1898.

Taylor, Gordon M. Topographical Plan, Hopedale, Mass., May 24, 1899.

Walker, George. *Map of the Town of Milford and Proposed New Town of Hopedale.* Boston: Geo. Walker, 1886.

Wheelock, W. C. Plan of the Sewers for the Hopedale Machine Company, Hopedale, Mass., April 1892.

Wheelock, W. G., Jr. Plan of Sewers, Hopedale, Mass., May 1894.

Wilder, A. H. Plan of the Hopedale Village Site. Worcester, Mass., Apr. 3, 1855.

Index

288
Index